MEETING HUMAN NEEDS
An Overview of Nine Countries

SOCIAL SERVICE DELIVERY SYSTEMS
An International Annual

Series Editors

DANIEL THURSZ
School of Social Work
University of Maryland—Baltimore

JOSEPH L. VIGILANTE
School of Social Work
Adelphi University

SOCIAL SERVICE DELIVERY SYSTEMS
An International Annual
Volume 1

MEETING HUMAN NEEDS

An Overview of Nine Countries

Editors
DANIEL THURSZ
and
JOSEPH L. VIGILANTE

 **SAGE Publications**   Beverly Hills / London

For information address:

SAGE PUBLICATIONS, INC.
275 South Beverly Drive
Beverly Hills, California 90212

SAGE PUBLICATIONS LTD
St George's House / 44 Hatton Garden
London EC1N 8ER

Printed in the United States of America

ISBN No. 0-8039-0314-6 (cloth)
ISBN No. 0-8039-0589-0 (paper)

Library of Congress Catalog Card No. 73-86705

FIRST PRINTING

CONTENTS

PREFACE

This book, the first in a series of several volumes, represents the concerns, interests, creativity, knowledge and drudgery of many people who were brought together (in print) by the editors. We all experienced the mutual excitement of launching a new venture. Our motivations were to learn about social service delivery in nations about which many of us knew precious little. The editors have learned a great deal. As we venture into the arena of international social welfare, we have made new friends, have been exposed to new concepts, and have been tested in our own ability to "stay loose" in order not to prejudge values or approaches.

We have had a great deal of support and we wish to acknowledge the help of social welfare leaders in those countries of the world which are represented in this volume and those to follow. The social welfare leadership in these countries, as well as the authors themselves, have been invaluable in our pursuit of new knowledge. We have had the aid of an outstanding Editorial Board. We are greatly indebted to our students with whom we have discussed some of the content, style, and some of the approaches for editing. We are especially grateful to the graduate students who have assisted us in the editorial process, particularly Rose Brown and Mary Adams.

The world knows that when two deans of professional schools, living many miles apart, attempt to undertake this kind of professional effort, the guidance, control, organization and monitoring of the effort is done by their respective secretarial staffs. We therefore acknowledge with utmost gratitude the contributions made by this secretarial group: from Adelphi University, Mrs. Evelyn Geddes and Miss Maria Georgiou, and from the University of Maryland, Mrs. Nancy Steele and Miss Sharon Backof.

We have kept up an ongoing correspondence with most of the authors of these works, and to the extent that it is possible for such a worldwide project to represent a team effort, we believe the project has done that. The team consists of two editors, ten authors, at least twelve social welfare leaders from all countries—including the U.S. Department of Health and Welfare, the Council on Social Work Education, and the International Association of Schools of Social Work —as well as students too numerous to mention. Whatever contributions this series may make should be credited to these individuals.

For whatever errors, mistakes in judgment, editorial and otherwise, which may appear, the editors assume total responsibility.

Daniel Thursz
Joseph L. Vigilante
Starlight, Pennsylvania
June 1975

A NATION'S RESPONSIBILITY TO THE HUMAN NEEDS OF ITS CITIZENS

Social services as institutional forms of providing help to families and individuals are rapidly becoming accepted as necessary components of the organization of industrial societies. Characteristic of the industrial, technological society are the necessity and the capacity for delivering human-oriented services to people whose needs are created or exacerbated by the phenomena accompanying industrial and technological development. The character of the social services developed as a response to the move from agrarianism through industrialism and eventually to consumerism will depend on a combination of factors ranging from differential resource availabilities to peculiar geographic and ecological factors as well as political and ideological stances.

Industrial and post-industrial societies, in addition to attempting to cope with the need for humanistic, individualized services, are also facing the demand for the delivery of services to masses of populations. The very concept of "service" has evolved to encompass interventions with families, groups, and whole communities. Instead of being limited to crises, social services in many parts of the world now include preventive activities as well as social education. As urbanism grows, population densities increase and social problems multiply. Having recognized the need to establish income maintenance programs for the masses, nations are developing mass delivery systems to provide supportive social services.

Industrialization rapidly followed the creation of many new nations at the close of World War II. These nations, as well as some pre-war countries, which were at that time basically agrarian, have been labelled in international political science language as "developing countries." They have been catching up with the established industrial countries both in the industrial production arena and in consumer absorption capacity. In the short space of 25 years, the income maintenance imperatives we first recognized have now become social service imperatives.

Information regarding income maintenance programs throughout the world has been generally available for many years as a result of work accomplished by the International Labor Organization and other organs of the United Nations. Similar information and research regarding social services has been scarce and rarely available in comparative or contrasting contexts.[1]

The editors have undertaken an initial effort to bring together in one place significant information about the nature of social service delivery systems in a variety of countries. This volume, together with a companion volume to be issued subsequently, offers descriptive articles dealing essentially with the "architecture" of these social services. We recognize that there are important variations among these national experiences—some caused by ideological factors and others by the unique history of a nation. As with all other aspects of national life, each account offers only a snapshot of an evolving subsystem within a constantly changing nation influenced by international and world forces. Most of the articles are written by leaders in social welfare. Although we did not have the opportunity to bring the authors together—and, therefore, each writes from his own perspective and priority considerations—it is fascinating to note the similarity in the approach of a number of them. The countries represented in both volumes were selected to provide a wide range of contrast and to include developing countries as well as those that have a long history of efforts to develop comprehensive systems of social service delivery. We believe that contrasting experiences with the organization of service delivery can be invaluable to both scholars and administrators in the continued search for more effective and rational ways of meeting human needs under a variety of circum-stances.

We are keenly aware of the relationship between culture and social service delivery systems. Approaches that seem self-evident in one setting can be catastrophic in another. Social welfare administrators, planners, and researchers who have worked on the international scene should have learned that programs are not easily transferable from one country to another. Nevertheless, our examination of the experiences reported in many countries reveals a commonality of concerns, value dilemmas, policy issues, and methodologies. These can contribute toward facilitating communication among social workers at an international level. We believe that even among national systems that are competing with each other—and, in some cases, are hostile to each other—there are mutual internal concerns and struggles that can provide a common ground for joint efforts and shared understanding. In our view, it would be helpful to the field of social work, and to the efforts of various groups throughout the globe, to know more clearly where commonalities exist and where differences begin. In time, the differences will have to be studied on a comparative basis to establish with some degree of certitude which approach is most effective for solving a problem.

As indicated earlier, we recognize the danger of assuming quick and effective transferability of programs across national and cultural boundaries. However, we are not prepared to assert that a program cannot be transferred. Methods need to be studied by which approaches developed in one setting can be utilized in another. In our view, there are ways by which transplants can work through particular adaptations and controlled procedures for assimilation. In time the "rejection" phenomenon in social service architecture will be solved just as it will be solved in the transplant field in medicine. There are enough social and cultural similarities among selected countries at various stages of development to suggest the possibility of some limited transferability even today.

Beyond the issue of the utility of a particular social service delivery system, outside of its initial national setting, is the paramount importance of increasing communication regarding social welfare systems across national boundaries. We believe that administrators, wherever they are, can learn from the experiences of others in coping with similar problems. A number of major phenomena creating social problems are present throughout the world. Cross-national migration, victims of international conflicts, cross-ethnic adoption, natural disasters, changing economies, physical and mental illness, individual tragedy, child abuse, senility, and unemployment all seem to be part of the lot of mankind; they appear in every community. Yet, the organization of response can be quite different and can provide useful insights to all engaged in such work.

Our expectations regarding these issues are confirmed as we review the articles in this volume. We note, for example, similarities in the authors' approaches to their tasks with respect to the identification of the family as the focus for designing delivery systems. We further note that in many countries, including the socialistic countries, the relationship between publicly financed and administered social services and private, nonpublic delivery systems is a matter of great interest, with little indication of the elimination of the latter. Further, countries tend to classify and categorize their approaches in two major ways: either from the point of view of social problems (juvenile delinquency, alcoholism, drug abuse, and the like) or from the point of view of the target population to which the service is directed (the aged, youth, families, immigrants, and so on). Most attempts at classification systems include both the problem and the target population orientations. Note, for example, the reference to decentralization both in the article on the United States as well as that on Italy. Decentralization is a popular phenomenon in the architecture of social services delivery. Also, throughout the world there is a common concern with day care and the role of women. Other difficulties, either implied or articulated in the articles, are manifest in the relationship between income maintenance and social services. Can these be separated administratively? What are the gains and losses of such a separation? There is also the recognition of the importance of education as a social service or as a separate kind of human service. Education as a social service is closely related to other forms of social services—such as day care, employment, and housing. The reader may note the absence of specific or detailed discussions of housing among developing countries compared to the more developed ones. And of course there is a recognition of the need for specialized training and for the development of specialized manpower systems for social service delivery.

We perceive a difference between the more sophisticated and developed countries and the developing countries, beyond the extent of services and resources. The articles from those countries which are moving from an agrarian to an industrial status tend to reflect their political and social histories; the authors chose to provide information about political and social history as a backdrop for understanding the social service delivery system. We suspect that some of the motivation for this kind of reporting may be related to the inevitable nationalism associated with socioeconomic development. It may represent an instinctive desire on the part of the author "to explain," as it were, why the service delivery system of his country may not be as sophisticated as those of the more developed nations. And, we believe, it symbolizes in a microcosm another commonality among nations, namely, that the social welfare delivery system is integrally linked with the economic and social system.

The editors wish to point out, in addition, that there is a wide range of available information within the countries reporting. In some countries there are few or no statistics. In others there is a large bank of available statistical information. In some countries there is no centralized information regarding administrative organization and structures, whereas in others this does not hold true. We are, nevertheless, satisfied that the materials presented here characterize the countries.

In conclusion, it appears to us that there is an expansion plain upon which social welfare scholars and administrators from communities throughout the world can meet. Differences in approach do not suggest to us difficulties in communication. On the contrary, they promise to provide a better turf for cross-breeding and cultivating knowledge.

Daniel Thursz
Joseph L. Vigilante
Starlight, Pennsylvania
July 1975

NOTE

1. We wish to acknowledge the assistance and stimulation of our colleague, Dr. Alfred J. Kahn, a member of our Editorial Board. His cross-national studies of social service systems have identified similar issues and complement this effort.

1

BASIC SOCIAL SERVICE NEEDS
FOR HUMAN COMMUNITIES

DANIEL THURSZ
JOSEPH L. VIGILANTE

It is not accidental that all industrialized and emerging countries are committed to the establishment and development of social services. Together with health and educational programs, social service activities highlight the concern for establishing a minimum floor to protect humanistic values of the community while at the same time continuing the search for methods by which a higher quality of life will be insured for all citizens. Whether ideologically aligned with the East or the West, whether an old, economically well-developed country or one just emerging from primitive isolation, the leaders of these countries share a major concern for the well-being of their citizens. Often, propaganda based on ideological or political conflicts tends to hide the truly universal nature of this general commitment, in theory, if not in practice as yet.

Although each country may be at a different stage in its quest for improving its national responsibility for the provision of social services, the problems of policy, organization, manpower, general strategies, and specific methodologies are shared by all. The patterns created following World War II for the transfer of policies and structures from developed countries to developing countries may have proved disastrous. Nevertheless, the search for better approaches to human need continues unabated.

It should come as no surprise that there are a large number of issues that seem similar in country after country even though the historical, political, economic, and social contexts are sharply different. There are common human needs that interpenetrate cultures and political systems. Human tragedy—on an individual or collective basis—knows no boundaries and ignores the frontiers established by nations. The impacts of war as well as natural disasters are felt to a surprising extent by peoples far away in all parts of the world. We should have accepted by now the economic interdependence of the world. There is also an increasing social interdependence that needs to be recognized. The policies and the structures by which social services are provided in one area will eventually affect other countries and therefore should be of high interest to social welfare administrators and scholars. Nations can indeed profit from the successes and failures of other nations in developing their social service systems, despite obvious differences in culture, geography, history, and other variables.

What are the basic social service needs of developing societies in the last quarter of the twentieth century? Do they differ from those of the more developed societies? An outstanding social phenomenon of the past quarter of a century has been the rapidity of change in "developing societies" due to a combination of improvements in transportation and communication, international cooperation through the United Nations, newly acquired economic wealth, the rapidity of expansion of international trade, strategic relationships with so called "Big Powers," and so on. Newly developing countries have not been content to wait for centuries or even decades of slow progressive change in order to obtain the consumer rewards of their more fortunate industrialized colleagues. Moreover, they have demonstrated that they do not have to. For even as technological advances have whetted the appetites of developing countries, so have these provided the wherewithal for the rapid attainment of consumer goods and perhaps more unfamiliar social services.

The spread of a more universal set of desires has brought with it, in many parts of the world, accompanying problems. Entry into the so-called modern world comes at a price in its impact on traditional family patterns, community and clan relationships, new mobility, potentially dangerous fads, cultural imitations based on movie and television re-runs with appropriate dubbing, and the like. We would add hastily that in certain areas of social service development, the emerging countries have made significant contributions from which the more advanced nations conceivably could profit. We have in mind as examples the social development experiments of the People's Republic of China, Ghana, and Kenya. The practical and low-cost approaches developed in Israel for the assimilation of new populations have already had a substantial impact on other new countries in the world, just as its program of international aid managed to avoid many of the pitfalls of the much more affluent AID program of the United States. We can expect many more constructive innovations in social services from such countries as well as from the professionalized and affluent industrial nations.

To set a background for an analysis of the basic social service needs of most societies, categories of widely understood social services ought to be established and considered. Essentially, social services can be classified in the following areas: those addressed to basic family needs; those designed particularly to serve youth and young adults; those related to the aged; those designed for violators of the law; those related to health care and mental health services; those concerned with housing; those concerned with community organization and development; those related to manpower and associated problems; and, finally, those related to childbearing and childrearing functions. The organizational patterns of service delivery in some countries make education a part of social services. For the purpose of this analysis, education will not be considered.

Family social services deal with the preservation and development of family life. The creation of such services is based upon a social value which emphasizes the family as a major unit of society and asserts the goal of maintaining this unit as the basic element for the preservation of culture and the transmission of existing values to new generations. The family services in industrialized countries have surpassed this simple description. In some situations, the preservation of the family in a healthy condition is seen as requiring limits on its size through birth control education and devices. Services to families may include activities related to marital health and prenatal care. They may deal with emotional problems specifically associated with family interrelationships. In countries where there is increasingly a need or opportunity for both parents to enter the labor force, the provision of day-care services is incorporated into the pattern of family social services. Increasingly, family life education programs are seen as essential aspects of family social services, together with family counselling and premarital counselling. An extension of family services may be seen in the establishment of family courts which function in many countries in a pseudo-social agency role.

Services for youth and young adults may or may not be incorporated into the structure of family social services. Together with services for the aged, the structure of social services in many countries tends to separate that population for specifically organized programs. Such services include adoption and foster care, protective services and counselling to prevent child abuse, counselling and other services to assist youth through the school experience, recreation and group work (including summer camps), youth organizations, and special institutions. Often programs dealing with both the control and prevention of juvenile delinquency are organized within this general umbrella, as are correctional facilities designed for youth.

A number of specific issues will emerge from a consideration of these services throughout the globe. To what extent is the incidence of foster care related to the stage of industrialization of particular societies? Is the family unit automatically threatened by the impact of industrialization or have some countries developed effective measures to prevent the weakening of family structure by the rhythms of modern life? How are various countries coping with the apparent increase in the incidence and prevalence of run-away youth, detached youth, and young people who are not affiliated with the traditional family unit as defined by the particular culture in which they live?

In the well-established countries, especially the United States, and apparently the Soviet Union, there seems to be a declining interest and identification with national purpose. Patriotism seems an old-fashioned and somewhat irrelevant phrase in some of the industrial countries today. Yet, this sense of commitment to a higher goal associated with a sense of mission has been a valuable conduit for channeling the concerns of youth and for transmitting values from generation to generation. Alienation is a major theme in studies of youth in some countries. Is this an actual problem for developing countries? Do they differ among themselves? Are alternatives being developed for old concepts that seem unfashionable these days?

A discussion of services for children and youth must include a recognition of relationships between preventive and remedial services, between services within the home and those outside, between foster care and institutional care, and finally with the increasing problem, apparently quite widespread, of youth unemployment.

When in 1958 the United States National Committee on Child Labor changed its name to the Committee on Employment of Youth, this action symbolized a profound social policy reversal, impelled, to be sure, by changing economic and social conditions. In brief, a highly prestigious national social organization in the United States was shifting its direction from and emphasis on protecting children from work to encouraging, in many situations, the employment of "young people." This may well have been an advance indicator of the direction that highly developed postindustrialized technological societies will inevitably follow.

Services to the aged have been identified as a special social service category since the publication of the English 1909 Poor Law Report, where services to the aged were separated from services to the poor. Industrialization and the refinements of technology have tended to increase the numbers at the opposite ends of the population curve. Through advancements in medical and bio-engineering sciences, human beings who otherwise may not have lived are being kept alive. Infant mortality has been reduced dramatically and the life span is constantly being lengthened. Advances in medical science, rehabilitation skills, and preventive activities have created concomitant social problems. As the size of the traditionally dependent populations has increased, societies have been impelled to create new systems for service. Concepts that were once the backbone of the community's response—such as filial responsibility—seem increasingly weak if not irrelevant to the problems of the aged as well as the sick and infirm.

Of special interest is the development in a number of countries of "gray power" groups which demonstrate the increased sophistication among some aged populations to articulate their needs in an organized manner, using the political process to insure adequate recognition for their needs. Modern youth movements are now paralleled by organizations of the aged who are demonstrating their abilities to influence decision makers and social policies.

Services to the violators of the law continue to be the source of a great deal of controversy throughout the world. The very term "corrections" used to define the field in the United States suggests an approach designed to affect the law violator and to end his inappropriate and illegal behavior. Yet, there is little evidence of success. Is this due to the fact, as many social workers suggest, that rehabilitation was really never given a chance in most countries? The tug of war between rehabilitation and punishment is reenacted each day in prisons and other correctional institutions in the Western world. The establishment of the National Conference of Charities and Corrections in the United States was early evidence of the response of industrialized society to the increased need to go beyond punishment in dealing with law violators.

Corrections services—such as probation and parole services as well as individual and group counselling within prisons, halfway houses, and other support activities for ex-offenders—are all part of the attempts of countries to prevent recidivism—the repeated or habitual relapse into crime. Special efforts focused on juveniles who commit crimes appear in the programs of most countries on the assumption that these youths are more malleable than older offenders and deserve a greater investment of social services to prevent a recurrence of such behavior. More recently, new programs have appeared in the technologically developed countries to provide social services to the victims of crime. Noteworthy are the various approaches now being tested for victims of rape.

It should not be surprising that in the emerging countries that are characterized by strong nationalist overtones, crimes against society are particularly repugnant. Therefore, social services tend not to be in great supply for law violators. Punishment, often severe, seems to be the treatment of choice. It has been argued that societies require a relative degree of affluence and technological security in order to exercise their potential humanism. Nevertheless, the gnawing question remains: is love really more effective than punishment in preventing recidivism? We would like to think so, although present approaches have been criticized for being unusually ineffective.

The fields of *health and mental health* have long demanded the attention of social services. As societies have recognized the close interrelationships between psychological, social, and cultural factors in the onset and character of illness, an array of medically and psychologically oriented social services have been developed. It is in these areas that possibly the highest level of preventive social service programming has been reached. It is also interesting to note that the United States has lagged behind many countries in identifying the social service component of health delivery. Legislation under consideration by the U.S. Congress leaves out of the health manpower field consideration of social workers. In the rest of the world, social services can be more widely observed in hospitals, out-patient clinics, community health centers and clinics, educational institutions, and industry. The range of these services is vast, and there is almost universal acceptance of the need for very concrete support provided by social services to the sick and recuperating individual as well as to the family. In brief, a physical illness has a specific and potentially hazardous social impact which requires as much expert management as does the physical illness itself.

Mental health services are most highly developed in the United States and Western Europe. From a fairly narrow perspective based on a single theoretical view of mental illness, the horizons have broadened dramatically to permit a wide variety of interventions designed to maintain mental health and to affect those who succumb to mental illness. Here social service personnel have played major roles in assisting individuals and their families to gain a better understanding of who they are as well as understanding of their needs with regard to each other and society. Individual and group counselling, role playing, patient government, community mental health centers, community homes, and other forms of intervention and treatment have accompanied the progress made in the use of biochemistry to assist individuals. However, there are complex problems that need highlighting. The de-institutionalization of mental patients can create havoc unless there are community structures and agents to assist such persons. The needs of the individual must be balanced with the needs of the family and of the community. In this area the transferability of one country's experience to another may be highly doubtful since cultural factors as well as economic issues may be crucial variables.

Dr. Eveline M. Burns, the world renowned social welfare economist, has suggested that *housing* is a major indicator of human need and a focus for the provision of social services. In some countries the provision of housing itself is seen as a major activity of the social service system. In most countries, public housing development, neighborhood renewal programs, privately sponsored housing, special housing for target groups such as the aged, and new planned communities are increasingly characterized by the addition of social services to deal with the wide variety of problems faced by the inhabitants and to assist in the integration of new populations. Social service personnel are often assigned to cope with the problems of dislocation and relocation as well as the unique problems experienced by special populations.

It has been alleged, but not always demonstrated, that the provision of social services in new public housing communities will not only help in the reorganization of the community but also prevent neighborhood deterioration. An outstanding example of the failure of this concept is found in the now infamous Pruitt-Igo project in St. Louis, U.S.A., where glorious visions of a new community of poor people were never realized and the buildings were finally razed. On the other hand, there have been notable successes in the merging of new housing with social services on a comprehensive scale, notably in Scandinavian countries.

A major problem in planning for publicly subsidized housing and new towns is the apparent inability in many countries to mix populations of varying economic classes. Racial integration seems feasible as long as the inhabitants are of a relatively high social and economic class, but major problems develop when such classes are mixed or when attempts are made to mix lower-class ethnic groups.

Perhaps the most significant social service required and used today by both developing and developed countries is *community organization.* It may even be suggested that some of the failures of social service delivery and of some dramatic approaches to the needs of people (such as the Pruitt-Igo Housing Project just mentioned) might be directly related to a lack of sophistication in planning with respect to community involvement and participation. It must also be recognized that architects, as well as other professionals such as physicians, often display an amazing lack of insight in the area of individual and collective human need. Issues of mix of populations, density, ownership, and income levels all have contributed to the failure of ambitious plans in which social service personnel were not consulted. Rather than planning for people, effective approaches require planning with people or, at the very least, with those who have intimate knowledge of the attitudes and needs of those to be served. Certainly, as newer nations have been struggling to "catch up" in the provision of basic social services, their reliance on and the development of community organization techniques have been imperative.[1]

Community work—a term often used to indicate the activities of community organization and community development—may be an area in which developing countries can provide valuable lessons to the well-established nations. In a number of countries of the Third World, as well as in the socialistic nations, some important experiments have developed in the establishment of service corps to which all young people are expected to devote a few years. We know very little about the community development movement in the People's Republic of China, especially in terms of organizational techniques. (A future volume will provide some insights.) Although aspects of nationalism, culture, and political organization make it most doubtful that the United States could borrow from these developments, they may have great value to other countries searching for ways of capturing the zeal and dedication of young people for the betterment of the society.

In our view, consumer participation in the planning and operation of governmental systems—especially those designed to provide health, education, and welfare services—is of paramount importance. Success in this activity depends on an effective structure and qualified *manpower* to direct such efforts. Amateurish attempts may serve to retard citizen involvement and create suspicion on the part of target populations as to the concern and legitimacy of the appeal for citizen participation.

Social planning—still the source of a good deal of controversy in the United States—represents an essential aspect of the structure of social services. Faced with limited resources and manpower, each country must identify priorities within a set of more generalized objectives. Recognizing that the present circumstances may make possible only a few social service programs, the architects of the comprehensive delivery system need to have a blueprint for the future in which the community has given some degree of sanction and support to what "ought to be" as compared to what "we can afford today."

A crucial aspect of the struggle to work within existing limitations and to make the most out of available resources is the assessment of the effectiveness of present programs. In meeting basic human needs, every expenditure must be demonstrated to be valid and effective, over a period of time. Of all aspects of social service delivery, it is in the area of evaluation and program monitoring that we find great weakness, even among the most developed countries. Although there are methodological problems to be solved in evaluative research, much more can be accomplished by sharing the advances developed in some parts of the world. We know too little in evaluative research but make use of only a fraction of what we do know.

The problems of lack of knowledge and unwillingness to use knowledge are not the only obstacles to research of social service delivery systems. There seems to be a resistance to organized data collection, and there is an even greater problem in getting various systems to use similar classification schemes. In the United States there is still no general pattern for maintaining social.statistics in a metropolitan area. Despite the existence of census tracks used by some social agencies for reporting data, other parts of the public social service system use postal zones, health districts, precincts, neighborhoods, and other geographical entities, thereby making it impossible to compare and study the relationship between such obvious factors as certain crimes and inferior housing or lack of recreational facilities. Simple statistics, such as the number of children served in a particular category of child welfare services in a particular location for a particular period of time, are very often impossible to obtain, as illustrated elsewhere in this volume.

Moreover, research has become identified in many instances with cost-benefit analysis. Evaluative research is a far broader concept than cost-benefit analysis. The latter is particularly difficult to apply to all aspects of social service systems. Some "benefits" cannot be "costed out." Does one put a dollar figure on ten uninterrupted talks with a potential suicidal adolescent by a case worker? A new level of absurdity is reached if one adds that the potential suicide was and probably would continue to be "on welfare." A strict cost benefit analysis would conclude that by preventing the suicide, the case worker adds immeasurably to cost over time!

Value overtones are the dilemma of social service research. The application of the scientific method to social service research may indeed be one of the major problems in developing adequate evaluations of the effectiveness of various interventions. But there are areas in which research can be undertaken, given the motivation and the provision of the necessary financial resources. Without specific financial allocations for evaluation and monitoring of programs, it is doubtful that even simple tabulations of service or elementary correlations will be done.

When research is undertaken, one of the many significant obstacles to be overcome is the generalized nature of goals of programs. Unless program goals are specifically defined, it is difficult to assess the degree to which goals are being met. Global approaches do not lend themselves to specific measurements. Although specific goals are not easily stated, there are ways in which valuable answers can be obtained. For instance, can we attribute a drop in the birthrate to an increase in knowledge of birth control, or does it result from changes in the economic picture in which an inflationary economy does not permit the expansion of family size? This is an important social policy question which is amenable to research with our present tools. Another example can be found in research on consumer satisfaction since it can be postulated that the degree to which clients are pleased with the efforts made on their behalf has some relationship to the efficacy of social service programs.

In this review of the broad classification for social service programs, we have attempted to highlight certain issues and problems that exist within each category. Although in no way exhaustive, these items suggest a degree of commonality among social service programs throughout the world. Rather than resulting from international discussions or even the contagion of one system upon another, it appears that these issues grow out of felt need and individual national experience, country by country.

In assessing the current architecture of service delivery systems in a number of countries, we have identified several key issues that administrators and planners are confronting. These issues, we believe, provide the fulcrum for comparing systems and for identifying target areas for increased research and development. They include:

Universalism versus Selectivity

It has been argued that services designed for the poor only inevitably become poor services. Yet, faced with very limited resources, countries are not able to provide universal services. To attempt to provide superficial services to the entire population might be worse than the provision of high quality services to a specific segment of the population of high risk, whether they are poor, children, aged, mothers at medical risk, or others. The dilemma between range and quality in the establishment of social service systems is at the heart of an agonizing process of social strategies.

Centralization versus Decentralization

Is a national approach to the delivery of social services more beneficial to recipients of service than one in which policies are developed at the local level with appropriate participation of the citizenry? It is ironic that in the United States those who have argued for community control in certain parts of the country in order to give more power to the disenfranchised are quick to argue national direction and intervention in other parts of the nation where community control would mean the application of values antithetical to their views. National approaches require the development of fairly complex bureaucracies and remove the decision-making responsibility to a distant and often unreachable level.

Decentralized operations with local options may not guarantee equity to all citizens. In this situation as with life in general, certain gains are offset by certain losses.

Public versus Voluntary Systems

Most countries recognize the responsibility of government to provide basic social services to its citizens. It is noteworthy that all governments also foster an element of voluntarism in this area; the patterns and extent vary considerably from nation to nation. There continues to be much controversy as to the respective roles of government and voluntary services—even if the latter are supported by government funds. Some writers suggest that the voluntary agencies ought to be at the frontier of new innovations while others see voluntary systems as serving as advocates for citizens in relation to government-sponsored social services. The range of possibilities is wide, and some creative tension is useful. Nevertheless, the inner-facing aspects of these two systems require far more clarity if they are to continue to exist side by side.

Manpower Issues

Who should provide social services? What kind of training is required, and under what circumstances should the personnel operate? The debate on professional training for social services is by no means ended even in the most advanced countries. At stake is not only the professional label to be used but also the degree to which the field is to be "professionalized" at the Master's or Bachelor's level. Of special importance is the relationship of paraprofessionals and volunteers to effective social service delivery systems. In some countries, a good value system as defined within the culture is all that is necessary to participate in this arena. In others, licensing is established by government edict, and levels of education are correlated to specific tasks. Autonomy of practice and potential risk to the population served continue to be helpful criteria by which assignments of various levels of workers can be made—provided a choice does exist within the country. In the United States the private practice of social work counsellors has become an issue of significance during the past five years. The concern will intensify as payments to private practitioners become more widespread under private and government health insurance schemes.

Community Care versus Institutional Care

We commented earlier in this chapter on the issues involved in attempting to reduce the extent to which citizens are removed from the normal community and sent to institutions. We know the terrible price paid by those who are placed in large impersonal institutional systems. Alternatives to institutions are difficult to develop and costly. Often there is opposition from the community in which halfway houses and similar programs are established. In the field of corrections, citizens are asking for protection from crime, and they see the more humane suggestions for open prisons and day work as dangerous ideas fostered by starry-eyed social workers. With evidence of the failure of large institutions and the possibilities created by modern medicine in the management of mentally ill persons, we predict an increased development of community care systems and a reduction in large institutional complexes. Unless there is a well-managed plan to work with the community in the establishment of this new care system, conflict will continue to rage between those who wish to have communities free of visible problems and those who advocate for a more humane way of dealing with the sick and the violators of law.

Relationship Between Bureaucracies and Political Leadership

Social services have become important aspects of a society. As a result they become increasingly part of the political process that exists around those features of a national approach that are of importance to masses of citizens. Increasingly large sums of monies are devoted to the support of social services requiring legislative and executive considerations. In brief, social services are too important to be ignored by the political leadership of a country. This means, in turn, that professionals in the field will need to engage in that process with the political leadership and to develop sophistication in areas that initially seemed unrelated to the specific aspects of social welfare for which they may have been trained. In a number of countries positions in social service systems are used for political patronage, with little consideration of the training requirements. The creation of standards for positions and a professional civil service may in time create new tensions between the political leadership and those responsible for social services. Nevertheless, if there is one universal principle applicable to all countries, it is that adequate social services depend essentially on political decisions reached by the leadership of the country.

Linkages with Other Social Systems

Although we have alluded to this in an earlier section of this chapter, we need to highlight the relationship between social services and other social systems. It is rare that social services can exist in isolation. Often they represent an aspect of a combined effort to improve the effectiveness of education, for instance, or adequate health care in hospitals, nursing homes, or similar institutions. The reality of social service is that it requires the most carefully executed adaptation of that system with other social systems. It also requires, on the part of social service manpower, an ability to work with other professionals such as medical personnel, lawyers, physical planners, accountants, judges, wardens, and so on.

Reference needs to be made to issues already described that involve the appropriate use of research and the general increasing requirement for accountability. In our view, this is not a development to be feared or avoided. Part of the task of social service administrators is to help the population at large and the political leadership to understand the nature of the social problems with which they are confronted and the degree to which particular interventions solve or ameliorate situations. A well-informed community may not make the choices which professionals might make individually. In the end, it is up to the professional leadership to interpret needs and to suggest alternatives for coping with social problems. It is up to the leadership and populace of a nation to decide how they wish to increase the quality of humanism of national service programs.

NOTE

1. For a discussion of the use of community organization in urban planning, see George Lockhart and J. L. Vigilante in "Community Organization: Factional and Social," in Community Development Journal—An International Journal for Community Workers 9, 1 (January, 1974). London: Oxford Press.

2

EGYPT'S SOCIAL SERVICE SYSTEM: NEW IDEOLOGY, NEW APPROACHES

HODA BADRAN

At one time in recent Egyptian history, it was questioned whether a social service system has a place in the new socialist society. The claim was that a social service system is a capitalist invention and only tranquilizes the masses to tolerate the injustices of society. Social workers, sociologists, economists, and planners took part in debates, and it was ultimately recognized that reforming political and economic institutions does not automatically create a utopia. Whatever the ideology of a society, social services contribute to the welfare of individuals, as far as such welfare is a major concern. The question now is no longer the necessity of a social service system, but rather how this sytem will be adapted to meet the needs of Egyptian society.

This chapter describes the Egyptian social service system as an integral part of the culture in which it works. The first part of the chapter gives the development of the Egyptian social service system and its existing framework. The second part gives a description of the important social services delivered to various groups.

The term "social services" still connotes different things in different countries and various meanings in the same country at different times. Moreover, the term is sometimes confused with other terms such as "social welfare" or "social work," and is used with them interchangeably. The difference in the scope of social services is particularly pronounced between developing countries and industrialized ones. Many developing countries include programs in independent fields such as health, education, and housing. Industrialized societies usually exclude these fields of activity from their lists of social services.[1]

In this chapter, social service is defined as "those activities that help change individuals and groups to achieve both adjustment and development and that help social institutions to meet individual and community needs more efficiently."[2] Social welfare is an "institution comprising all those policies and programs by which government guarantees a defined minimum of social services, money and consumption rights."[3] Social work is "a profession based upon scientific knowledge and skill in human relations. It uses certain strategies and tactics to involve individuals, groups or communities in achieving adjustment and improving living conditions."[4] Accordingly, "social welfare" is the institution, "social services" are certain types of activities or programs, and "social work" is the profession involved in providing these services.

Services such as public health or education are considered as programs within the social welfare institution but will not be included within the list of social services. The latter are services in which social work strategies and tactics are used, although they may be located in other institutions such as school social services, medical social services, or industrial social services.

DEVELOPMENT OF THE SOCIAL SERVICE SYSTEM IN EGYPT

Before 1939, the social service system in Egypt was completely a voluntary effort. The socioeconomic condition was at that time characterized by hopelessness and demoralization. A rigidly stratified society existed, with a predominantly agricultural economy and a very low standard of living. Sectarian social agencies provided services to their own groups, including education, money, and religion. Non-religious agencies served foreign communities through their own schools and hospitals. Members of the royal family and the upper economic class established charitable agencies for publicity and as leisure activities. A few services were organized by professionals educated abroad. They transplanted programs administered in England and the United States, regardless of their relevance to the needs of the culture. Services were financed through contributions, donations, and charity parties. No qualifications were required for social service personnel, and in most agencies board members volunteered to carry out administrative and professional work.

In 1939, the Ministry of Social Affairs was established as the governmental agency responsible for social services. The decree establishing it stated that the social service system could not be left to mere chance or to conflicting forces. Rather, there should be an official agency responsible for the social life of the individual and his family. The ministry started with eight general departments: Co-operation, Rural Development, Labor Affairs, Prisons Supervision, Publicity, General Manners, Research, and Administration.

Several changes have occurred in the structure and scope of the ministry's responsibilities. A social security program was initiated in 1939, proving that Egypt belongs among modern nations. Voluntary agencies worked side by side with the government, and the number of these agencies increased to 3,000 working in various fields. The first law to regulate voluntary agencies was passed in 1945. Graduates of newly established social work institutions started working for the Ministry of Social Affairs and for voluntary agencies.[5]

In 1952, the revolution erupted and the new regime immediately undertook many tasks. The economy was transformed from monopolistic private enterprise, with an unfavourable distribution of income, into a publicly controlled system.

The Ministry of Social Affairs reviewed its program in the light of new developments and defined four fields of action for itself:

(1) To promote the welfare of the labor force.

(2) To encourage the cooperative movement as a means of raising the living standard of the population.

(3) To provide services to villages and to develop the rural areas.

(4) To cooperate with voluntary efforts to promote social welfare and guide social development.

The ministry took initial steps towards decentralization of services in 1943. The country was divided into four regions to implement, on a local level, services which the ministry formulated and planned centrally.

In 1954, the ministry's work was reorganized into nine general departments and 18 regional branches. The head of each regional branch was responsible for implementing the ministry's plan within his region. Throughout the country, 498 local offices of social affairs were opened to provide direct services under the supervision of the regional branch.

In 1958, when Syria and Egypt united, two structures were responsible for social services. The Central Ministry of Social Affairs was responsible for policy-making and planning for the two countries, while the Egyptian Executive Ministry and its regional departments were charged with implementation within the country.[6]

Another reorganization of the ministry was undertaken in 1962 after the separation of Syria from the Union. The Ministry of Social Affairs remained to form policy and planning, leaving implementation to the departments of social affairs on the governorate level.

Certain activities of the ministry were transformed into independent structures, such as the Ministry of Youth or Labor. Other ministries have also recognized the need for a social services component and have established special offices for these activities within their own structures; these include the Ministry of Health and the Ministry of Education. Accordingly, the Egyptian social service system today includes the activities of the Ministry of Social Affairs, social service offices within other functional ministries, and voluntary social agencies. This totality is referred to when this chapter discusses the conceptual framework of the system, the personnel the system employs, and the structures providing services.

THE CONCEPTUAL FRAMEWORK FOR THE
SOCIAL SERVICE SYSTEM

The conceptual framework for the Egyptian social service system remained, until the sixties, a mixture of the early charity orientation and the values underlying the American social work system. In 1962, the Charter of Egypt, a document which spells out national policy in all spheres of life, laid down the conceptual framework for the whole social welfare system including the social service system. The following points were emphasizes in different chapters.

1. Economic and social development are two sides of one coin, each contributing to the other:

The aim of production is to widen the scope of services and services—in turn—are a driving force turning the wheels of production. The relations between services and production and their rapid, smooth running movement creates a sound national blood circle vital to the life of the people wholly and individually.[7]

2. Opportunities should be equal for all citizens to obtain a fair share of the national wealth. This necessitates increasing production and

> on the other hand, fair distribution calls for planning programs for social action, programs that enable the popular working masses to reap the benefits of economic action and create the welfare society to which they aspire and struggle to promote.[8]

3. Citizens' participation as an expression of democracy and as a way of distributing responsibilities is a necessity. The charter states:

> to shape his destiny, to define his position in society, to express his opinion and by means of his thought and experience and hopes to take an active part in leading and directing the evolution of his society is an inalienable human right which must be protected by law . . .

> the responsibility of each individual in this action must be clear to him, so that he may, at any time, know his exact position in the national action.[9]

The necessity of explaining the costs of realizing the masses' hopes is stated in another part of the charter.

4. The family is the important unit in society; it helps society achieve desired goals. Women should be freed from remaining shackles and children should be socialized to carry out future responsibilities. Family planning deserves the most sincere efforts, supported by modern scientific methods, to face the problem of an increasing population.

Within this conceptual framework, the first and second five-year plans (1960-1970) formulated programs for the service sector of the country. In the July 1971 celebration of the nineteenth anniversary of the Egyptian Revolution, accomplishments in both the production and service sectors were reviewed, and new directions were pointed out. The National Working Program presented by President Sadat on this occasion underlined gaps in development efforts. The following points which he made relate directly to the functioning of the social service system:

(1) The population lacks awareness of planning.

(2) There are gaps between national goals and the behavior of the masses; these gaps affect development. Such behavior includes spending patterns and family size.

(3) In spite of the expansion of services, they are still insufficient to meet the needs of the population.

The National Working Program has also outlined projects in the social sector to be included in the present ten-year plan. Two basic projects were particularly emphasized: the reconstruction of Egyptian villages and the establishment of housing schemes for industrial workers.[10]

THE SOCIAL SERVICE SYSTEM WITHIN NATIONAL PLANNING

Planning in Egypt operates essentially on three levels. The cabinet of the government decides overall political and socioeconomic policy. On the same level, the Ministerial Committee for Planning provides a direct link between political authority and technical ministries. The social service system is never treated as a whole or as an entity separate from other services in overall policy or planning. Accordingly, when the cabinet of the government decides on policy for social services, this policy refers to all social welfare institutions, including housing, health, education, publicity, and defense.

The Ministry of Planning, established in 1960, sets the framework in accordance with policies emanating from the cabinet, and lays down economic and social parameters and alternatives. The Institute for National Planning undertakes the research needed to prepare plans. The Ministry of Planning has sectoral divisions which correspond to the functional ministries, and from discussions with those ministries projects are prepared within the plan framework. The Ministry of Social Affairs, with its corresponding unit, formulates its own projects. Social services as components of other ministries' activities do not get adequate consideration within their ministries' overall plan, nor are they treated in an integrated form. The third level of planning involves the relationship between the functional ministries and their departments of planning, and the productive or direct service units. A two-way process of communication takes place between the central authorities and the lower levels.

The Department of Planning, within the Ministry of Social Affairs, formulates projects and activities for the ministry on the basis of requests submitted by different central departments and by direct service units. Research to identify social needs and to evaluate programs as bases for planning is carried out by the Research Department of the Ministry and by the National Centre for Social Research. The centre is now carrying out a national survey to get a profile of Egyptian society. Data collected will help identify gaps in social programs, including social services. Social offices within other functional ministries work out projects with the planning departments within their ministries.

The Social Workers' Union, established in 1973, has spelled out for the first time the overall goals of the social service system in Egypt. They are:

(1) To increase the social awareness of the population in order to increase economic production, improve the standard of services, and strengthen the socialist ideology of the country.

(2) To study contemporary social problems and outline solutions and recommendations for relevant government structures.

(3) To organize efforts to contribute to national goals and to cooperate with popular organizations in implementing the development plan of the country.[11]

In addition to these goals, the union's existence is considered a major step in clarifying many issues related to social service system personnel.

SOCIAL SERVICE PERSONNEL

Social service workers already in the field have various educational backgrounds and experiences. Personnel of the planning unit responsible for social services in the Ministry of Planning include two social workers, one with a Master's degree in sociology, and the other with a B.A. in social work and seven years' experience in the field. The unit also includes a lawyer and clerks, and it is headed by a graduate of the Law School who has twenty years' experience in the social field.

Most of the early workers still on the staffs of voluntary social agencies have no educational degree but have a wealth of practical experience. Another group employed by the Ministry of Social Affairs includes graduates of almost all departments of the university and of social work institutes. Many of these graduates have two degrees, one in agriculture and another in social work. These people hold most of the higher positions in the Ministry of Social Affairs. While the educational backgrounds of the personnel in this ministry vary, workers in social service offices within other ministries generally have a B.A. in social work or sociology.

Now that a Union for Social Workers has been established, new social work positions cannot be filled except by those who are members of the union. To qualify for membership, one has to hold a B.A. degree from the Institute of Social Work or the sociology or psychology departments of the University. Graduates of the Intermediate Institute of Social Work have to have a minimum of four years' practice to qualify for membership.

Graduates of other university departments who already work as social workers qualify for membership if they have a minimum of five years' experience. An honorary membership may be awarded to selected individuals who make special contributions to the field, though they may not meet the standard qualifications.

Among major objectives of the Union are:

(1) To coordinate efforts of social workers in Egypt and in all Arab countries, and to establish relationships with international organizations within the field.

(2) To cooperate with Arab, African, and Asian countries to study common problems, and to participate in international conferences dealing with these problems.

(3) To follow developments in the profession abroad, and to undertake necessary changes within the Egyptian system of social services.

(4) To participate with other authorities in formulating plans for development.

(5) To organize all aspects of the social work profession, and to encourage research.

(6) To provide special services to members of the union, including financial assistance, health insurance, and other social services.

STRUCTURE FOR SOCIAL SERVICES

According to national policy, all university graduates, including those of social work institutes and sociology or psychology departments, are placed in jobs through the Manpower Department of the Ministry of Labor. All functional ministries submit yearly requests to the Manpower Department indicating the number of social workers they need to employ for the next year. Accordingly, social workers get employment in almost all ministries, although most go to the Ministries of Social Affairs and Education. Except for those ministries with no departments within the local government, all ministries distribute new personnel, including social workers, among their departments in different governorates. Each department is then responsible for placing its new personnel in direct service units according to its programs. The Department of Social Affairs usually places its social workers among the local Social Affairs offices all over the country. The Department of Education places its social workers in schools, priority being given to secondary and preparatory levels. Social workers of the Department of Health work in MCH centers, family planning centers, school health units, and hospitals. Those in the Department of Labor work in the local labor offices. The Department of Youth uses social workers in youth centers and clubs. A few are appointed by the Ministry of Industry to work in industrial firms, and a very few are appointed to the Ministry of Defense, either in its central department of social services or in the veterans' hospitals.

Grades, salaries, and promotions of social workers in various government structures follow the national scale for university graduates. They are appointed on the seventh grade level, and they get promoted to a higher grade within about four years. Workers get into supervisory positions after a minimum of eight years. Voluntary agencies are free to give salaries and promotions, and there is great variation among them.

The cost of social services administered by various ministries is met through the national budget. The size and type of programs are controlled by the central ministry more than by local government. Legislation regulating certain services, such as social security, public assistance, and some industrial social services, applies nationally. There is still a gap between the theoretical autonomy of the local bodies and the strong control which each functional ministry exerts over its local departments. The budget for all social welfare services within the present ten year plan amounts to L.E. 215 million. L.E. 7 million are allocated to social and religious services together. Budgets for social services within other ministries are not specified. That social and religious services are combined as one item reflects the charity image of the social services held by planners.

The voluntary sector within the social service system is still active, despite confusion about its role caused by ideological changes in the 1961 Socialist Acts. The Ministry of Social Affairs has primary responsibility for organizing activities of this sector through legislation, supervision, and technical assistance and financing. Several laws were issued to regulate voluntary agencies, the last of which is Law No. 32 of 1964. This law includes several terms and provisions aimed at:

(1) Stressing the importance of voluntary agencies.

(2) Organizing their activities on geographical and functional bases locally and nationally through specific structures whose creation the law stipulated.

(3) Consolidating their financial resources by means of subsidies.

(4) Confirming the efforts of agencies in relation to services needed by communities. The law specified seven fields of action, including family welfare; child and mother welfare; care of the aged; services to the handicapped; social aids; religion, culture, and science; and community development.

(5) Strengthening social agencies and giving them a special standing that immunizes them from judiciary execution on their property, or expropriation of such property for public utility purposes.

The ministry provides supervision and technical assistance by observing the activities of all voluntary social agencies and by evaluating their efforts. It also helps plan their programs. To raise the standard of services, the ministry provides agencies with material and advice. Supervision is sometimes overdone. The boards of certain agencies are dominated by ministry staff.

The ministry also provides subsidies to most agencies to supplement their own resources. The ministry has established an Aid Fund responsible for allocating such subsidies. Resources of the fund include:

(1) Proceeds of extra fees charged according to the law on benevolent services.

(2) Appropriations in the national budget for subsidies to voluntary agencies.

(3) Proceeds of lottery allowed by the law.

(4) Proceeds of donations offered by banks, companies, or other organizations.

A board chaired by the Minister of Social Affairs decides on policy, and on ways of distributing money to agencies. Subsidies are given the agencies yearly to assist them in carrying out their overall responsibilities, or are given for special projects. At times, subsidies are given for construction purposes. Subsidies are justified on the basis of a study at a maximum of 75 percent of the total cost of the service, but not exceeding L.E. 5,000.

Besides efforts by the Ministry of Social Affairs to organize and coordinate voluntary activities, other structures play a major role in this sphere. The Regional Council for Social Agencies, which includes representatives of agencies from each region, carries out the following responsibilities:

(1) It formulates social programs in the region.

(2) It conducts research in different fields of activities.

(3) It defines standards for various services.

(4) It coordinates efforts of social agencies in the region.

(5) It offers technical assistance to agency members.

Other councils of social agencies work within specified fields, and include as members people from all agencies working in the field. The General Federation for Voluntary Agencies includes representatives of regional councils, functional councils, the Arab Socialist Union, and selected individuals. The Federation is chaired by the Minister of Social Affairs and, with the Ministry of Social Affairs, is responsible for formulating the overall policy for voluntary social services in Egypt. The Federation is not equipped, however, to carry out this function.

TRAINING SOCIAL SERVICE PERSONNEL

The first social work school was established by the Greek community in 1936 in Alexandria. In 1937, another school was opened in Cairo by the Egyptian Association for Social Studies, and the Greek School was Egyptianized. The government opened a third school of social work in 1946. Today, there are four university-level institutes of social work, two in Cairo, one in Alexandria, and the fourth in Kafr el-Sheikh. Graduates get a B.A. in social work after a four-year course of study. Three other intermediate institutes offer two-year courses after high school, and grant a social aid certificate. One of these institutes is in Cairo, another in Alexandria, and the third in Aswan. About 3,500 students graduate every year with a B.A. in social work, and about 2,500 students graduate each year from the intermediate institutes. Graduates of the departments of sociology from the six universities total about 6,000 students per year. About 70 percent of these get social work jobs. The Higher Institute of Social Work in Cairo, run by the government, offers Master's and Doctorate courses. About 50 students are in the Master's program, and about 15 study for a Doctorate degree.[12]

The curriculum for a B.A. has been revised several times to meet the demands of the field. It now places greater emphasis on the community organization method, both in the classroom and in field work. Casework content still leans heavily towards therapy, and group work still centers on clubs and youth centers. No real integration among the methods of social work has been achieved, and neither the behavioral nor the social sciences component is coordinated with methodology. The behavioral and social sciences components are also taught with different orientations. While an economics course is given within a socialist framework, sociology courses represent different schools of thought. Depending on who teaches the course, students may get their information according to the old French school or to leftist theoreticians.

Students on the B.A. level are admitted according to their standing in the Secondary School Completion Examination. The required standard for admission is relatively low and, accordingly, the quality of candidates, plus their large numbers, make adequate training difficult to achieve. Placing such great numbers in field work is almost an impossible task. Some agencies are used, although they may not give the type of experience desired by the institutions.

Various ministries organize in-service training for their social workers to increase efficiency within a specialized sector. The most important training programs are those administered for the personnel of the Ministry of Social Affairs. These include pre-service training and in-service specialized training. The pre-service training course comprises 14 weeks of theoretical classes giving knowledge about the ministry, its objectives, its administrative structure, and the services it provides. The same course includes two months of supervised field work in rural and urban areas under the Local Social Affairs Offices. Specialized in-service training is organized on two levels: courses for direct service workers, and others for supervisors and heads of services. These courses are given to public assistance workers, personnel of delinquents' institutions, workers with the handicapped, workers in family guidance offices, and workers in family planning units. About 500 workers attend the various types of training every year.[13]

TYPES OF SOCIAL SERVICES

Egyptian social services can be classified according to fields of action, such as family welfare, delinquency, and youth, or according to methods used, such as casework, group work, and community organization. They can also be classified according to source of financing—public, private, or semi-public. This chapter views the social service system within the context of national development. A major purpose of social services is to help the people make maximum use of their own capabilities and of various systems and structures to achieve an increase in economic production. Accordingly, social services will be classified by their contribution to economic development. A continuum may be established, with those services making a maximum contribution to economic development at one end, and those contributing least at the other. Services will be classified as those making a direct contribution to development, those making an indirect contribution to development, and those to special groups. Certain services can be grouped under more than one heading.

The major elements affecting the economic development of Egypt since 1952 are the Land Reform Scheme, nationalization of industry, trade, high dam construction, the Yemen War, and the 1967 and 1973 wars. Agriculture occupies an important position in the economy, providing 62 percent of export earnings. Industrialization has played a dominant role in development strategy since 1957.

I. SOCIAL SERVICES WITH DIRECT CONTRIBUTION TO ECONOMIC DEVELOPMENT

Services in this category include those industries in the land reclamation scheme, vocational training centers, family planning efforts, and the productive family program.

Social Services Within Industry

In 1952, industry was essentially private. This was gradually superseded by government control throughout the early and mid-sixties. At present, there are nine public sector organizations responsible for about 160 companies. The companies are grouped according to similarity of industrial undertaking. Government policy for industrial development focuses on import substitution and export promotion of manufactured items. Problems affecting the realization of this policy include the low quality of consumer goods available for internal consumption, and the low productivity among certain important export industries. Several factors contribute to these problems: manpower deficiencies at the lower and middle levels, poor maintenance of machines, scarcity of technicians, lack of research, and the social attitudes of the industrial working class.[14] It is particularly in relation to the last factor that social services within industry can make a contribution to increased productivity.

As part of the social welfare program within the industrial sector, social services aim at raising the productivity of laborers by assisting the worker in adjusting to the factory, and by raising the standard of living for workers and their families.

Most social welfare programs are established by legislation, and apply to all industrial firms. The programs include forbidding arbitrary wage fixing; setting minimum wages; limiting working days; and insuring against hazardous conditions, illness, death, and old age. Factories in remote areas must provide housing and transportation facilities. Factories hiring 100 females or more have to establish a day care center. Working mothers also get a leave of one hour daily to feed their babies.

Social services as defined in this chapter vary according to the size of the firm, the type of industry, the strength of the labor union branch, and the average worker's salary. In general, such services cover the following areas:

(1) Receiving new workers and introducing them to the work community, including informing them about work regulations, responsibilities and privileges, and available services.

(2) Keeping a record for each worker, including a brief summary of his social background, work history, and patterns of behavior inside the factory such as his punctuality, productivity, and promotions.

(3) Organizing group meetings with departments to discuss work problems and to strengthen relationships on different levels.

(4) Organizing social and sports groups and helping them carry out various recreational and cultural activities, including picnics, summer camps, festivals, and conferences.

(5) Helping to coordinate the work of different structures within the firm, including the labor union, the unit of the Arab Socialist Union, and the administrative committees.

(6) Providing casework services to workers referred by various departments because of absenteeism, accident proneness, low productivity, and other individual problems. Such services are also provided to workers and their families in cases of sickness and hospitalization.

(7) Helping to organize literacy classes and encouraging workers to join and continue to attend.

(8) Determining eligibility of workers for financial assistance or loans given by the labor union or special funds.

In firms with housing for their workers, the social worker helps to establish eligibility for an apartment. The social worker helps tenants adjust to the new environment. In factories operating a day care center, the social worker has overall responsibility for the service, assisted by one or two aides.

In theory, all workers are eligible for any available social service. When demand is greater than supply, each firm establishes conditions for receiving the service. The services of disseminating information, receiving new workers, and keeping records apply to all workers. Participation in social groups is usually limited to younger age groups, 20 to 30 years old. The demand for financial assistance or loans is usually greater than funds can cover. The social worker then studies the case of each applicant and decides eligibility on the basis of need. Because of the pressures of work, social workers usually cannot provide help for workers with personal or family problems.

In a study of social services in the El-Nasr Company for Automobile Manufacturing, it was found that about 70 percent of the workers benefit in one way or another from social services, and that financial assistance covers 59 percent of those who apply. Sixty percent participate in recreational activities.[15] These figures represent the situation in most other companies.

To finance welfare services in the industrial sector, the law requires an allocation of 15 percent of the net profit from each factory. Ten percent has to be paid for national programs to the Central Department of Social Services within the Ministry of Industry. The additional 5 percent is used for local programs. As for the insurance system, the employer contributes 3 percent of the worker's salary to cover medical treatment or rehabilitation for work-related injuries. Workers contribute 8 percent of their salaries, and the employer contributes 14 percent of salaries paid for insurance against death, old age, or incapacitating illness. For insurance against unemployment, the worker pays 1 percent of his salary, and the employer pays 2 percent of salaries paid. Unemployment compensation covers a maximum of 28 weeks.

Units in factories providing direct services to laborers are called social work sections, personnel departments, or industrial relations offices. The social worker in any of these structures is not necessarily called a social worker. He may be called a public relations officer or a personnel specialist. The Central Department of Social Services within the Ministry of Industry is responsible for the overall policy and planning of services. Social service personnel are appointed and promoted according to national regulations for civil service employees. The private sector of industry is not using social workers at this time.

No effort has been made either within the factory or on a wider level to evaluate the services' effectiveness. Very few social workers systematically record their activities. Although the basic assumption is that social services contribute to satisfactory work relations and to the improvements of social attitudes, both of which should lead to higher productivity, no research has been done to demonstrate this. Apart from those services prescribed by legislation, planning for various programs does not depend on studies of need or adequate data. A recent research study emphasized the need for a continuous assessment of social services to help planning. Among the important recommendations of this study were:

(1) Better training for social workers in the industrial sector.

(2) Special budget for the social service system, separate from welfare budget.

(3) Involvement of the workers in planning social services.

(4) Improvement of the standards of services to encourage wider participation.

(5) Education of the community about the role of the social service system in industry.[16]

Social Services Within the Reclaimed Areas

Agriculture dominates Egypt's economy. The main objectives for agricultural development are the attainment of maximum land productivity, self-sufficiency in food commodities, diet improvement, higher farm income, a reduction of imports, and an increase of exports of agricultural products. To achieve these objectives, the government emphasizes three main areas:

(1) Expansion of production through land reclamation and irrigation schemes.

(2) Expansion of production through greater use of fertilizers, improved seed, pest control, and diversification of production.

(3) Improvement of institutions, including better credit facilities, research training, modernization of farm management, mechanization, and marketing.[17]

Though initial returns from land reclamation are low, alternatives are limited. The government is allocating L.E. 86 million for land reclamation under the current ten-year plan. This provides for the investment of some L.E. 1,000 million to increase agricultural production by 50 percent. The target is to reclaim 604,000 feddans (one feddan equals 1.038 acres) for 60,000 families or 300,000 persons. Social services in relation to agricultural development are particularly significant as a component of the Land Reclamation Scheme.

The already reclaimed new communities are distributed in eleven zones, divided into farms of about 5,000 feddans each. There are central villages where various welfare programs are offered. For each village of about 200 houses, there is an agricultural cooperative society for every 200 families; relevant health and educational facilities, including schools, health units, and clinics; and social services.[18]

The social service system in new communities aims at accelerating the adjustment of the settlers and their families, and at creating a social milieu which can maximize their economic production. To achieve this, the Egyptian Authority for Formation and Development of New Communities has established a variety of social services, including day care centers, vocational preparation classes, rural women's clubs, youth clubs, girls' workshops, and community development associations.

Day care centers serve children three to six years old of both settlers and employees of the Authority. A nominal fee of 50 piastres is paid by the family. The center is used to care for the child, and to teach the mother better child care. The vocational preparation program includes literacy classes, and helps children out of school to prepare for work.

The rural women's club is a gathering place for mothers, offering home economics classes, nutrition information, health education, and child care information. Group work services are provided through youth clubs and recreational activities. Girls' workshops usually include knitting and sewing classes for girls 10 to 20 years old. The Community Development Association works through various citizens' committees with the help of the social worker. The committees study community problems, formulate plans, and participate with the Authority in carrying out these plans.

In addition to helping settlers benefit from the above services, social workers in the Authority play an important role in the following areas:

(1) Selection of families immigrating to new communities.

(2) Acquainting selected immigrants with living conditions awaiting them in the new communities, through home visits and group meetings.

(3) Helping immigrant families during their first weeks in the new environment. This includes assistance in getting children to school and information on how to utilize services.

Social workers also play an important role in discovering leaders in the community, in involving these leaders in various activities, and in devising training facilities for the refinement of their leadership skills. Casework services are provided whenever family or individual problems arise.

All settlers are eligible for these social services. They are encouraged to use them as long as they are living in the community. Girls' training programs and boys' vocational preparation classes take two years to complete. Girls' and boys' workshops accommodate about 30 percent of the relevant population. Day care centers serve only about 20 percent of the eligible children. About 60 percent use the services of the youth clubs, and women's clubs serve about 30 percent of the eligible population.

The Egyptian Authority for Cultivation and Development, part of the Ministry of Land Reclamation, has overall responsibility for all activities in reclaimed areas. On the national level, the Authority, headed by a general director, is divided into seven departments, including the Department for Community Development. This department has three divisions: the resettlement of immigrants, the administration of social welfare programs including social services, and research. The Department outlines policies and plans for the social service system in each project. On the zone level, the same three divisions are represented, and each zone supervises the implementation of services within its domain of about seven to thirteen productive units. Each unit of two to seven villages is headed by a social worker responsible for coordinating work within the unit. In addition to the coordinator of services, villages receive direct services.

The social service system of the Land Reclamation Scheme is financed through two channels: the budget of the Ministry of Land Reclamation, and allocations from ministries to their own units serving the area, such as the MCH of the Ministry of Health or the clubs of the Ministry of Youth. Meanwhile, the World Food Program (WFP) of the United Nations contributes indirectly to the financing of the system. From 1970-1974, WFP has provided commodities worth $45 million to the Land Reclamation Authority. Savings to the Authority, as a result of using food as part of wages, are used in buildings for various services. The United Nations Children's Fund (UNICEF) has also contributed about $1 million in equipment, supplies, and training facilities to the social service system.

Social workers in the reclaimed areas are either employed by the Land Reclamation Authority as directors or coordinators of productive units, or are employed by the ministries providing services. The United Nations Development Programme (UNDP) has assisted the government in establishing a training center for workers in resettlement areas. Special courses are organized by the Center for Social Workers. Six courses, serving 635 social workers, were organized during 1972.

Until recently, no adequate recording system had been established to achieve an objective assessment of the social service system. In 1973, a statistical guide was issued showing the number of service units working in various villages. There is no information, however, about the number of beneficiaries of certain programs, such as youth clubs or vocational preparation classes. The Community Development of the Ministry is trying to build a system to assess the effectiveness of services.

Few studies have been undertaken, and these were not limited to the social service system. An evaluation of WFP assistance (made in 1972) included an assessment of social services. Another study was undertaken to understand the role of settlers in the Community Development Associations. A research project of the Social Research Centre of the American University in Cairo is producing a study entitled "Rehabilitation Process in the Newly Settled Communities in the North Western Delta." One part of the study, which is not yet completed, investigates the functioning of the Community Development Association, leadership, popular participation, community solidarity, and decision-making on a community level. A survey of sociological factors in family planning is also being undertaken by the Social Research Centre.

Vocational Training and Preparation

Social services within this sphere are rendered as part of the Labor Offices' activities within the Ministry of Manpower and Labor, or as part of the vocational preparation classes of various ministries. The Labor Office is the unit of the Ministry of Labor giving direct service to local communities. Besides observing the application of work legislation by different production units, the local Labor Offices carry out special programs for vocational training. The offices help unemployed youth 18 to 30 years old to get training in factories and workshops. The program is called "Learn and Earn" because trainees get a nominal wage (10 piastres a day) from employers as an incentive during training. Trainees are usually employed in the same factory after completion of training. Social workers carry out surveys to discover training opportunities in each locality. They also follow up on trainees until they get employment. One pilot project has also been started on an experimental basis in one of the Labor Offices, giving vocational counselling to applicants before placing them in factories.

Applicants for training have to be unemployed residents of the geographical area served by the Labor Office. The training period is determined by each production unit according to the skill required. Training facilities are far below demand since the service covers about only 10 percent of those requiring it. The program is planned on a national level, and the relationship between the Ministry of Labor, units or production, and trainees is specified by the law. The program is administered locally, however, through the Labor Offices in various districts. The Department of Labor in each governorate bears the administrative costs of the program, including salaries of social workers and incentives to the trainees through appropriations from the Ministry of Manpower. Social workers work in direct service and on higher levels according to civil service regulations on appointment and promotions.

Assessment of procedures or evaluation is not carried out on a regular basis. Offices keep records of registered applicants, number of trainees, and training opportunites.

Vocational preparation classes aim at helping school dropouts acquire knowledge and skills to enable them to compete in the labor market. Besides skill classes, trainees attend programs designed to impart social and general knowledge and to help them acquire proper work attitudes. Social workers in the program help in selecting trainees, and organize various group work activities for them. They also provide casework services whenever necessary. Children 12 to 18 years old are eligible for the program. Applicants have to pass a reading examination and a medical checkup. A selection committee includes the director of the vocational preparation center, selected instructors, and the head of the village council in rural areas. Training courses take nine to fifteen months. The number of those served by the program includes a very high percentage of school dropouts.

The National Committee for Vocational Preparation is the national structure responsible for the policy and overall plan of the project. The Committee is chaired by the Minister of Social Affairs and includes under-secretaries of state for the Ministries of Education, Youth, Social Affairs, Industry, and Agriculture, and other national experts. Departments on the governorate level supervise the program within the regions. Units are located within schools, social agencies, or youth centers, depending on the sponsoring ministry. Each six workshops constitute one center of vocational preparation headed by a director.

The service is free for all trainees, and each ministry is responsible for the administrative costs of its program. UNICEF has an agreement with the three ministries, through which they receive equipment and transportation for supervisory purposes. The head of each unit is a professional social worker with a B.A. in sociology, social work, or physical education. Several complaints have been expressed about training content and equipment, but no study has been carried out to assess the situation.[19] The real problem with the vocational preparation classes is lack of coordination between the program, which does not really turn a trainee into a skilled laborer, and the Ministry of Labor's "Earn and Learn" program. The original plan was to use those who finish vocational preparation classes as trainees for the other "Earn and Learn" program, which is more advanced. The link has not been established.

Family Planning Services

The population of Egypt, about 33.4 million, has been increasing at an annual rate of about 2.5 percent during the past five years. Nearly 45 percent of the population is under 15 years of age, and 3.5 percent is above 64 years of age. Only 51.5 percent of the population is of working age, resulting in a heavy burden on the economy of the country.

A population policy was adopted by the Egyptian Government in 1962, and a national family planning program was started in 1965. Social workers within the program promote family planning education, encourage women to use the service, and follow up on cases of dropouts. Although the concept of family planning includes spacing of children and treatment of sterile parents, it is usually used in a narrower sense to mean reducing family size.

All married couples 14 to 45 years old are eligible for the service. A medical examination is performed before specifying the type of contraceptive to be used. Despite efforts to encourage the use of contraceptives, only 14 percent of the eligible population is using the service, according to 1972 statistics.

The Supreme Council for Family Planning is the national structure with responsibility for the program. The Council is headed by an executive and by a secretariat composed of the Ministers of Health, Local Government, and Social Affairs. Through its departments, the Council draws up the national plan and supervises its implementation; coordinates efforts in the field and organizes training courses for personnel of family planning units; and conducts and encourages research related to the problem.

On the governorate level are the Executive Bureau and the Governorate Committee for Family Planning. Great overlap exists between the two. The Bureau is the link between the Council and the Governorate Committee. It provides contraceptives to the clinics and reports on the activities of family planning in the governorate to both the Council and the Governorate Committee. Staff of the Bureau, consisting of medical, social, and religious personnel, supervise the work of the clinics. The Governorate Family Planning Committee is headed by the governor and includes the heads of departments of ministries on the governorate level: Health, Education, Social Affairs, Information, and Religious Affairs. It also includes a representative of the Arab Socialist Union, the director of the Executive Bureau, and two interested leaders. The functions of the Governorate Committee include: following up and supervising the program in the governorate; finding solutions to difficulties which may face the program; planning the program on the regional level; and reporting on the program and carrying out studies on the local level. On the local level, there are family planning clinics working through various organizations, including maternal and child health centers, health offices, hospitals, combined units, and rural health units.

The above structure parallels that of the Egyptian Family Planning Association. The Association coordinates the work of the voluntary social agencies in this field within the general policy and plan of the Supreme Council for Family Planning. The Association has 22 branches all over the country. Each branch is registered as an independent entity and is responsible for supervising the work of the family planning clinics run by social agencies within its geographical area.

The Egyptian Family Planning Association, as a national structure, has the following functions:

(1) It plans family planning activities for voluntary social agencies within national policy.

(2) It encourages voluntary efforts to carry out family planning programs, gives technical and financial assistance to such programs, and helps coordinate them.

(3) It follows up, supervises, and evaluates the activities of its branches, helps them in carrying out their work, and undertakes related studies and research.

(4) It organizes training courses for personnel and board members of voluntary agencies working in the field.

The family planning program in Egypt is financed through various channels. Appropriations in the national budget are provided through both the Ministry of Health and the Ministry of Social Affairs. The United Nations, including UNFPA, UNDP, and UNICEF, contributes to the budget. The Egyptian Association for Family Planning gets about L.E. 100,000 as an annual subsidy from the Ministry of Social Affairs. The Association gives grants to clinics operated by voluntary social agencies through governorate branches. Intrauterine devices are inserted free, and oral contraceptives are sold at a reduced price to users. The proceeds are distributed among the medical and para-medical personnel. Not all centers, however, have used such an incentive system for employees. The system is being reviewed because it encourages the distribution of pills without a doctor's prescription. It also encourages first insertions of the loop and new cases, at the expense of follow up and general care.[20]

Each clinic reports monthly on its activities to the regional branch. The branch reviews, reports, and gives a summary evaluation of the activities within the region to the national Association. The work of the clinics is also evaluated according to various criteria, including the number of contraceptives distributed and the per capita costs.

The Association carries out comparative studies on clinics, describing variations in number of cases, type of location, and efficiency of personnel. KAP surveys are carried out in different communities to estimate the impact of the program. Other related research, on attitudes and behavior in the governorate of Menoufia, has been carried out by the Social Research Center of the American University in Cairo. The Center is also participating in action research in the inner city of Cairo with the Family Planning Association of the Ministry of Social Affairs. This special research focuses on the training of social workers for family planning services. Studies have also been done on the characteristics of persons who accept the family planning concept and on dropouts. Several studies were undertaken to find out important variables related to the size of the family, particularly women's employment.[21]

The Productive Family Scheme

This scheme aims at helping members of the family who are unemployed or underemployed to use their time productively. With loans, and sometimes training, many families are able to start a small enterprise. Families apply either to the Social Affairs Office in the district or to any of the voluntary social agencies participating in the scheme. A social worker studies the case and determines eligibility on the basis of need for extra income and ability to participate. Eligible applicants work out with the agency the type of enterprise they can undertake. They may be referred, if necessary, to training centers affiliated with the scheme. Families receive appropriate tools, machines, and raw materials, and social agencies help in marketing the product. After one year, families pay back the loan in installments as profit allows. The number of families participating in the program has increased from 18,040 in 1969, to 34,291 in 1971. Because of limited funds, only about 40 percent of the eligible applicants are accepted to join the scheme.[22]

The project is carried out on the district level by selected voluntary social agencies. The Productive Families Organization on the governorate level coordinates work within each region with the help of the Department of Social Affairs of the governorate. The Ministry of Social Affairs has overall responsibility through a special department. The scheme is financed almost completely by the Ministry of Social Affairs from the national budget. The Ministry of Local Government contributes about 1 percent and voluntary agencies about 7 percent of the costs.

Personnel at the direct service level are social workers affiliated with the voluntary agencies. Supervisors either on the district or on the regional level are recognized as social workers, but they do not necessarily have academic qualifications. Each agency keeps records on the project participants, types of projects, and the status of returning loans. A yearly report is submitted to the Productive Family Organization on the governorate level as to the quality and quantity of work done. The Ministry of Social Affairs gives information about the number of families participating in the project in its yearly statistical report.[23]

II. SOCIAL SERVICES WITH INDIRECT CONTRIBUTION TO ECONOMIC DEVELOPMENT

Services within this category include those in the youth sector, those in the health sector, day-care centers, and community development projects.

Social Services for Youth

Youth is of major concern to the government for the following reasons:

(1) Youths constitute about 40 percent of the total population, and they have the energy which, if well directed, can contribute immensely to national development.

(2) Youth is the period between dependency and independent adulthood. The degree of maturity one acquires depends on socialization during adolescence and early adulthood.

(3) In a developing country such as Egypt, where development depends largely on human resources, the preparation of this group is crucial in achieving goals.[24]

Social services for youth aim at providing social conditions to help them develop their potential. Such development will enrich their personal lives, on the one hand, and ensure their participation in realizing development goals, on the other hand. To achieve this, programs are designed for youth in urban and rural areas, whether in schools, factories, or in independent centers.

Social services in schools started in 1949 when a group of graduates of the Higher Institute of Social Work were appointed to positions in a number of secondary schools. Using casework, group work, and community work, they try to achieve the following objectives:

(1) To help students form healthy relationships with teachers, colleagues, and the administration to maximize their educational opportunities.

(2) To help discover the students' abilities and to refine them through extra-curricular activities.

(3) To help students solve problems which affect their educational achievement.

Community work in schools includes programs to link the school with the community, such as involving students in cleanup campaigns or encouraging them to volunteer in community agencies. The student union participates in planning these programs and cooperates with the parents' association. On the group level, students are encouraged to join hobby groups, picnics, and camps. The students' union is used to train students in election procedures and in democratic forms. It is also used to identify and develop leaders. Students are encouraged to establish and run consumer cooperative societies to acquire qualities needed for team work. Sport teams are used to train students in various positive social qualities.

School clubs are opened during the summer vacation to provide a variety of social and sports activities. On the individual level, the social worker contacts students who may encounter special difficulties. He may refer cases to outside agencies, or he may be able to offer them service in the school. Financial and casework services are provided.

The services described above are available in schools on all levels, primary, preparatory, and secondary. Services for university students include hobby and sports groups, camping, and organizing community projects. A special program for spending summer vacations abroad is also available.

All students are eligible for services, and they are encouraged to make free use of them. The number of students on the university level who have benefited from one service or another amounted to 49,425 students in 1972, about 20 percent of the total university student body. No statistics for the number of beneficiaries of social services in primary, preparatory and secondary levels are available, but it is estimated that about 60 percent of students use such services.

Social services for youth in rural areas outside schools include a number of projects. The skill development experiment involves rural youth in agricultural projects to give them experience acquiring proper attitudes and knowledge. A farm is used to train youth in agricultural techniques, rural industries, marketing, poultry raising, and dairy techniques. With the help of the social worker, trainees organize different cultural and social programs. Villages selected for this program have to be near an agricultural unit and a youth center with an active social worker. To be eligible to join the program, youths have to meet the following criteria: they must live in the village, be members of the youth center between 15 and 25 years old, have finished the sixth grade, and attend a training course with success on the final examination.

The project is carried out by the Ministry of Youth, with the cooperation of the Ministry of Agriculture and Land Reform. The Ministry of Youth, with its departments on the governorate level, has the overall responsibility for the project in terms of policy-making and financing. The departments select social workers and indigenous leaders who act as directors for the farms. They also organize training courses for the participants, follow up the experiment, and evaluate results to modify planning accordingly. The Ministry of Youth will plan the application of the experiment on a national level if it is successful. The Ministry of Agriculture participates, through its local centers, in the training courses, especially the agricultural ones. The ministry provides equipment, animals, and poultry, and supervises the technical aspects of the project. It also participates in the assessment and evaluation of results. The two participating ministries are responsible for the preparation of publications and for organizing recreational activities and exhibitions for marketing products. The overall budget for one farm amounts to L.E. 10,000.

Another project organizes rural youth volunteers to plan and implement public projects for their villages. Such projects may include filling swamps, levelling roads, planting trees, or organizing literacy classes. The Ministry of Youth formulates the overall policy for the project and a committee on the governorate level plans implementation. The committee, headed by the Director of the Youth Department, includes heads of other departments. The committee decides the types of community projects in different villages in the governorate and defines the role which agencies play in these projects. The committee follows up projects and evaluates results. The volunteers' village office, headed by a social worker, carries out the project on the local level. The office studies the needs of the community and decides priority among projects to be undertaken. It specifies criteria for selecting volunteers and plans areas for voluntary work.

The social worker, as the head of the volunteers' office, is assisted by a committee including the head of the health office, the head of the agriculture center, the cooperatives' specialist, and selected teachers. The Department of Youth on the governorate level supervises the work of the office and appoints its social worker. The budget of the whole project comes from the Ministry of Youth through its governorate departments.

Social services for out-of-school youth are also provided through youth centers in both rural and urban areas. Besides sports, the centers organize work camps, picnics, and various other social and cultural activities. All activities are used as tools to assist members in acquiring relevant social attitudes and forming healthy relationships with others. Youths 12 to 30 years old are eligible to use the services of the centers. They pay a nominal fee for the services. There are 1,685 youth centers in the country serving about 817,970 young people. This number represents about 15 percent of those eligible for the service. Each center is staffed with a social worker, a physical training specialist, and sports trainers.[25]

The Council for Youth and Sports is the national structure

responsible for planning the social service system serving youth. The Department of Youth Welfare in the Ministry of Higher Education is responsible for implementing policy for students at the university level. Offices for youth welfare within university departments provide direct services to the students. The Department of Youth Welfare in the Ministry of Education is responsible for implementing policy towards students in schools below the university level. The Department is assisted by a number of committees responsible for different programs. For example, there is a committee for cooperatives, for student unions, and for school clubs. The Department of Education on the governorate level supervises the programs within the region, and the social work offices in the school provide direct services to students. Services within schools or universities are financed by the Ministry of Education through its departments on the governorate level. The Council of Youth pays subsidies for certain activities such as school clubs and summer camps. Although education is free through the university, students pay a nominal fee for social services each year.

Departments of Youth on the governorate level are responsible for planning and supervising programs for non-student youth. Youth centers are the local units which provide direct services. The follow-up system for these services is well planned. Each local unit has to submit a report, including statistical information about the participants in various activities. The report also includes qualitative data about the programs, groups, and the community. The report gives data about plans, expenditures, problems, and new needs. The Department of Youth in the governorate keeps records for each local unit, including information submitted by the unit itself and reports on the supervisors' periodical visits. Each department submits a summary report of the activities within the region to the Planning Department of the National Council of Youth twice a year.

Several studies have been undertaken within the youth sector. The important ones are:

(1) The relationship between sports activities and social attitudes, published by the Council for Youth and Sports, 1968. The study pointed out that types of sports vary in their contribution to desired social attitudes. Accordingly, priority should be assigned to sports with a maximum contribution.

(2) Priority needs among university students, published by the Council for Youth and Sports, 1970. The results pointed out needs within different

areas and emphasized the relationship between family problems and students' academic achievement.

(3) Membership in youth centers, published by the Council for Youth and Sports, 1966. The study helped define factors related to participation in centers' activities. The study emphasized members' roles in planning activities and the importance of keeping records for members and activities.

Social Services Within the Health Sector

Social services were introduced in the Ministry of Health in 1948, when the first social worker was appointed to the University Hospital of Cairo. In 1953, a special department for Social Health was established within the Ministry with 15 social workers. After the reorganization of the ministry in 1961, the number of social workers amounted to 1,200.

Social service within this sector aims at creating health awareness among the population in order to reduce mortality and morbidity and maximize health and productivity. To achieve such objectives, the following services are provided:

(1) Health education programs as a component of the services of MCH centers, hospitals, family planning clinics, and other health units.

(2) Casework services to citizens and their families to help them utilize, and benefit from, various health services, and the organization of recreational activities for patients.

(3) Cooperation with different structures inside and outside the organization to solve citizens' problems and raise the standard of services.

(4) Provision of free medical supplies when needed.

Except for the last service, efforts are made to cover the whole population, particularly in health education programs. When medical supplies are needed, the patient has to provide documents showing his inability to pay. A special committee within the district hospital, consisting of the director of the hospital, the social worker and two other staff members, determines eligibility.

The social service system in the health sector functions on three levels. The Department of the Medical Social Services within the Ministry of Health is responsible for policy and planning. There is a special section for social services within the Department of Health on the governorate level. Each section is headed by a director and assisted by three supervisors. On the local level, each health unit has an office for social services with at least one social worker. The ministry allocated L.E. 10,300 for social services in 1972, besides L.E. 41,700 for supplies for students. During 1972, 793,670 people of various groups were served.

Recently, a questionnaire has been designed to obtain information from patients about services. Results are discussed twice a year by a special committee consisting of heads of departments of health on the governorate level, and supervisors and heads of social service departments. Efforts are made to use the results in planning and modifying services. Part of a study of the existing health system considered the role of social workers in health units. A group of specialists from the health and social field constructed a manual for social workers which helps identify their roles in hospitals, health clinics, and MCH centers.

Nurseries

Nurseries in urban areas are usually established to care for children of working mothers during their absence from home. In rural areas, the problem is not so much the absence of the mother as it is the mother's inadequate socialization. The nursery is used there to provide adequate care for the child and to educate his mother. Children in day nurseries are accepted from three to six years old, if they pass the medical examination. The child learns some basic lessons about reading and arithmetic, but most of his time is spent in playing under supervision. Most day nurseries provide a meal for the child, while others require the child to bring his own food. Children are supposed to be checked daily by a nurse to avoid spread of diseases, but this is not the case for all nurseries. Some nurseries have transportation facilities, while others expect the mother to bring the child every morning and pick him up at noon. There are 1,020 nurseries in the country, 13 of which are residential. The service covers about 51,341 children, or 5 percent of those eligible for the service. It has been estimated that Cairo alone needs 595 new nurseries.[26]

Nurseries are administered either by voluntary agencies, by the Ministry of Education, or by individuals as private business. It was not until recently that the Ministry of Social Affairs issued a law regulating the establishment and administration of nurseries and requiring certain standards as to physical facilities and staff qualifications.

Nurseries which are administered by voluntary social agencies get subsidies from the Ministry of Social Affairs. Others depend on fees paid by the family of the child. Few nurseries are completely free, and these are financed by the Ministry of Social Affairs. Staffing varies greatly from one nursery to the other. The director of the nursery may have training in education, or may not have any acknowledged training or degree. Supervisors and workers may have no formal qualifications or may be graduates from the Intermediate Institute of Social Work. Records as to the number of children are not accurate for some of the nurseries. The ministry is undertaking a survey of the service to find gaps in the services and plan accordingly.

Community Development Projects

Until very recently, community development projects were mostly undertaken in the rural areas. The objective of these projects is to involve the people in making the decisions which affect their own lives. A combined social unit is the major structure carrying out these projects. Each unit consists of a health unit, an agriculture extension office, a primary school, and a social section including a day care center, a youth club, and girls' training classes. There are 327 combined social units in the country and 863 units are projected in the Ten Year Plan. Each unit serves 15,000 people, and is operated by the villagers themselves through a number of committees. They study community problems, plan for them, and contribute to implementation with money, work, and follow-up. In some villages, the unit has been able to activate the villagers to build schools, dig canals, fill swamps, and finance various needed services. Recently, three governorates began establishing urban development offices to experiment with projects of community development in urban slums. The governorate, through its sectoral departments and with the help of citizens of the communities, cooperates in outlining comprehensive plans to improve the slum. Citizens also participate in implementation of the plans at various stages.

The Ministry of Local Government is the body responsible for formulating the overall policies and plans for these community development projects. It also provides some finances. On the regional level, the governorates initiate these projects, assign staff to them and supervise the work. On the local level, the combined unit in the rural areas, or the social center in the slum, works directly with the citizens to plan and implement projects. Different ministries contribute indirectly to these projects by financing services within their own domain through their department in the governorate. UNICEF is assisting the Urban Development Project because of its interest in alleviating the consequences of the slum on the lives of children. Assistance is in the form of equipment, transportation, and technical advice.

Administrators of the program in the Ministry of Local Government, and supervisors on the governorate level, are professionals with agricultural education and experience in administration. Those carrying out projects on the local level and having direct contact with the citizens are social workers with degrees in social work and experience in the social field. The unit submits to the governorate data about the number of committees, volunteers, and the type of projects. No real supervision is given to these community development projects, and the degree of success in any of them depends to a large extent on the enthusiasm of the worker.

A number of research activities are undertaken in relation to these projects. The Ministry of Local Government has contracted with the National Academy for Research to carry out a survey and an evaluation of rural development programs to outline a comprehensive plan for developing the rural areas. The Ministry of Social Affairs is also carrying out an action research project in a selected number of villages to experiment with approaches to community development and citizens' participation. One social work dissertation has dealt with the issue of public participation in rural development projects, and has discussed characteristics of participants and their motivation to participate. The experiment in urban development involves keeping records as a means of evaluation, in addition to periodic reporting.

III. SOCIAL SERVICES TO SPECIAL GROUPS

Services of this category are particularly designed for high-risk groups in the population. Provision of such services shows that society can tolerate weakness and vulnerability and give support when needed. Services within this area cover children's residential institutions or foster homes, family counselling offices, social defense services, rehabilitation of the handicapped, and old age programs.

The overall responsibility for these services lies within the domain of the Ministry of Social Affairs. The administrative structure of the ministry consists of nine departments: social security, productive family, family and child welfare, rehabilitation of the handicapped, social defense, social development, voluntary agencies and coordinating councils, and two departments for services for veterans' families. Each department studies the needs within its area, formulates policy for services, and follows up the implementation of services. The department also reviews related legislation and carries out related research. The ministry has a special department for statistics and research with the following responsibilities:

(1) Keeping a general and continuous statistical register about the activities of the ministry and its divisions, and issuing periodical statistical reports.

(2) Designing statistical forms in collaboration with different departments, and investigating and analyzing results.

(3) Assisting the planning sections of the ministry in designing research projects and studies undertaken by these departments.

(4) Establishing a statistical library to provide technical departments with data needed for planning programs.

The Department of Statistics has three sections: the service section, which is concerned with data about types of services; the administrative section, which is concerned with data about the ministry's personnel; and the documentation section, with responsibilities related to publication of data and library work.

On the governorate level, the statistical unit within the Department of Social Affairs collects data on the various activities. The data is sent to the Statistics Department of the ministry. Heads of departments and of the statistical unit attend a special training course to understand the function of the unit.

On the local level, forms are filled in by social workers in offices of social affairs or in voluntary agencies. Forms are submitted to the governorate to be summarized in a governorate statistical report. No qualitative data is recorded. Except for social security and public assistance services, which are provided through the local social affairs offices in different districts, all other services are implemented through voluntary social agencies. As mentioned before, the work of these agencies is regulated by a law which specifies ways of establishing agencies, administrative procedures to be followed, and forms of relationship with the ministry. The ministry pays subsidies to the agencies and has great control over their boards of directors and the content of their work. The ministry supervises the work closely by appointing its personnel as board members, and by sending inspectors through its local offices of social affairs. Agencies use personnel with social work degrees on the direct service level. Because no qualifications were previously specified for social service personnel, the old employees now in supervisory positions or higher administrative posts do not necessarily have professional qualifications. The situation is changing now, and qualified social workers are being promoted to higher posts in agencies and in the ministry.

The budget of the Ministry of Social Affairs is a part of the national budget. The ministry allocates money for its departments on the governorate level to carry out pilot projects and to subsidize voluntary social agencies implementing services in the governorate. Voluntary agencies are also financed through contributions, fees for services, public campaigns, and selling lotteries.

The following is a summary of the major social services for special high-risk groups.

Residential Institutions for Children

Institutions of this type are established for children who either do not have families to live with, or who live in a damaging family atmosphere. There are 176 institutions serving 13,807 children over six years of age. The staff of the institution includes a social worker, a nurse, a part-time psychologist, teachers, and workshop instructors. Children receive social, vocational, and educational services. They are helped to get employment after learning relevant skills. Children return to their homes whenever their families are ready and able to have them. The social worker helps the child and his family in the adjustment process.

Institutions accept children six to eighteen years old from broken families, if they pass the medical examination. The child or his guardian applies to the institution on a special form. The social worker studies the case and reports to a special committee which reviews the applications and decides eligibility. The average period of stay is three years.

Foster Homes

The foster homes program is designed to provide a normal family life for illegitimate children, for children who cannot locate their families, and for orphans who lack adequate care. Families apply to participate in the foster care program. Social workers make a thorough study for each family to ensure a healthy atmosphere for the children. The study is submitted to a special committee on the governorate level to decide whether the family can provide adequate care. Families accepted in the program sign a contract periodically. Social workers also pay home visits regularly to the participant families. While some foster families get paid from the Department of Social Affairs, others provide the service free. According to 1972 statistics, 1,996 children were placed in foster families. Allowances for families range from 35 to 85 Egyptian pounds annually according to the age of the child. The maximum age at which children have to leave the family is 25 years old.

Family Counselling Offices

Family counselling offices run by voluntary social agencies provide casework services for families to help them solve social and psychological problems. The first office was opened in 1963, and there are now 35 offices in the country. Each office employs a social worker and a psychologist, and both help parents to improve the home atmosphere for the benefit of adults and their children. The office helps the civil court in studying cases of divorce. Theoretically, the offices should be organizing family education activities on the community level, but such a component is rarely found. Offices are financed through public contributions, in addition to subsidies from the Department of Social Affairs of the governorate. During 1972-1973, 4,392 families were served by the offices.

Services for the Aged

Services for the aged include, besides social security, residential care facilities. An aged person can apply to a residential institution if he or she is over 60 years of age with no relatives. A few institutions are completely free, while others require a monthly fee that ranges from 10 to 50 Egyptian pounds. Services provided by institutions include, besides the dormitory, health check-ups and medical care, meals, and recreational activities. Clients must be free from contagious or incapacitating diseases. Applications are reviewed by the board of the institutions to determine need on the basis of a social worker's case study. There are 26 institutions accommodating 1,329 cases. All these institutions are in urban communities. In rural areas, the aged are always considered important, and are cared for by members of the family. Although the number of the aged who need these institutions is far greater than those who are using the service, a need for more institutions has not been expressed. The service covers about 1 percent of those who need it. The Ministry of Social Affairs gives subsidies to the institutions through its departments on the governorate level.

Social Defense Services

Services in this area are regulated by the law, which has specified a minimum standard for health, educational, psychological, and social services provided to delinquents.[27] Programs for delinquents include a comprehensive social unit and reformatories. The former includes a reception center, an observation home, a social work office, and a hostel. When a youngster is brought to the police station for an offense, a social worker either talks to him or sends for his parents and warns them, allowing the youngster to go home. The case may be referred to a special attorney for delinquency; the latter may bring in the parents, give a reprimand and let the youngster go, or the case may be filed for the court.

Cases filed for trial are referred to the reception office, where an intake interview is done to determine the youngster's needs. The youngster is then referred to the observation home, where he stays until the date of trial. During this period (usually about one month), he is observed and studied by the staff, with the cooperation of the social work office. Interviews with the youngster and his family are undertaken to understand his problem and to plan for treatment. The observation home and the social work office also cooperate in the treatment process.

After trial, the youngster may be sentenced to a period in a reformatory, or he may stay in the hostel until his family is ready to receive him back. The treatment plan is continued in either case. The reformatories provide social, educational, psychological, and vocational training, and have various workshops where juveniles can be trained for handicrafts and small industries. The staff team helps in meeting the needs of every case and a placement officer helps in finding employment after release.

The National Committee for Social Defense is responsible for studying the problem, formulating overall policy, planning different services, and training those working in the field. During 1972, 12,748 cases were served through 24 units. Services cover all those who need them.

Rehabilitation Services

Rehabilitation services include programs for the blind, the deaf, the mentally retarded, the physically handicapped, and the aged. Critical developments have occurred in this area since 1952, and efforts have increased tremendously. Eighty organizations are working in this field. The principal ones are the Demonstration Center for the rehabilitation of the blind, the Kasr el-Aini Center for the physically handicapped, the Veterans' Rehabilitation Center, the Egyptian Association for the Deaf, and the Mental Retardation Center. All rehabilitation projects are staffed by a physician, a social worker, a psychologist, vocational specialists, a placement officer, nurses, and instructors.

The center for the blind includes a school where children can get a high school certificate, a braille printing house, a home teaching department, and a vocational department. There is also a sheltered workshop attached to the center.

The center for the physically handicapped has a special workshop for manufacturing prostheses and appliances, a boarding school, social and vocational services for children under 20 years of age, and a counselling office for adult cases.

All other centers and agencies provide a combination of physical, educational, social, and vocational training services. Clients obtain a special certificate upon completion of a rehabilitation course which qualifies them for work in industrial firms or in sheltered workshops. A vending stands project for the blind has been operating successfuly since 1955. A decree was issued in 1952 obliging industrial firms employing more than 50 workers to accept 2 percent of their work force from the rehabilitated handicapped.

Public services for the handicapped also include reduced transportation rates, tax exemption for certain materials, and priority in marketing their products. Several action research projects have been undertaken during the last five years to determine new comprehensive approaches for rehabilitating various types of handicaps.

SUMMARY AND CONCLUSIONS

Within the context of national development, the goals of the Egyptian social service system are to help create a social milieu to accelerate the process of development, to alleviate the problems which may accompany development, and to maximize the benefit to the masses of development. Although all social services help in one way or another to achieve these goals, some services contribute more directly and more effectively than others. Services to industrial laborers are, for example, meant to increase productivity and hence accelerate development, while urban community development projects help alleviate the problem of urbanization which usually accompanies industrialization. Medical social services help people to use health services more effectively.

Due to limited resources, priority should be given to those services making a direct contribution to the development process. In Egypt, however, policy makers, planners, and laymen still perceive the social service system as including only those services related to high-risk groups. Other services which contribute strongly to development are usually considered outside the social service system and, consequently, personnel involved in those services are not usually called social workers. To change this perception and to maximize the contribution of the social service system to development, the values and conceptual framework of the system have to be revised. An overall policy and plan for social services as an integral part of the national plan has to be outlined and translated into programs. The training of social workers must be made relevant to the tasks implied in these programs.

Some efforts have been made to discuss the conceptual framework of the social service system in terms of relevance to the Egyptian culture, its problems, and needs. More efforts are needed to decrease the influence of irrelevant western values on the system. Some of the social work principles that are taken for granted need to be tested, explained, modified, or qualified. Schools of social work can make a great contribution towards this end. Practitioners in various settings should also make use of their experience and systematize their experiences.

Although the social service system is fragmented among the Ministry of Social Affairs, other sectoral ministries, and the voluntary sector, an overall policy for the system should be outlined by one structure. There was some hope that the new National

Council for Social Services would be the responsible structure, but membership of the Council did not include any social workers. The Social Worker's Union is the most relevant existing structure available to crystallize the system's overall policy. To implement the overall policy and incorporate it within the national plan, an effort should be made to help planners perceive the social service as an asset to the development process and not as a burden. A cost benefit analysis for certain services would back the argument.

To outline an overall plan for social services, the Ministry of Planning will have to reorganize so that charity activities and social services will not be treated as one package, and parts of the social service system located within various ministries will be integrated in one plan. Budgets for financing social services within the functional ministries are not clearly specified. The amount spent depends to a great extent on the attitude of each minister towards social services. In some cases, where the minister has had a negative perception of the value of these services, almost no budget was allocated. To avoid this problem, costs of social services within different ministries should be specified clearly and spent accordingly.

The role of voluntary efforts in a socialist society such as Egypt is not completely clarified. The Ministry of Social Affairs needs to review its relationship with the voluntary agencies and should put more effort into encouraging voluntarism. Payment of subsidies to the agencies should not lead to domination of their boards and activities.

Training of social service personnel is a very important issue within the constraints imposed on schools of social work. These schools have made some achievements in adapting the curriculum to the problems and needs of the society. More efforts are needed to integrate methods of practice in dealing with problems within defined areas. More integration between the methods courses and the social sciences is needed. Students on the B.A. level can hardly make such an integration on their own. Opening courses for Master's and Doctorate studies will help raise the standard of practice and of teaching. It also gives hope for more scientific research.

NOTES

1. A. J. Kahn, *Social Policy and Social Services.* (New York: Random House, 1973), p. 19.

2. Ibid.

3. Ibid., p. 24.

4. Ibid.

5. *Ministry of Social Affairs Twenty-fifth Anniversary* (Cairo: Government Printing House Public Relations Information Service, 1964).

6. *Ministry of Social Affairs in Eleven Years, 1952-1963* (Cairo: Government Printing House, 1963).

7. *Charter of the United Arab Republic* (Cairo: Government Printing House, 1962), p. 46.

8. Ibid., p. 44.

9. Ibid., p. 70.

10. *National Working Programme* (Cairo: Government Printing Office, 1973).

11. *Official Paper of the Cabinet* 14, 23 (June, 1973), p. 243.

12. *Report* (Ministry of Higher Education Statistical Department, 1973).

13. "Training Workers in the Social Field," (Cairo: Ministry of Social Affairs, 1971).

14. "Country Programme Background Paper for the Arab Republic of Egypt," *United Nations Development Programme Publication* (Cairo, February, 1972), 30-32.

15. M. Tawfik, "Evaluation of Welfare Services in El-Nasr Company for Automobile Manufacturing," unpublished thesis (Cairo: Higher Institute of Social Work, 1972).

16. Ibid., pp. 495-561.

17. "Country Programme Background Paper," United Nations, 16-18.

18. "Development of New Communities," (Cairo: Egyptian Authority for Land Reclamation, Ministry of Agriculture, 1969).

19. "Vocational Preparation Classes," (Cairo: Ministry of Youth Public Relations Department, June, 1969).

20. H. Shanawany, "Management of an On-going Programme of Family Planning," paper presented to the Conference on Family Planning and National Development, organized by the Indonesian Planning Parenthood Association and the International Planned Parenthood Federation of Southeast Asia and Oceania Region, 1-7 June, 1969, p. 7.

21. *Plan of Action for the Second Year* (Cairo: National Council of Family Planning, 1972).

22. *Annual Report of the National Association of Productive Families* (Cairo: Ministry of Social Affairs, 1972).

23. Ibid.

24. M. A. Hashem, "Training of Professional and Voluntary Youth Leaders in the UAR," paper presented to the Inter-regional Seminar on Training of Professional and Voluntary Youth Leaders, Holte, Denmark, 1969.

25. *Report of the Council for Youth and Sports* (Cairo: Ministry of Youth, 1972).

26. *Al-Ahram,* 10 October 1971.

· 27. Hoda Badran, "Social Work Programmes in Egypt," *International Social Work Journal* 14:1 (1971): 13-16.

3

SOCIAL SERVICES IN GREAT BRITAIN: TAKING CARE OF PEOPLE

H. GLENNERSTER

THE TERM "SOCIAL SERVICES"

In Britain, the term "social services" generally includes all income maintenance provisions, medical care, and education provided through public agencies, public housing, and social work services including residential care facilities, whether publicly or privately provided. The Central Statistical Office excludes housing from its definition of social services, but academics who study social administration have usually included it. In Britain, then, the term has a very broad definition, approximately equivalent to the American term "social welfare." However, in recent years, following the example of a government committee of enquiry, we have come to adopt the term "personal social services."[1] This covers a range of activities which correspond more closely to the American category "social services." The addition of the adjective "personal" can scarcely be defended on logical grounds, but it is the label used throughout this chapter to avoid confusion with the broader term.

In 1972, the total public expenditure in the United Kingdom on social services, excluding housing, was £11,800 million. With the addition of public expenditures on housing, the total was £13,300 million.[2] This sum was equivalent to nearly 25 percent of the Gross National Product. A broadly comparable figure for the United States was 17.6 percent, according to the *Social Security Bulletin*.[3] Thus, these services are small in monetary terms when compared to education or the National Health Service.

STATUTORY AND VOLUNTARY SERVICES

Another distinction should be made at the outset—the difference between statutory and voluntary services. Although many of the present social services can be traced back to the work of charitable organisations in the nineteenth and early twentieth centuries, personal social services are provided today largely by various public agencies.

Since the United Kingdom is a unitary state, all local authorities and public agencies are the creations of Parliament and their powers and duties are specified by statute. No local authority can undertake any activity unless the specific power to do so is laid down in an act of Parliament. Not infrequently, these will be stated as duties, and if a local authority does not perform them, the central government can step in and undertake the functions itself. This has recently happened to one local authority in relation to its housing powers. In short, the term "statutory service" in Britain has a very precise and much stronger meaning than that implied by the more permissive grant-giving functions of the American federal government.

There are two kinds of statutory bodies responsible for the delivery of social services in Britain: elected local authorities and appointed bodies. Locally elected councils have a legal responsibility to exercise powers and duties delegated to them by Parliament. The relevant laws give the appropriate secretaries of state specific duties, which include overseeing the way in which local authorities are performing their functions. A secretary of state chosen by the Prime Minister becomes a member of the Cabinet and is responsible to Parliament for the work of his department. Those who are concerned with social services in England and Wales (Scotland has rather different arrangements) are:

(1) the Home Secretary, who is concerned with the Police Service, the Prison Service, the treatment of offenders, the Probation and After Care Service, and who has certain responsibilities for a small programme of community development;

(2) the Secretary of State for Health and Social Services, who is responsible for the National Health Service, the whole of social insurance and supplementary benefits, and personal social services;

(3) the Secretary of State for Education and Science; and finally,

(4) the Secretary of State for the Environment, who generally oversees local government and housing, town and country planning, and transport.

All of these individuals and their departments have the task of ensuring that the acts of Parliament concerning their fields are carried out effectively. This means that there are inherent tensions between secretaries of state responsible to Parliament and local councils responsible to local electorates. Although these tensions sometimes produce conflict, if not deadlock, for the most part they have been constructive. Local councils have brought innovation, pressure to expand services, and local commitment. However, in the end, a large element of control resides in the hands of the secretary of state, or more accurately, in those of his departmental civil servants.

The structure and boundaries of local authorities have recently undergone a radical change—the first major change since the basic pattern of local government was established nearly a century ago. The new councils took up their duties on April 1, 1974. Their responsibilities vary depending on the area they serve. The large urban-industrial regions with continuous built-up areas are called Metropolitan Counties, and their local authorities have overall town planning and transport powers, as does the Greater London Council. Within these metropolitan areas are Metropolitan Districts, which are responsible for providing education, housing, and personal social services. The pattern in London is somewhat similar, where the London boroughs provide personal social services.

Outside the urban regions, the pattern is quite different. Here the county councils, 47 in England and Wales, are responsible for the most important range of functions: planning, major highways, fire, police, education, and personal social services. However, they are not responsible for public housing. Thus, public health, minor roads, and other powers are the responsibility of district councils covering much smaller subdivisions of the counties. The precise internal organisation of local authorities is decided by each council. However, the normal pattern is that each divides its responsibilities among specialist committees. Increasingly, councils are adding a top-tier coordinating committee, usually called a "Policy and Resources Committee." However, councils are required to appoint certain committees. The 1970 Local Authority Social Services Act specified that the appropriate councils (now County and Metropolitan District councils) must appoint a Social Services Committee and a Director of Social Services. This latter individual is the principal officer responsible to the committee and the council for the work of the social services department (and whose powers we shall discuss in detail below). His appointment must be approved by the Secretary of State for Health and Social Services, who will look for a candidate with appropriate qualifications and experience.

With the exception of housing, there are no specific central government grants to local authorities for financing particular social service programmes in Britain. There is nothing equivalent to the U.S. federal government's matching grants for personal social services. Instead, the central government gives general support to local authorities' incomes, akin to the new revenue-sharing process in the United States. Local councils receive what is called a "Rate Support Grant." Rates are a local property tax, and virtually the only form of revenue available to local councils apart from central grants. This meets just over half of the councils' expenditures. An overall sum is fixed nationally, depending on the economic prospects. Once decided, this sum is then divided among local areas according to a complex formula based on the age and needs of the population. Areas with large numbers of children and the elderly, for example, receive larger sums than areas with smaller numbers. This income supplements a local council's revenue. It is spent on a wide range of activities, of which education takes the largest share. Personal social services must compete for resources with all the other specialist committees.

Quite distinct is the National Health Service, with a separate administrative structure and system of finance. Yet many of its functions overlap or are closely related to the personal social services. This system, too, has undergone a major reorganisation which also took effect on April 1, 1974. There are now 15 regional health authorities in Britain whose members are appointed by the secretary of state and who are responsible to him for regional health planning and resource allocation. Beneath these are area health authorities which are appointed by and responsible to the regional authorities. These areas are coterminous with the county and Metropolitan Districts which administer the personal social services. The Health Service is entirely financed by the central government. Hence, the degree of central control over resource allocation is very substantial.

These, then, are the two sets of statutory agencies provided by non-profit or charitable organisations, and, in some cases, by private profit-making concerns such as those which administer old persons' homes. The charitable or voluntary groups are often financed in part by public funds and their facilities may be subject to government inspection, but they are not statutory bodies created by Parliament.

They still, however, perform an important and changing role in the provision of social services.

Before attempting a detailed description of the delivery of social services, it will be helpful to glance back to the different strands in the development of these services which have come together to form the pattern of provision as we know it today. Many apparently odd features of and public attitudes toward the services themselves can only be understood from this perspective.

THE ORIGINS OF PERSONAL SOCIAL SERVICES

The Statutory Services

The origins of personal social services are disparate, but they may be grouped together to simplify matters. First, and most important, is the legacy of the Poor Law; second are the responsibilities placed on local authorities by successive Children's and Young Persons' Acts for the care and protection of children; third are the various powers and duties accumulated through health legislation, including that on mental health; and, fourth are the services related to correctional or law enforcement activities. These represent four overlapping historical patterns that have developed over at least a century and a half and which have fused only in this decade with the passing of the Local Authority Social Services Act in 1970.

The Poor Law Legacy. The most important statutory origins of the personal social services are the Poor Laws and, in particular, the 1834 Poor Law Amendment Act. Originally, local Boards of Guardians were responsible for the care of orphaned children, many of the elderly, the mentally and physically handicapped, the sick, and the able-bodied unemployed. Their responsibilities arose not from any special powers related to the needs of these groups but from an overall duty to provide for the destitute poor. However, the particular nature of that legislation established a threefold division in the system of welfare priorities that emerged after 1948. The first division is the emphasis placed on the provision of housing and public attitudes toward it. The Guardians were supposed to give relief to able-bodied adults only if they were prepared to give up their homes and live in the harsh environment of the workhouse. It was not until much later that they began to provide separate accommodations for groups such as the elderly and the sick, as distinct from the able-bodied unemployed. This was the beginning of specialised residential care, but it carried the stigma of pauperism. This administrative history has been a very real part of old persons' experiences and resulted in their attitudes toward "being sent into a home."

The legacy of the Poor Law extended beyond the powers to provide residential accommodation; it also left a number of large barrack-like Victorian buildings. Even as late as 1960 about half of all local authorities' accommodations for elderly persons consisted of old Victorian workhouses, almost all of which housed over 100 persons and the majority of which had over 250 beds each.

Paradoxically, the Poor Law was also responsible for the "splintering" of care (once monolithic) among separate departments. So great was the hostility toward the Poor Law that its functions were eventually divided in 1948 among children's departments. The provision of funds was transferred to a central government agency. The separation of cash aid from social work supportive services is part of this legacy. In the end, however, the stigma and the ethos remained. Even after 1948, those administering services, especially welfare services, continued to see this type of aid as a last resort.

Between 1948 and 1970 all of these aspects began to change. There was a growing emphasis on support at home rather than institutional care. While the stigma began to disappear, however, the fragmentation remained.

Protection and Care of Children. The parish, the Guardians, and public assistance authorities had major responsibilities for the care of illegitimate, orphaned, and neglected children until 1948.[4] However, at the end of the nineteenth century a second strand of legislation appeared as courts were given powers to prosecute parents for willful cruelty and to commit children to the care of "fit persons," including local authorities. In time, the local authorities also acquired powers to prosecute parents for neglect or ill-treatment.

Because of considerable criticism of the way in which local authorities were administering their powers and duties, the 1948 Children's Act gave statutory responsibility to a local authority Children's Committee and Children's Officer. These departments were intended to employ trained social workers, and the government set up a Central Training Council in Child Care to recognise and promote courses.

Health Services. The third broad area of statutory provision comes from health legislation which began with powers to treat infectious and contagious diseases and developed through health insurance to comprehensive care. This lies largely outside the scope of this article. In order to assist families and individuals in overcoming difficulties caused by ill health, and, in particular, to enable individuals to continue to be cared for at home, a number of domiciliary services have been developed. These include home nursing, health visitors, and domestic help for the sick, the disabled, and elderly, as well as social workers helping those suffering or recovering from some mental disorder, and hospital and psychiatric social workers employed by local authorities. Until very recently these services were provided by the health departments of local authorities or were adjunct hospitals.

Law Enforcement. Children who come before the courts after committing offences have always presented particular difficulties and required changing responses in terms of care and treatment. Reform and industrial schools in the nineteenth century, and later approved schools and community homes, have constituted a residential solution. Supervision at home is another response. Probation services, which received statutory recognition in 1907, became the first field of social work to require approved professional training.

In the early days, court missionaries did supervision for the court. They were attached to or worked for religious organisations. Their powers gradually extended to cover social enquiries for the court, matrimonial counseling, and after-care of ex-prisoners or those who had been at approved schools and Borstals. In 1925, probation committees, comprised of local justices of the peace (lay magistrates), were created to administer this service, as they still do. Training courses were begun following a committee of enquiry in 1936. Throughout, the Home Office has been the central government department responsible.

The Seebohm Reorganisation in England and Wales

These, then, were the four main strands of legislative development. Each gave rise to separate administrative arrangements. During the two decades following World War II, separate local departments and their committees of elected representatives were responsible for children's services, welfare services—mainly the residue of services left from the Poor Law—and health services. Education and housing departments also employed welfare workers, while hospitals em-

Table 1: Changing Organisational Structure for Statutory Personal Social Services in England and Wales, 1970-1974

Types of Social Services				Statutory Authorities Responsible		
Field Work	Residential Care	Day Care	Other Services	Pre-1971 Local Authority Committees	1971 to 1974 Local Authority Committee	April 1974 onwards Local Authority Committee
Preventive work with families	Reception centres for young offenders[a]		Advice centres	Children's	Social Services	Social Services
Receiving children into care, supervising children in care, finding foster homes and supervising foster parents, adoption work, work with offenders	Children's homes[a] Approved schools[a] Remand homes[a]		Financial and material help to children coming into care or before a juvenile court			
Domiciliary care of the elderly, the physically handicapped, teachers of the blind, deaf and dumb, work with problem families	Residential care for the elderly and disabled	Clubs for the elderly and handicapped	Meals on wheels, laundry service for the elderly, adaptions to houses for the aged and handicapped	Welfare		
Workers with mentally ill, social work with the after care of people suffering illness, home helps	Hostels for the mentally ill and mentally handicapped	Day nurseries, junior and adult training centres for the mentally handicapped		Health		

[76]

	Residential	Day care / clinics	Other			
Domiciliary care and education from health visitors, home nurses, midwives, occupational therapists, physiotherapists		Registering of child minders. Clinics and infant welfare centres, health centres	Family Planning		*National Health Service*	*National Health Service*
Education welfare officers, social workers in schools	Boarding schools, especially for the handicapped	Special day schools for handicapped	Youth service, child guidance clinics	*Education*	*Education*	*Education*
	Medical social work in hospitals. Psychiatric social work in hospitals			*National Health Service*	*National Health Service*	*Social Services*
Probation Officers	Probation Hostels			*Home Office and Probation and After care Committees*	*Home Office and Probation and After care Committees*	*Home Office and Probation and After care Committees*

a. These have been reorganised into a single system of community homes (see text).

ployed medical social workers. The probation service was separate. This pattern is set out in the fifth column of Table 1. Different aspects of a family's welfare were the responsibility of various statutory agencies. Despite professional and academic criticism of the situation, it did not really arouse political interest until concern with juvenile delinquency in the late 1950s led to the appointment of a committee of enquiry which made some hesitant and minor proposals about coordination.[5] The Labour Government in 1965 outlined more far-reaching proposals.[6] Further debate led to the appointment of another committee under the chairmanship of Frederic Seebohm. In 1968 this committee produced the Seebohm Report, proposing a major reorganisation in England and Wales.[7] (For the situation in Scotland, see below.) The functions performed by the Children's Departments, Welfare Departments, and many of the functions of the Health Departments were to be merged. The 1970 Local Authority Social Services Act enacted these recommendations, and the new departments came into operation in 1971. Those functions which became the responsibility of the new departments can be seen from Table 1; they will be discussed in more detail below.

Apart from these structural changes, the writers of the report hoped for a change of emphasis and philosophy which would make a final break with the legacy of the Poor Law. The new departments were to seek out those in need in order to stimulate demand for the services and, at the same time, to change former attitudes toward the department functions. This was not easily done, although, to their credit, many departments tried to comply with the proposed changes. One organisational change suggested in the report was that departments split their social work staff into area teams, each covering populations of 50,000 to 100,000 with easily accessible offices. This proposal has in fact been adopted in most places where accommodations can be found. These departments, therefore, represent the fusion of 140 years of legislative tradition. In what follows, then, we are providing a brief overview of a rapidly changing situation.

Scotland had undertaken a similar reorganisation two years earlier than England and Wales. The Social Work (Scotland) Act of 1968 gave certain local authorities in Scotland the responsibility of appointing social work committees and a director of social work. These authorities and the social service departments in England and Wales differ in that the Scottish authorities include the probation department.

The recent reorganisation has gone a long way toward placing most statutory personal social service functions under one administrative unit. Yet there are still significant areas where closely related services are offered by different authorities or departments.

The Voluntary Services

Most, if not all, statutory services owed a great deal to voluntary societies in their formation and continue to work closely with them in some fields. This is probably most true in the child-care field, where as many as a third of the places in children's homes are provided by voluntary groups (such as Dr. Barnardo's).

Many old persons' homes are provided by charitable organisations. However, the role of local authorities has steadily grown so that voluntary bodies now fill a residual role in terms of their share of the provision of services, although in many cases they are pioneering new kinds of care. It is in the care of the disabled that voluntary organisations have been most prominent in recent years, partly with new services, partly in offering help and advice, but more often acting as pressure groups pointing out deficiencies in existing services, pressing for the extension of legislation, or urging the implementation of existing powers. For example, the Disablement Income Group recently succeeded in persuading the government to introduce an allowance for those who look after disabled relatives.

Finally, there are a number of experimental and pioneering ventures and groups seeking to provide material aid and support. Perhaps the most important shift of emphasis in recent years has been the growth of organisations pressing the claims of neglected groups: handicapped children, disabled persons and their relatives, claimants for supplementary benefits, and homeless families. A colleague, Adrian Webb, has appropriately called this development "assertive self-help."

SERVICE PROVISIONS TODAY

The previous section has described the gradual fusion of different administrative systems and legislative traditions. This section begins from the standpoint of different social groups and the services provided for them. A caution on the word "service" is perhaps needed. Many statutory activities are not necessarily viewed as services by their immediate recipients. The probation officer is lucky if his work is viewed by the offender as a service. School children may not welcome the education officer's attentions, but we shall continue to call them services.

Services will be described under seven broad headings:

(1) care and protection of children and support for families;

(2) services for and work with adolescents and young persons;

(3) services for the elderly;

(4) care of the physically handicapped;

(5) care of the mentally ill and handicapped;

(6) work with the courts; and

(7) general work with communities and advisory activities.

In each case a brief description of the service available and those eligible is followed by some assessment of needs. The administrative structure, staffing, and financing of each group of services is described briefly under each heading, though the reader is advised to refer to Table 1. Education and training are discussed in a concluding section.

1. Care and Protection of Children and Family Support

Care and Protection of Children. Under various acts of Parliament, the new local social service departments safeguard the interests of four groups of children. First, there are children who are received into care because they are deprived of a normal home life. This may be either because the parents or guardians die or desert them, or because, for various reasons such as inadequate housing or home-lessness, their parents cannot look after them. Many children are taken into care for only short periods because the mother is either having another child or she is ill and there is no one to look after the family. In 1972, one-third of those under care were admitted for these reasons (see Table 2). One or both of the parents can apply for a child to be received into care, as can friends or relatives who look after the child. The child himself can apply, as can others such as the family doctor. There are no eligibility requirements except residence in that local authority. The social workers concerned have to be sure that there is no reasonable alternative, and whenever possible the child remains with his or her parents or relatives. The decision lies

Table 2: Why Children Were Taken into Care of Local Authorities During 1972, England and Wales (in percentages)

Reception into Care	
Abandoned or lost	0.8
Death of or deserted by mother;	
father unable to care	5.7
Incapacity of parent or guardian:	
Confinement	4.4
Short-term illness or incapacity	15.6
Long-term illness or incapacity	1.1
Child illegitimate: mother unable to provide	2.0
Parent or guardian in prison or in custody	0.9
Family homeless:	
Through eviction	1.2
Other reasons	1.8
Unsatisfactory home conditions	3.5
Committal to Care	
Care orders	9.6
Interim care orders	10.4
Other reasons	6.7
Total admissions to care	63.7

SOURCE: *Social Trends, 1973*

with the local authority. The local authority returns the child as soon as possible, and the parents can ask for the child's return (the local authority can only prevent this by a court order). Parents can visit the child, and the social worker must keep the parents informed about the child's progress. If the child is received into care and no other arrangements can be made, he or she will remain in care until 18 years of age. The parents, if there are any, must contribute to the cost of care until the child is 16, on a sliding scale related to their income. Children in care may be placed in residential community homes run by local authorities or voluntary organisations, or they may be placed in ordinary households, with foster parents who are specially chosen by the authority's social workers and are paid a contribution to cover the cost of maintenance. The amount varies among local authorities. Roughly one-third of all children in care are boarded out with foster parents (see Table 3).

The second group of children, those under 14 and young persons 14 to 17, can be committed to care by the courts. Officers of the National Society for the Prevention of Cruelty to Children (NSPCC) may investigate reports of cruelty, and local authority social workers must investigate reports of neglect. On the other hand, the child or young person might commit an offense. Where supportive measures

Table 3: Children in Care at Year End, England and Wales (in percentages)

Types of Accommodation	1961	1972
Boarded out	29.1	29.9
In lodgings	1.8	2.3
Local authority children's homes	19.5	21.6
Voluntary homes	3.6	5.7
Accommodation for handicapped	2.0	2.3
Hostels	1.0	1.6
Remand homes and approved schools	–	8.2
Under charge and control of parent, guardian, relative or friend	2.4	15.2
Other	2.8	3.8
Total in care	62.2	90.6
Total in care as a percentage of population under 18	0.5	0.6

SOURCE: *Social Trends, 1973*

either fail or are likely to fail, the local authority, the police, or the NSPCC may bring care proceedings. The courts in England and Wales have to be satisfied that one of the following applies:[8] (a) the child's proper development is being prevented, his health is impaired, or he is being ill-treated (this will probably be the case with another child in a family for which a care order already applies to his brother or sister); (b) the child is in moral danger; (c) the child is beyond the control of the parents or guardian; (d) the child is of compulsory school age and not receiving education; or (e) the child is guilty of a criminal offense, excluding homicide.

If a court is satisfied on one of these counts, then it may make a care order, placing the child in the local authority's care without the parents' consent. These care orders can last for a period of 28 days or less in the case of interim care orders, or for longer periods. Alternatively, a court can make a supervision order under which the child remains at home and is supervised either by a social worker from the local authority or by a probation officer from the court. Other kinds of orders can be made, but they do not directly involve the social service department. Each year, roughly one-third of all new cases are committals to care by the courts (see Table 2).

A child or young person can also be brought before the court not under care proceedings but under criminal proceedings. If found guilty of an offense, the child can be placed in care or fined, ordered to pay damages or sent to a Borstal (an institution for 16 and 17 year olds). In the near future, children under 14 may be excluded from criminal proceedings altogether.

In Scotland different provisions apply. Under the Social Work

(Scotland) Act of 1968, court proceedings forr young people have been replaced by what are called Children's Hearings. These are comprised of three volunteers from the local Children's Panel, and hearing are administered by paid officials called reporters. They bring children before the hearings only when compulsory care is necessary.

The third category of children includes those who are placed in the care of a local authority as the result of matrimonial proceedings —such as a divorce.

Finally, there are children who are sent to foster homes by private arrangement. We have seen that local authorities place children with foster parents, but many children are fostered privately. These arrangements must be made known to the local authority if they are to last for six days or more and if a person regularly takes foster children, or after 27 days if the person is a relative or is only temporarily looking after the children. All registered foster children have to be visited regularly by social workers.

In 1972, the total number of children under local authorities' care in England and Wales was just over 90,000, slightly more than one-half of 1 percent of the population under 18 (see Table 3). Care for children constitutes a large part of the daily activities of field workers in the social service departments. The type of accommo- dation and care provided is also set out in Table 3. Under the Children's Act of 1969, local authorities must combine to produce regional plans for approval by the secretary of state, providing community homes of different kinds.

In addition to these basic duties, social service departments must provide advice and support to families to prevent children having to be taken into care. This statutory duty dates only from 1963, though some authorities had begun such work several years earlier. Depart- ments can undertake case work, and they can also give financial assistance, such as payment of rent arrears, when this may prevent a family from breaking up. Social service departments also have powers to arrange adoptions.

Various studies have examined the relationship between levels of provision and the need for services. Yet the nature of the service makes it difficult to measure quantitatively. Decisions about what constitutes sufficient grounds for accepting a child into care vary among social workers and among departments with different policies or practices. There is a wide divergence in the number of children cared for by different local authorities.

Packmann (1967) pointed out that in 1963 the number of those being cared for per 1,000 population varied from 1.8 in Anglesea to 12.4 in London.[9] However, using a sample of 42 authorities, she found that these wide variations were not easily explained by differences in social conditions, or by the exisstence of voluntary provisions or private foster care arrangements. She explained much of the difference in terms of the varying policies of different departments. The most sophisticated attempt to examine the reasons for variations in child care services (Davies, 1972) reveals that the relationships between need, demand, and provision are highly complex.[10]

Spending levels are associated with the political party in control of the council. The size of the authority is independently important but it is related to the social disorganisation of the area. In turn, this factor is related to demand and the difficulty of recruiting staff. High levels of demand seem to produce different types of responses by individual departments. An extreme case can be found in the different practices that Children's Departments adopted in the face of the demand for substitute care that arose from West Indian mothers.[11] Lacking the normal British inhibitions about having their children taken into care, such mothers quite correctly saw that the authority provided better facilities for their children then they could themselves. Their demands on the service were therefore greater. Yet social workers in different departments held different views on how to respond to the additional demand, some giving greater weight to the need for care generated by poor housing conditions, others giving greater weight to the need to keep the family together.

Local authority homes are usually in short supply, and the supply rises very slowly because of competition from more attractive demands for capital. Hence departments have responded by using other forms of care, voluntary homes, or, most often, by keeping children in care for shorter periods. In short, no attempt to invent target numbers in need has much meaning here. We are still a long way from understanding how agencies respond to the demands on them and what determines the nature and the extent of available resources.

There have been relatively few attempts to evaluate the outcome of child care work. Apart from general work on the development of children deprived of a normal life and of institutional care, attempts have been made to isolate factors associated with successful foster care as opposed to the institutional care of children, and to produce tables forecasting the likelihood of success when placing children from given backgrounds with families of given types. Although some success has been gained by validating such predictors in the same authority, using the methods across departments has proved unsuccessful.[12] Professor George has argued that realistic performance measures must take into account the standard of the staff, the work pressures, the availability of resources, the quality and quantity of support for foster parents, and many more factors.[13] Such a study would entail a great deal of arduous research, and from what we know about such studies in other fields, it is unlikely to produce clear findings very readily. Yet hardly any studies exist which supervisors or senior staff can use to form an assessment of child care.

Family Support. Another major field of social service responsibility concerns support and care for children under five. Provision for this age group is confusing and complex. Three authorities are responsible. The health authorities provide infant welfare clinics which oversee the health of young children, dispense advice and welfare foods to mothers, and immunise and vaccinate the children. Health visitors, employed by the health authorities, are the key workers here. They visit all children under five regularly, especially in their first year, to give advice to the mothers.

The social service departments now have responsibility for day care of those under five. This means two things: the provision of day nurseries, and the inspection and registration of play groups and child minders who look after young children in their own homes.

Day nurseries are in very short supply. They provide day care, not education, for children under five. Their facilities are open sufficiently early in the morning and late at night so that working mothers with full-time jobs can leave their children all day. They are designed to meet the special needs of mothers who work, or whose children are living in unsuitable conditions or are mentally or physically handicapped.

The British equivalent to U.S. welfare, the Supplementary Benefit Commission, provides cash support to single mothers with school-age children. The assumption is that this will enable these mothers to stay at home. There are currently only 23,000 places in local authority nurseries. This is equivalent to 0.5 percent of all children under five. Some local authorities provide no nurseries at all. The support of a family doctor or social worker is often necessary for a successful application. There are no formal eligibility rules. The authority has complete discretion. Maximum charges, depending on income, range from a few shillings to several pounds a week, according to the local authority. Quite distinct are nursery schools and classes for preschool children provided by education authorities. These are staffed by trained teachers. At the moment only about 12 percent of the appropriate age group receive such education, but here need is not usually taken as a criterion. The more knowledgeable parents tend to get their children on the long waiting lists first, and proportionately more high-income group children benefit than do low-income group children. A gradual expansion of facilities by the education authorities is planned so that by the early 1980s part-time nursery education for children whose parents demand it should be available. There is no comparable planned expansion of day nursery facilities for working women.

There are no reliable estimates of need, but very long waiting lists indicate a substantial lack of day nurseries. Moreover, the *1973 General Household Survey* reveals that about two in five women with schoolchildren (16 percent) are at work and that two in five of them would have liked to go to work earlier if day-care facilities had been available.[14] This compares with the 0.5 percent of children of preschool age in local authority day nurseries. Whether the state should make such provision is the subject of some debate. Clearly, a demand exists.

In addition to providing these very limited facilities, social service departments must inspect play groups, private day nurseries, and individuals who care for children. The number of registered nurseries and babysitters increased sharply in recent years as new requirements took effect. Even so, the majority of babysitters are probably not registered, and, in many cases, the children are looked after in appalling conditions.

For children of school age or younger who are mentally or emotionally disturbed, there exist child guidance clinics. Parents may take children on their own initiative, though probably in most cases children are referred either by the family doctor or by schools. These clinics are staffed by psychiatrists, educational psychologists, and social workers who assess the children's difficulties and advise parents on how to help their children. In some cases, they may recommend that the child return regularly, attend boarding school, or live in a residential establishment. These clinics are run either by the National Health Service or by local education authorities. Again, there are no reliable estimates of need for this service, but clinics normally have long waiting lists.

Handicapped children are the particular responsibility of education authorities. They have a duty to ascertain which children require special education, and they have a right to medically examine children to determine whether they have one of the handicaps listed below. Parents have the right to ask that their child be examined, if they feel he or she ought to be receiving special education and is not. In either case, the parents can appeal to the secretary of state against the authority's decision to give or withhold special education. The children considered in need of special attention are the blind or partially-sighted, the deaf and partially deaf, the educationally subnormal (those with an IQ below 70), the epileptic, emotionally disturbed or maladjusted, the physically handicapped, those with speech defects, the deaf-blind, and the autistic and delicate children. Need is difficult to establish. At one end of the spectrum, the blind and deaf are clear cases where need is most fully met, but the educationally subnormal and maladjusted categories are much more vague. The maladjusted child might merely be a child with whom an ordinary school cannot cope. A good deal of controversy exists about the high number of West Indian children who are classified as educationally subnormal on the basis of test scores. The only pronouncement on national levels of need in this field was made by the Ministry of Education immediately after World War II. It was then said that 10 percent of all schoolchildren were in need of special education, but only 1 percent should be in separate special schools.

More recently, survey work has suggested that these overall figures are far too low. The number needing some kind of special education has been estimated at 17 percent in one London borough. A survey in the Isle of Wight, of nine to eleven year olds with one of only four of the major handicaps, concluded that one child in six had a chronic recurrent handicap. In particular, the cases of severe maladjustment were about twenty times higher than previous measures. Clearly, quite different measures of severity and need are being used by teachers or administrators knowing the available resources and by independent researchers adopting ideal measures. Ideas are also changing about the need for separate schools as distinct from specialist units within ordinary schools. Currently 1.4 percent of the school population is in separate special schools.

Finally, there are children who are mentally handicapped, who were previously considered ineducable and who had been the responsibility of health departments. Since 1971, their care has become the responsibility of education departments.

Homeless Families. Local authority social service departments must provide accommodations for homeless families as welfare departments previously did. The problem is acute in large cities, especially in London, where high rents and property values have made it more and more difficult for young families on low incomes to find housing. Until the mid-1960s, local authority discouraged the potentially enormous demand for temporary accommodations by splitting families up, not housing the husband, and generally providing only the most meagre facilities. These practices have begun to change, following some well-publicised protests and central government pressure. The Seebohm Report recommended that these powers be transferred to housing departments since homelessness was essentially a housing problem. This is now happening. There are also special units designed to help difficult families readjust to an independent existence. Temporary accommodations for single persons, "down-and-outs" or "persons without a settled way of living" as the legislation calls them, are provided by a central government agency, the Supplementary Benefits Commission, which also gives cash benefits. The Commission took over an old Poor Law responsibility and its buildings. These are now called "reception centres" and are to be found in or near the major centres of population. The aim is to give food and shelter, medical attention, and help and advice if these persons want jobs or seek more permanent accommodations.

2. Services for Young Persons

Local education authorities have a duty, under the 1944 Education Act, to secure adequate facilities for leisure activities for young persons. Local authorities can make grants to voluntary organisations which maintain youth clubs or sports facilities and employ youth workers. The central government also financially supports national youth organisations. In 1971-1972, however, the sum involved amounted to only about £0.5 million. Both local education authorities and the central government's spending amount to only 1 percent of the total education budget devoted to the Youth Service. This proportion has remained virtually unchanged over the last 12 years. At the local level there is usually a youth committee consisting of representatives of local organisations and those from the local authority. This committee coordinates local activities. Provision of activities depends largely on the existence and enthusiasm of local part-time workers from churches and other charitable organisations.

In large urban areas with particularly serious problems, other facilities have grown up. Some areas have developed a Young People's Counselling Service where young persons can go for advice on personal problems. Advice on contraception is available at clinics and advisory centres; again, these are run on a voluntary basis. Finally, voluntary groups and a few local authorities run hostels for homeless young persons. The local social service department also gives advice and help to young persons.

There are, in short, no really comprehensive statutory services for young persons. There is instead only a patchwork of statutory and voluntary assistance which is steadily growing more coordinated. There is undoubtedly room for much more extensive and varied provisions.

The Seebohm Report stated, "We do not regard any of the present services as satisfactorily meeting the needs of more than a minority of the young peoople" (par. 252). Little has changed since the Report.

3. Services for the Elderly

By far the most important of the personal social service in terms of manpower and spending is the care of the elderly. Most of the residential care provided by local authorities is for old persons, and three-quarters of all their residential staff are employed in these homes. Moreover, most of the home help's time is spent with old persons, as is an unknown but large portion of the field worker's time.

About nine million persons, or 16 percent of the population, have reached retirement age, though only about eight million have actually retired. The number of elderly persons will increase by more than three-quarters of a million between 1971 and 1981. The average age of the group will also rise as will the percentage of single elderly women over 75.

Division of Administrative Responsibility. The services available to the elderly fall into four broad groups: support of the elderly in their own homes; the provision of independent units of accommodation designed for or allocated to the elderly; residential care outside the hospital; and hospital care. In practice these categories overlap somewhat.

Three separate administrative units are concerned with the delivery of these services. First, there are the local authority social service departments and the lower units in the rural counties. Second are the district councils, which are responsible for housing but which also provide recreational facilities and meals, and give grants to voluntary groups concerned with the welfare of the elderly. The third administrative unit involved is the National Health Service and, in particular, the area health authority. The administrative restructuring of the 1970s has not done a great deal to simplify this threefold division. Indeed, in some respects the division of responsibility is now more complex than ever. Previously, functions such as the provision of district nurses to attend people in their own homes was the responsibility of a local authority health department. This was a separate department from the social service department, but both were part of the same local authority. Since 1974, however, health services, including district nursing, have been the responsibility of health authorities and outside the sphere of the locally elected council altogether.

The most serious division of responsibility occurs in the care of the most severely handicapped. The NHS is responsible for old persons who need hospitalization, while the local councils are responsible for residential care in special homes and for supportive domiciliary services. Numerous studies of old persons in hospitals have shown that many of them could, on medical grounds, leave the hospital and live in a less institutionalised setting. One major barrier to such movement is the lack of any family support in many cases and the absence of suitable accommodations. For more than a decade, it has been the declared aim of successive governments to shift emphasis from institutional or hospital care to community care. Community care is thought to be the less expensive of the two programs.

Clearly any major shift of responsibility requires a degree of planning and coordination which the many administrative divisions make difficult. Even more important is the financial factor. The NHS, and hence hospital care, is wholly funded by the central government. The other services are funded from the local authorities' resources. The central government does provide a substantial supplement to the local property tax, yet this sum is received on the basis of population size and other factors unconnected with the numbers of old persons in residential care. Thus, even if a local authority increases its supportive services, it will not receive a larger central government grant. It merely takes on a larger burden. Without any financial inducement, local councils have not been eager to shoulder these additional burdens as the hospital sector would wish, especially because during the 1960s the population aged 65 and over increased by nearly one-fifth in England and Wales. In short, while the NHS has an incentive to press for community care, the local authorities have every incentive to resist. The financial structure actually hinders cooperation. We now turn to describe the four broad types of service in more detail, and begin with the supportive services.

Supportive Services. Support for old persons living in their own homes or for younger persons caring for their elderly relatives can be provided by local social service departments under general powers both to promote the welfare of the elderly or under powers and duties to provide specific services. Under the legislation, local authorities can not only provide a wide range of activities but also can give grants to voluntary groups. The following list (adapted from one previously compiled) gives some impression of the types of activities (those provided by at least some local authorities are followed by asterisks): aids for the infirm* (loan of gadgets); boarding out for short periods in lodgings*; chiropody clinics*; clubs*; day centres*; day sitters-in (giving relatives the chance to get out and leave old person); domestic help* (done by local authority home helps); employment and job finding services; entertainment*; hairdressing and shaving (now done by some local counties, e.g., Camden); handicraft and other classes*; holidays*; home nursing equipment*; house decorations and repairs; housing*; informatioon and advice*; laundry services*; libraries (often mobile)*; meals delivered to the home* (Meals-on-wheels) and lunch clubs; night sitters-in*; odd jobs (also done by local authority home helps)*; outings*; reading and letter writing; residential courses*; safety precautions*; transport*; visiting; and radio and television sets. In most areas there are old person's clubs of one kind or another and these are run by voluntary efforts but financed in part out of public funds. Even so only about one in ten old persons belongs to a club.

One of the major tasks of the social service department is to put old persons in touch with the wide range of provisions that are available and to seek out those in particular need. Under the previous administrative arrangements the task fell to officers in the welfare department. For the most part these officials had no formal social work qualifications. Today they perform similar tasks in the new social service departments. Some areas have sought to build up a comprehensive register of all old persons, with some kind of visiting.

Since compiling a register is a task far beyond the scope of local authority social workers, most authorities rely on relations, neighbors, doctors, or clergymen to refer cases in need of help or advice. Most authorities also recognise that any widespread attempt to reach all old persons would give rise to more demands for some services than they could cope with. Whether this is an optimum strategy as far as the elderly are concerned is a rather different matter.

Under the duties originally laid down in the 1946 National Health Service Act, and made more specific in 1968, new social service departments must provide domestic helpers who do cleaning and shopping for the old person who cannot do these tasks adequately, but who is, in general, sufficiently mobile to live alone. These workers are mainly women with family responsibilities of their own who, working part-time, probably do more to keep the elderly living in the community than any other group of workers. They also make regular friendly social contact with old persons and hence relieve a great deal of loneliness. Nearly one-half million people were visited regularly by home helpers in 1972. There are always more people wanting this kind of help than there is help available. In each area home help organisers have the job of assessing priorities, and a doctor's certificate is needed to ensure service in many places. However, an elderly person can apply directly to the local social service department. Charges are made for the service on a sliding scale. Most old persons do not have to pay much, if anything.

The British home helper has no training; he or she is merely someone who can provide a limited range of domestic help. Gardening, spring cleaning, and electrical repairs are not things that helpers are supposed to undertake. Various observers have suggested training and increased status for home helps. Higher pay would seem more immediately appropriate. When local employment is high, local authorities have the greatest difficulty recruiting helpers.[15]

Another important practical support is the meals-on-wheels service which originally was handled by volunteer groups, generally since World War II. This service is often still performed by voluntary organisations which are funded by local authorities, but it can be performed directly by the local authorities themselves. They provide hot midday meals to old persons in their own homes about twice a week for a very low charge. In 1972 over 150,000 meals were served in Great Britain in one week, mainly by volunteers. There are no formal eligibility rules. Old persons may be referred by doctors or social workers or may apply directly.

New legislation also makes it a duty for local authorities, once again through their social service departments, to adapt homes in which the disabled or handicapped live, including the elderly. Handrails for the bath and toilet, ramps for wheelchairs, or kitchen fittings can be provided. Those with sufficient income have to contribute to the cost.

Other services are provided through the health authority. Particularly important are district nurses. They can give regular treatment, injections, bathe the patient, or renew dressings. The nurse is responsible for ensuring that laundry is provided if the local authority supplies this service. The nurse can therefore help many families who would otherwise find the strain of regular care for their elderly relatives too great.

In a few areas old persons' clinics have been established where advice is given—about diet, for example—and facilities exist for treating or advising treatment of bad feet or poor eyesight and other normal disabilities of old age. There is evidence that the eyesight of old persons is, in fact, improving. Many more health authorities and some voluntary agencies provide a chiropody service. There is a small charge (about a third of the normal cost) for each visit. In many areas it is possible to arrange home visits. Again, old persons merely have to apply, though in some places there may be a long wait. Moving further along the spectrum toward more intensive care, day hospitals and day centres now exist where old persons can attend on a regular basis for a day, a week, or more often. Physical and occupational therapy is also available. Very similar work has been done by the NHS in a few hospitals and by local councils in day-care centres. Both exist in only a few areas.

Geriatric units provide short spells of hospital care after which the old person can be returned to the care of the family with outpatient attendance. There are about 200 such units in existence.

Finally, the family doctor spends a large amount of his time meeting the old persons' health needs. Men aged 65 through 74 see their doctor about one and one-half times as often as men of all ages and nearly twice as often after they reach 75.[16]

Supportive services are thus provided primarily by local social service departments and voluntary bodies with area health authorities also playing an important supportive role. The 1973 General Household Survey gives some idea of the extent to which these various supportive services are reaching old persons. Table 4 shows the estimated number of old persons visited at home by one of the workers.

Table 4: Supportive Services Received by Old People
(1973 General Household Survey)

Service	Number per 1000 Population	
	Age 65-74	Age 75 and Over
Health visitor	7	16
District nurse	17	58
Chiropodist cutting at home	8	42
Home help	24	98
Meals on wheels	10	27
Welfare officer	8	17

Housing. Under the housing acts, local housing departments can provide housing for old persons. Most units are one-bedroom flats, few of which are designed to meet old persons' special needs. Many authorities provide sheltered accommodations. These are a group of old persons' bungalows or flats with a warden on call in case of need. Sometimes shared eating or recreation facilities may be available, but the old person still leads an independent life. Housing facilities are provided by local district councils, a lower level authority than the social service department in country areas but the same level in the very large urban areas. The wardens are paid by the social service department and this dual responsibility has sometimes made such schemes difficult to arrange. With many housing authorities facing large slum clearance programmes and long waiting lists for young families, old persons' housing has had a low priority.

Residential Care. Care for the elderly and disabled in special homes is the local authorities' most expensive task, even though only about 3 percent of all old persons actually live in such accommodations. Under the 1948 National Assistance Act, as amended in 1970, the social service departments must provide accommodation for any old person deemed in need of care, without regard to his or her financial circumstances. They must, however, charge according to income for the residential care they provide. The standard charge is very low compared to the actual cost even when the full fee is charged. About three-quarters of the old persons in these homes are over 75. In 1972, there were 120,000 old people supported by local authorities in residential homes, 18,000 of these in private and voluntary homes paid for by the local authority. Any private or voluntary home should be inspected by the local authority and the central department whether or not any of the residents are supported by public funds.

The quality of care, psychological as well as physical, is of the greatest importance, as is the process by which old persons give up their independence. The attitude that they have toward the move will affect their lives in the institution, whatever the physical conditions or the quality of the care. We have very little recent information about the quality of care in this critical area. The first systematic national survey was undertaken by Professor Townsend nearly 15 years ago.[17] It revealed not only widespread low morale and a poor quality of life in social terms, but also very poor physical amenities. Over half of the homes were very large institutions housing 250 people or more in poorhouse accommodations. At least, since that study was undertaken, the number of large homes has fallen by about half, and the great majority of places are now called medium-sized homes; these house between 30 and 70 persons.

Hospital Care. Finally, about 15 percent of all hospital beds in Great Britain are occupied by old persons or the chronically sick. Roughly one of every five non-psychiatric and maternity beds are filled by women aged 75 and over. The general emphasis on reducing the length of stay in hospital has applied to old persons as well, but at the same time more old persons have been admitted to hospitals. Between 1957 and 1970 the overall level of utilisation for the over-65 age group increased by 30 percent while the size of the age group rose by only about 20 percent. The admission of elderly patients to mental hospitals is also high compared to other age groups. Admissions per 1,000 population in 1970 were 41 for men and 74 for women. The comparable figure for those aged 75 and over were 71 for men and 76 for women. Altogether, 60,000 old persons were in mental hospitals in 1970.

Total Aid for the Elderly. Provision for the elderly, in terms of accommodation or care, is therefore very large within the whole range of activities we call the personal social services. Yet none of the supportive work would be possible without adequate income maintenance. The most important of the maintenance provisions are national insurance, retirement and widows' pensions, and what are called "supplementary pensions" provided by the Supplementary Benefits Commission. The latter gives additional benefits which bring the basic insurance pension up to a subsistence level. Roughly two-thirds of all those on supplementary benefits are old persons. It is a scheme very like the new U.S. federal supplementary security income scheme. It supplements a basic flat-rate pension which is currently set below what has been fixed as a basic minimum income by Parliament, and about a quarter of all pensioners draw it to supplement their state pension. Probably half again as many could apply for such a supplement and would be entitled to receive it because their incomes fall below the entitlement limit, but they fail to do so—partly through ignorance of their rights, partly through pride and the dislike of the means test, and partly through a desire to manage on their own.

Altogether, total expenditures on the elderly in Great Britain under all the headings we have considered amount to about 7 percent of the GNP, but only a small part is related to the personal social services, probably not more than 0.5 percent of the GNP.[18] Having considered the nature and scope of the services for the elderly it is now necessary to consider the adequacy of these services if only briefly.

The Needs of the Elderly. In 1968, the Social Survey, an agency of the central government, compiled a study of needs and provisions in 13 local authority areas.[19] In an attempt to assess the need for home helps, the government social survey team collected details from a sample of old persons about their capacity to undertake housework or get out to do shopping. They ascertained how far help was available from relations and neighbours, and from a detailed questionnaire they made an assessment of whether the person needed a home help. The proportion of households who needed but did not have a home help varied from about 25 percent in some areas to 90 percent in others. Over all, roughly 50 of every 1,000 elderly households had a home help, and nearly twice that number needed and qualified for help and would have received it had it been available.

A national sample survey in 1962 estimated that just over 1 percent of all old persons received meals on wheels,[20] and the Social Survey of 10 local areas in 1968 concluded that a similar proportion of old persons in these areas were receiving meals. National statistics have only recently been collected. The *1973 General Household Survey* indicates a similar figure for the 65 to 75 age group but a higher one for the over-75 group. the newly available national figures of people served indicate an increase between 1971 and 1972. How does this compare with possible levels of need? Here again the Social Survey gives some limited idea. It estimated that in samples in 12 authorities, 2.4 percent of those 65 and over could not get even one cooked meal a day without difficulty. This is more than twice the percentage actually served. However, more meals are now being served to old persons outside their own homes in clubs at a low price.

Approximately one in six old persons has his feet examined through the health service. The survey referred to already concluded that 20 to 30 percent of old persons had their feet attended to either through private or public provision. However, local authorities often only provided for visits every two months, while most private patients went more frequently. No more specific indication of unmet need was available.

None of the services described so far has explicit eligibility rules, but since housing is in such short supply more explicit eligibility rules are applied to ration the scarce accommodations. Authorities have waiting lists, sometimes separate ones for the elderly. Most local authorities have residence criteria of some kind. Those who have lived in the local authority area for a longer period are given preference. Indeed, living in the area for too short a time could disqualify an old person altogether, although this may now be less common. In the mid-1960s only 3 percent of those housed in Sheffield had resided in the town for less than 40 years. The required length of residence in the local area varied with the demand for accommodations but it was the deciding factor in obtaining a place in most areas. Given this basic qualification, there were wide variations in the allocation procedure. The only universal way to be sure of a house was to live in an area being demolished by a local council, which would then relocate those moved out. Existing local authority tenants who are living in overlarge accommodations after their families have left have high priority, for the obvious reason that their leaving frees needed space for another family. But on the opposite end of the scale, overcrowding, lack of amenities, ill health, or the sharing of amenities are all factors in assigning priority points to families or individuals. The long waiting lists in many areas show the need for more housing. The national level of unmet need for one-bedroom accommodations, quite apart from specially equipped housing, is something that many commentators have emphasized for the past 20 years.

The needs for more residential care are again difficult to measure, but the 1968 Social Survey proceeded by examining waiting lists and eliminating those who no longer wanted accommodations. It also included a figure based on its survey interviews, where respondents were asked whether they wished to enter homes or had considered it. Their circumstances were then assessed. This produced a figure of need nearly 70 percent higher than the number of places in the 11 studied areas in Great Britain. It is not entirely clear how far this figure reflects inadequacies in housing or needs that might be met in other ways, nor does it mean that, even if the need were met, others might not seek help, but it does suggest a significant area for concern.

4. The Physically Handicapped

Until comparatively recently, the physically handicapped were given low political and professional priority. The first statutory responsibility for the blind was assumed in 1920. It was not until 1960 that welfare authorities had a duty to promote welfare for the deaf and other classes of handicapped persons. The outstanding work done by various voluntary groups and by the Disablement Income Group and other pressure groups led to growing political awareness. Eventually a comprehensive act of Parliament was passed in 1970, thanks to the efforts of a single member.

It is worth summarising that act, for it now forms the basis of the statutory services for the handicapped. Local authority social services departments have a duty to find out how many disabled persons they have in their area, to maintain a register, to publicise the services available for such people provided by the local authority, and to inform them of other services that are available. The act specifies a long list of facilities that the social service departments must provide where they deem it necessary for a particular individual: practical assistance in the home; radio, TV or library facilities, lectures, outings and other recreation; transportation; adaptations to the home and a telephone; holidays; and meals at home or elsewhere.

Local housing authorities have a duty to take account of the needs of the disabled in providing future housing. Local authorities that provide any kind of public facilities—from public conveniences to libraries and schools—must make the buildings accessible to disabled persons. The young chronically sick and disabled must, as far as is practicable, be treated separately from those aged 65 and over in hospitals and homes. Information on this must be submitted regularly to the secretary of state.

Although the local social service department is meant to compile a register, it is up to the individual whether his name is entered. The person's own doctor will say whether his patient falls within the category of substantially and permanently handicapped. This includes blindness, deafness, injuries or deformities, diseases (including those affecting the heart or lungs), and mental disorders.

Many local authoorities have kept registers for a long time but they have been far from complete. Since 1970, numbers on the registers have grown more rapidly.

Another kind of register is for employment. The Department of Employment, a central government department, keeps a register of those disabled who are seeking work in each of its local offices. This register is divided between those who can work in ordinary conditions, and those who can only work in sheltered or special work situations. It is the job of the Disablement Resettlement Officer (DRO) to read the medical report from the family doctor and assess a person's eligibility to be put on the register. There is a DRO in every local office. The advantage of being registered is that each firm with 20 or more employees is supposed by law to employ some disabled persons, and they cannot be dismissed without good cause. There are over half a million people on the register, and 80 percent of them are employed.

A special company set up by the old Ministry of Labour employs 7,000 disabled persons in sheltered workshops. Voluntary organisations do the same. Local authorities also have the power to provide sheltered workshops. For those too incapacitated to continue working, local authorities have responsibilities similar to those for the elderly. They must employ welfare officers who visit the disabled person at home to help, advise, and give practical assistance.

Finally, the central government Department of Health and Social Security will supply invalid tricycles, give grants toward converting private vehicles, and less frequently supply a car to someone who is so severely disabled that he cannot walk or has great difficulty in walking and is in full-time work. A recent report has recommended that the tricycles be phased out and replaced by converted cars. Housewives looking after a household are similarly eligible.

In the provision for the disabled, voluntary effort has always played a very large part and continues to do so. The Royal National Institute for the Blind is one example. It publishes books in braille, has a talking book library, and runs workshops, residential homes and schools. There is an equivalent organisation for the deaf, and a Central Council for the disabled coordinates the activities of a large number of specialised groups.

The 1970 act and the publicity that surrounded it, as well as the educational work done by voluntary societies for the disabled, have all led to a significant increase in the demand for local authority services. In some areas the number of disabled being referred to social service departments has doubled since 1970. Yet in the same period, the number of workers available has not increased commensurately. Some delays, disappointments, and frustrations have followed. Yet, to be fair, much has been achieved, and departments are beginning to catch up with the demand. The deaf, and more so the blind, are better served as their special needs have been recognised for a much longer period. For the blind, there are welfare officers or their equivalent who have a specialised knowledge of aids and facilities, and the blind and partially sighted population in need is very largely registered. Other handicaps are not being helped as fully. In 1968 and 1969, the Government Social Survey conducted a national survey of the handicapped and the impaired; the results were published in 1971.[21] The survey began with a national sample of households contacted by a postal questionnaire asking specific questions about the presence and extent of handicap in the household. This was followed by a detailed personal interview of all those under 65 with handicaps and one in four over 65. Tests of the severity of the handicaps were administered. The conclusion was that there were approximately three million people in Great Britain, excluding children, with varying degrees of handicaps out of a total population of nearly 55 million. These people are further categorised in Table 5.

Of the 157,000 very severely handicapped, 26,000 men and 90,000 women are aged 65 and over, but those aged 16 to 19 were more represented than other age groups, apart from those 75 and older. The serious handicapping conditions most commonly seen are summarised in Table 6.

The survey also showed how few of the disabled were registered or had even heard of the register. It found that 82 percent of the handicapped and impaired had never heard of the register, and only 5 percent were actually registered. Eighteen percent of the very severely handicapped were registered, as were 11 percent of the severe cases. The fact that such people were not registered does not

Table 5: Distribution of Handicapped by Severity of Disability (Government Social Survey of 1968-1969)

Degree of Handicap	Number
Very severely handicapped, needing special care	157,000
Severely handicapped, needing considerable support	356,000
Appreciably handicapped, needing some support	616,000
Impaired, but needing little or no support for normal everyday living activities	1,942,000

Table 6: Most Commonly Seen Handicapping Conditions

Condition	Percentage Suffering Who Are:	
	Very Severely Handicapped	Appreciably Handicapped
Multiple Sclerosis	65	13
Parkinson's Disease	52	19
Strokes	52	19
Paraphlegia/Hemiplegia	34	22
Spastic	24	21
Arthritis	20	28

mean that they fail to get services, for 30 percent of the total used at least one of the personal social services. Home helps attended 16 percent of the severely and very severely handicapped and 40 percent of the very severe cases are attended by a home nurse. They visit two-thirds of those needing day and night care usually once a week. Over half of the severely and two-thirds of the appreciably handicapped received no on-going local authority support or service, though some have had mechanical aids, ramps, and other fittings paid for or installed by the local authority. As we have seen, registration has improved since this report was undertaken, but there is no way of knowing precisely by how much care and support has increased. It has sometimes been said that welfare officers have been more concerned with creating a tidy card index of names on a register than with providing material support. The pressures of the last few years, unmatched by equivalent resources, must have increased the temptation to do this.

5. The Mentally Ill and Handicapped

Social service departments are involved in the admission of patients to hospitals, the after-care of those who have been to hospital, and the continuing care of those who remain in the community but who need help and whose families need support. The National Health Service, in the form of the new area and regional authorities, is the other major statutory service involved.

The legislative foundation for mental health care services is the 1959 Mental Health Act. The act distinguished four categories of mental disorder, but we shall distinguish only two broad categories: mental illness, and mental handicap or retardation. The act, and the ministerial pronouncements following it, emphasised the importance of voluntary admission to hospital where hospital care was necessary, and a shift toward greater emphasis on community care. This meant the local authorities would take responsibility for the care of more of the mentally disordered in residential homes or with their families. Specifically, local authorities had five duties. The first involved appointing mental welfare officers whose task it was to help and advise the mentally disordered and their families and to arrange for admission into hospitals. Application for compulsory admission had to come from either a relative or a mental welfare officer. These functions are now performed by a designated social worker in the social service department. Compulsory applications must normally be supported by two doctors, but in an emergency case, one doctor is sufficient. There are opportunities for either the patient or the relative to appeal against such compulsory admission through a system of Mental Health Review Tribunals. However, the whole emphasis under the present service is that entry should, if at all possible, be voluntary. In 1971 only 6 percent of patients in mental hospitals were compulsorily detained. Second, the authorities must provide residential accommodation for those who have no family, or halfway houses for those who have recently left the hospital but who are not ready to take up a fully independent life in the community. Many will need some degree of residential help all their lives. Third, authorities must provide training or occupational facilities in a sheltered environment, and offer mentally handicapped adults and youngsters over the age of 16 the opportunity to acquire some skill and work experience that will enable them to enter the labour market and live independent lives. Similarly, sheltered workshops will help to accustom those who have been in hospitals to a working environment. Fourth, authorities must provide supportive services —such as clubs, recreational facilities, and discussion groups, as well as supportive casework. Finally, the authorities act as guardians for anyone so handicapped as to be unable to look after his or her own interests and having no one else prepared to do so.

Linked with and supplementing a local authority's own services will be those of voluntary organisations, the most important of which is the National Association of Mental Health which has numerous local associations affiliated with it. The national body produces information and advice while local associations provide the practical help and support. It also runs some residential homes. Another new body is the British Association for the Retarded.

Since the mid-1950s the total number of in-patients in mental hospitals or within general hospitals has declined. The number of

Table 7: In-patients and Admissions to Mental Hospitals and Units, England and Wales (number per 1,000 population)

	1949	1959	1965	1969	1971
Admissions during year	1.3	2.4	3.3	3.6	3.6
In-patients at end of year	3.35	3.15	2.69	2.38	2.25

SOURCE: *Social Trends, 1973*

admissions, including re-admissions, continued to rise until recently. The figures in Table 7 indicate these trends.

This pattern of shorter stay reflects the changing treatment patients receive, and the result is that local authority services are shouldering more responsibility. The figures in Table 8 show the scale of this change.

It is hoped to decrease places in hospitals even further, possibly to less than half the present number, and increase the number of hostel places. This will mean a substantial degree of cooperation between the health authorities and the locally elected social service authorities. The financial and the administrative difficulties discussed above in relation to community care for the elderly persist here, and are only heightened by social attitudes to mental illness. There are long waiting lists for hostels and training centres, and there are wide variations in the availability of such services among areas. However, in 1971, following an initiative begun by a Labour secretary of state which was followed by his Conservative successor, significant additional funds were allocated to services for the mentally handicapped and an important white paper, "Better Service for the Mentally Handicapped," was published. This reviewed the scale of the problem and the deficiencies in the existing services, and set targets for local authorities and the Health Service for places in residential institutions, training centres, and hospitals.

Between 1971 and 1974 local authorities were urged to plan for 10,000 new places in adult training centres, 750 places in homes for

Table 8: Numbers of Mentally Ill in Local Authority Care, England and Wales (number per 1,000 population)

	1961	1966	1970
Under care	40.2	75.1	91.8
Attending training centres	0.4	1.4	3.0
Resident in homes and hostels	0.7	1.9	2.7
Boarded out at L.A. expense	0.02	0.06	0.37

SOURCE: *Social Trends, 1973*

children, and 3,500 places in adult homes. Space limitations prevent an evaluation of the move from institutional to community care in the field of mental health. Please refer to the Bibliography for sources of information in this field.

6. Work with the Courts and Prison After Care

The Probation Service in England and Wales has remained outside the formal structure of the local authority personal social services, although in Scotland it has become a part of he social work program. The probation officer's task can be divided into at least six different activities. The first is the preparation of social enquiry reports for the courts in criminal cases. Probation officers also provide reports in affiliation proceedings and where arrangements have to be made for the children in cases of divorce or separation.

There is, second, the original task of supervision in the community, which can usefully be divided into supervision of offenders aged 17 and over, and supervision of juvenile offenders aged 10-16. The probation order now applies only to those aged 17 and over, and lasts for a period of one to three years. Conditions such as receiving medical treatment or residing in a certain place (often a hostel) are frequently added to basic requirements relating to regular employment, contact with the supervising officer and "good behaviour." As a result of the 1969 Children and Young Persons Act, the probation order has been replaced in the juvenile courts (dealing with the 10-16 age group) by the supervision order, which was previously reserved for non-criminal cases (e.g., failure to attend school, care and protection cases). The supervision order can now be applied in criminal and non-criminal cases, and does not differ substantially from the probation order it replaced, except that it can incorporate provisions for the offender to engage in certain activities, usually of a recreational or educational nature, for limited periods during the currency of the order. These activities can take place either while the young person is living at home or, if necessary, at a residential centre. This concept, which did not exist in a formal sense prior to the 1969 act, has come to be known as "Intermediate Treatment," although this phrase is not used in the act. Intermediate treatment programmes have been slow in developing, and their effectiveness has not yet been evaluated. The division of responsibility between the probation officer and the social worker from social services departments is drawn by reference to age (those under 14 would not normally be supervised by the probation service) and prior involvement of a particular worker (probation officer or social worker) with the case.

Third, the probation officer is involved in marriage guidance work. Couples or individuals may be referred from court or come on their own, either for legal advice or for ordinary guidance. As other forms of legal aid have improved and other sources of help become available, too, this aspect of their work has probably declined. Marriage guidance is undertaken by voluntary workers who belong to local marriage councils which are coordinated nationally. Yet the bulk of such work is probably still undertaken by the probation officer.

Fourth, they are concerned with the care of offenders who have been released from prison or from Borstals. Prisoners may be released on the condition that they undergo supervision by a probation officer, or they may seek help voluntarily. Probation officers also work in prisons where they are called prison welfare officers. In the past, officers have been more available to undertake social case work with persons who sought help or with whom officers came into contact as part of their work. This dates from a time when they were virtually the only trained or generally available social workers in many areas. Now these general tasks usually fall to social service departments.

Finally, officers work with volunteers, especially in helping to organise after-care and resettlement. The National Association for the Care and Resettlement of Offenders coordinates the activities of local groups helping prisoners and their families.

7. General Services for the Community

The most widespread general service for the population at large that provides advice and information is the Citizen's Advice Bureau (CAB). Most offices are run by voluntary organisations, usually a local Council of Social Service or a local authority itself. A national organisation provides summaries of legislation and guidance and organises training. The aim of the CAB is to reply to any kind of query, and it will refer a member of the public to the appropriate agency. Some local authorities, especially in areas of housing stress, are providing housing and advice centres. Urban centres with a high proportion of poor and transient residents or with slum clearance programmes have begun employing more community workers.

Traditionally, such workers have been employed in new housing areas and especially new towns, but, as a result of growing concern about the potential violence and racial tension in urban centres, the Home Office has begun a series of pilot community development programmes with 12 such areas. Various official reports from government departments in the late 1960s argued that community workers should be appointed in a number of different contexts. Youth work and town planning are two examples. It is an ill-defined area of work at the moment, but all the signs are that it will grow.

STAFFING AND EDUCATION

The organisation of social work in Great Britain is currently undergoing a major upheaval. Before 1970, professional training was available in a multitude of courses in different kinds of institutions. The Central Training Council in Child Care approved courses which led to a certificate of recognition in child care. The Probation Advisory and Training Board began approving courses in 1946. There were courses for hospital social workers, psychiatric social workers, and, dating from 1962, courses run outside the universities under the auspices of the Council for Training in Social Work. There were courses in residential child care, and university courses in generic social work called courses in applied social studies leading to diplomas or to higher degrees. In 1961 just over 300 field workers qualified for degrees in the United Kingdom, but by 1972 the figure had risen to over 1,900.

At the same time as the new general social service departments were created, the social work training programme reorganised. There is now one Central Council for Education and Training in Social Work (CCETSW) which is in the process of taking over the functions of all the previous training councils. In the future, all social workers who qualify will gain a certificate of qualification in social work, but only from a course that has been approved and given recognition by this body, created by Parliament with statutory authority. The Council is planning to encourage the expansion of both graduate (one year) and non-graduate (two year) courses, so that about 3,000 students will qualify as social workers each each from the mid-1970s. However, at the moment many social workers have not undergone full professional training (see Table 9). Nearly two-thirds of the field social workers employed by local authorities are not qualified. This is

Table 9: Staff Employed in Personal Social Service Departments, 1972

Type	Numbers	
	Actual	Whole Time Equivalent
Social Work Staff		
Senior staff total	3,219	3,207
qualified	1,883	
unqualified	1,336	
Social workers	9,689	9,328
qualified	3,537	
unqualified	6,152	
Trainee social workers	1,428	1,428
Welfare assistants	1,150	1,118
Total Social Work Staff	15,486	15,081
Day Care Staff and Supportive Staff		
Adult training centre staff	2,731	2,709
Day centre staff	1,122	1,038
Day nursery staff	5,849	5,787
Home helps	75,976	36,382
Miscellaneous	20,866	16,973
Total Day Care Staff	106,544	62,889
Residential Staff in Homes for the:		
Elderly and physically handicapped	50,305	40,171
Temporary accommodation	500	416
Mentally disordered	3,065	2,306
Children:		
Residential nurseries	2,731	2,284
Homes and hostels	14,455	11,377
Total Residential Staff	71,056	56,554
Total Staff	193,086	134,524

even more true of residential work, where only 18 percent of those working in children's homes hold a certificate in residential child care. The National Institute for Social Work, an independent body, has provided advanced courses and courses in management, and now the Local Government Training Board and the CCETSW are developing courses for managerial levels.

The basic courses are a move away from specialised training for work in separate agencies or specialist types of work. It is hoped that "qualified workers will emerge from training with a common core of knowledge and skill, but with some variety of expertise."[22] The rapid advance of professionalisation these changes imply is not a development whole-heartedly acclaimed by all those involved, but many see it as a logical outcome of the kind of changes the services have undergone.

OVERVIEW

We began by illustrating the diverse legislative traditions which have only in this decade partially fused to give us a single local authority department responsible for the delivery of social services. The actual legislative responsibilities did not change much. We have subsequently seen that, even after this reorganisation, the care of different groups within the community is still fragmented, especially between the health care system and the new social service system. While this coalescence of functional responsibilities was taking place, local authorities and the medical care authorities were also reorganised, and many disappeared altogether. In addition, there has been a complete restructuring of social work education on a generic basis. Departments themselves have attempted to shift the emphasis of their work following the concept of a comprehensive family service which the Seebohm Report recommended. The Report argued that "a family or individual in need of social care should, as far as possible, be served by a single social worker." The attempt to achieve this situation with a staff which has very different backgrounds and is used to working with children, old persons, or the mentally ill, has been a traumatic experience and the outcome is in some dispute. It is not a dispute we intend to pursue here but it does provide further evidence of the upheaval. Finally, the size of the new departments and the consequences of size on organisational structure have created tensions of a different kind.

It would be wrong, however, to fail to emphasise that a great many positive consequences have followed despite the costs of change. The work these departments do has now taken on a political importance that scarcely seemed possible 10 years ago. Social work is acquiring greater professional standing with other professional groups, such as doctors and planners, without which cooperation among agencies and individuals is unlikely. The new departments are defining their roles in a much more active way than their predecessors used to do. Although low in relation to expressed demand, cash was flowing faster until the most recent crisis. The figures in Table 10 illustrate this.

The new committees and the new directors have begun to develop the planning functions and the research and intelligence roles that the Seebohm Report advocated. While they leave much to be desired in many cases, it is an emphasis largely lacking before. These activities have been stimulated by a request of the central govern-

Table 10: United Kingdom Public Expenditure on the Personal Social Services
(£ millions—actual price)

1962	1965	1968	1970	1972
75	105	158	276	384

SOURCE: *National Income and Expenditure, 1973*

ment asking the new authorities to prepare ten-year plans for the development of their services, which they are doing. One further direct result of the Seebohm Report was that in 1973 a new government appointed advisory body was created called the Personal Social Services Council. Its purpose is to advise the secretary of state and local authorities on policies relating to the personal social services and to undertake research and development. It is as yet a small organisation but it is an interesting new institution which could prompt new departures and policy developments. These services have not only changed but are likely to change further.

NOTES

1. *Report of the Committee on Local Authority and Allied Personal Social Services* (Seebohm Report) (Cmnd. 3703, HMSO, 1968).

2. *National Income and Expenditure, 1973* (HMSO, 1973).

3. That is, social welfare expenditure from public funds as a percentage of GNP. *Social Security Bulletin* (Washington, D.C.: December, 1972).

4. *The Report of the Committee on the Care of Children* (Curtis Report) (Cmnd. 6922, HMSO, 1960).

5. *Report of the Committee on Children and Young People* (Ingleby Report) (Cmnd. 1191, HMSO, 1960).

6. *The Child, the Family and the Young Offender* (Cmnd. 2742, HMSO, 1965).

7. *Seebohm Report.*

8. Section I of the Children and Young Person's Act, 1969.

9. J. Packmann, *Child Care: Needs and Numbers* (London: Allen and Unwin, 1967).

10. B. Davies et al., *Variations in Children's Services* (London: Bell, 1972).

11. K. Fitzherbert, *West Indian Children* (Occasional Paper in Social Administration) (London: Bell, 1967).

12. R. Parker, *Decision in Child Care* (London: Allen and Unwin, 1966).

13. V. George, *Foster Care: Theory and Practice* (Routledge, 1970).

14. Central Statistical Office, *1973 General Household Survey* (London: HMSO, 1973).

15. For a full survey of the home helps tasks in different areas, see A. Hunt, *The Home Help Service in England and Wales* (Government Social Survey, London: HMSO, 1970).

16. *General Household Survey.*

17. P. Townsend, *The Last Refuge* (Routledge and Kegan Paul, 1960).

18. *Social Trends, 1972* (London: HMSO, 1973).

19. A. I. Harris, *Social Welfare for the Elderly* (Government Social Survey, HMSO, 1968).

20. P. Townsend and D. Wedderburn, *The Aged in the Welfare State* (1964).

21. A. I. Harris et al., *Handicapped and Impaired in Great Britain* (Social Survey Division, Office of Population Census and Surveys, HMSO, 1971).

22. *First Report of the Central Council for Education and Training in Social Work* (1971-1973).

BIBLIOGRAPHY

Basic Texts

Rodgers, B., and Stevenson, J. *A New Portrait of Social Work*. London: Heinemann, 1973.

The Seebohm Report. *Report of the Committee on Local Authority and Allied Personal Social Services*. London: HMSO, 1968.

Slack, K. *Social Administration and the Citizen*. London: Joseph, 1966.

Willmott, P. *Consumers Guide to the British Social Services*. Middlesex: Penguin Books, 1973.

Specialised Studies on Children

Davies, B. *Variations in Children's Services*. London: Bell, 1972.

George, V. *Foster Care: Theory and Practice*. London: Routledge, 1970.

Heywood, J. *Children in Care*. London: Routledge, 1959.

King, R. *Patterns of Residential Care*. London: Routledge, 1971.

Packmann, J. *Child Care: Needs and Numbers*. London: Allen and Unwin, 1967.

Parker, R. *Decision in Child Care*. London: Allen and Unwin, 1966.

Pringle, K. *Residential Care Facts and Fallacies*. London: Longmans, 1967.

Pringle, K. *Adoption: Facts and Fallacies*. London: Longmans, 1968.

Specialised Studies on the Elderly

Goldberg, E. M. *Helping the Aged*. London: Allen and Unwin, 1970.

Harris, A. I. *Social Welfare for the Elderly*. London: HMSO, 1968.

Marris, P. *Widows and their Families*.

Meacher, M. *Taken for a Ride*. London: Longmans, 1972.

Raynes, R., D. King, and J. Tozard *Patterns of Residential Care*. London: Routledge, 1971.

Shanab, E. *The Elderly in Four Industrial Societies*.

Townsend, P. *The Family Life of Old People*. London: Routledge, 1961.

Townsend, P. *The Last Refuge*. London: Routledge, 1964.

Townsend, P. and D. Wedderburn *The Aged in the Welfare State*. 1964.

Tunstall, J. *Old and Alone*.

Webb, A. and R. Hadley *Old People and Young Volunteers*. DHSS.

Specialised Studies on the Physically Handicapped

Harris, A. I. *Handicapped and Impaired in Great Britain*. London: HMSO, 1971.

Sainsbury, S. *Registered and Disabled*. 1970.

Specialised Studies on Mental Illness and Handicaps

Apte, R. *Halfway House*. 1961.

Better Services for the Mentally Handicapped. London: HMSO, 1971.

Bone, M. *Plans and Provisions for the Mentally Handicapped.* London: Allen and Unwin, 1972.

Freeman, H. and J. Farndale *Trends in the Mental Health Services.* London: Pergamon, 1963.

Freeman, H. and J. Farndale *New Aspects in the Mental Health Services.* London: Pergamon, 1967.

Greenland, C. *Mental Illness and Civil Liberty.* 1970.

Jones, K. *A History of the Mental Health Services.* London: Routledge, 1972.

Martin, F. W. and G. Rehin *Patterns of Performance in Community Care.* London: OUP, 1968.

Morris, P. *Put Away.* London: Routledge, 1969.

Tizard, J. *Community Services for the Mentally Handicapped.* London: OUP, 1964.

Wing, J. K. and H. Hoffner *Roots and Evaluation.* London: OUP, 1973.

Specialised Studies on Education and Training

Central Council for Training and Education in Social Work, *Report No. 1 Social Work: Setting the Course for Social Work Education,* 1973.

4

TWENTIETH-CENTURY IRAN: SOCIAL SERVICES IN TRANSITION

SATTAREH FARMAN-FARMAIAN

INTRODUCTION

Government provision of social services in Iran is of fairly recent date. Only within the last 50 years has responsibility for social welfare been incorporated in various ministries. Formerly, social welfare services had been performed by individuals or by private groups, mostly within a religious context. These private or group charities have gradually been taken over by organized agencies and institutions. At present some half dozen government agencies, 12 semi-private social organizations, and a number of private institutions are active in the field of social services throughout the country.

The Plan and Budget Organization, a government agency, sets national policies and goals and allocates government expenditures for social and economic development. It determines which groups are to receive priority in the development and expansion of welfare services, what is the nature of each group's needs, and what services are to be provided.

In addition to low income, the social significance of the groups and the degree of their disability and vulnerability are considerations in determining priorities. Priority is currently being given to rural villagers and, in urban areas, to recent migrants from rural areas (low income), as well as to children and teachers (social significance), and the physically, mentally, and socially handicapped (disability and vulnerability).

Eligibility

Eligibility criteria for specific programs are determined by the executive bodies of the agencies themselves. Private agencies, for the most part, predate government intervention in the welfare field and continue to administer and set criteria for their programs, even where they receive government funding. Government-run agencies determine eligibility within national guidelines. Since direct financial aid is rarely provided, service provision is determined by other need factors, medical, educational, and so on. Administrative difficulties may also determine eligibility criteria, as in the case of rural social security, which presently can only be extended to members of rural cooperatives.

Increasingly, social workers are being used to do family and individual studies so that psychological factors are taken into account and assignments are determined on the basis of emotional needs and ability to benefit from the programs. Those agencies which do not employ social workers and which have limited facilities often accept on a "first come, first served" basis.

Duration of Services

Because direct financial aid is rarely provided and most services are medical or educational, the limits of service provision are generally determined by the time during which service is required. Certain services do set age limits; for example, in the area of rehabilitation, where facilities and trained personnel are limited, preference is given to younger applicants.

Percentages of Various Population Groups
Served by the Various Programs

As is true in many developing countries, exact figures are difficult to obtain. The size of many groups, such as the disabled, orphans, and so on, can only be estimated. For social policy and planning, populations are generally grouped as follows: children and families, laborers, rural residents, and special groups. For the various disabled and handicapped (special) groups, no figures are available. The percentages of the labor force and of the rural populations receiving benefits will be discussed below under the appropriate ministries. In the area of child and family welfare, the following figures have been published in the Fifth National Development Plan: of the nation's urban children, it is estimated that 400,000 could use day-care facilities. In 1972, 10,000 children between ages three and five, and 24,000 six year olds, were enrolled. It is also estimated that 300,000 of the nation's urban families will be receiving family welfare services by 1978, the end of the Fifth National Development Plan period.

Administrative Organization

As already noted, provision of social welfare services has only recently become a governmental responsibility. Service provision is now divided among six government agencies and a number of semi-private national charitable societies funded by the government as well as by private welfare organizations.

The Plan and Budget Organization of the Imperial Government of Iran is the agency responsible for the formulation and finalization of national development plans. In its Fourth National Development Plan, the Plan and Budget Organization included social welfare goals and planning in national development policy for the first time.[1] The executive agencies concerned with social development and welfare formulate projects in consideration of needs and problems, based on data and statistics within the framework of national growth models and within the resources available. Targets and priorities are decided and financial allocations are made by the Plan Organization in close collaboration and active association with the executive agencies. International and United Nations experiences and findings also are considered in fixing targets and in establishing criteria for priorities. Each ministry and private agency receiving money from the Plan Organization is then responsible for the execution and administration of its programs under the supervision of the Plan and Budget Organization. The administration of individual agencies is left to their governing bodies under the supervision of the appropriate government or public agency. Administration has tended to be centralized, but the general policy of the last two development plans has been toward decentralization, particularly in having local authorities take responsibility for programs. Because health and welfare services were lacking for so long in most provincial areas, no infrastructure has been available to handle these services.

According to the Fourth Plan, the responsibilities and functions of the government at the national level are as follows: planning and formulation of general policies and assignment of priorities; allocation and distribution of credits in various regions, on the basis of requirements and the relative level of development; coordination, establishment of standards, and supervision; framing of regulations; education and research at the regional level; estimation of regional requirements and assistance in planning; coordination at the regional level; and supervision and implementation where social and private organizations are not able to meet urgent local demands.

In order to achieve coordination, establish planning discipline, and prevent overlapping of duties, as well as to avoid wasting human and financial resources, a High Council for Social Affairs has been established. Included in the membership of this planning body are all executive, governmental, social, and private bodies concerned with welfare services. The High Council is presided over by Her Imperial Majesty the Empress of Iran. The Secretariat of the Council is handled by the Plan and Budget Organization. The Council has a general assembly, composed of the representatives of all the above bodies; a central committee, composed of the representatives of major welfare agencies and the planning body; a technical secretariat; and the following technical committees: social insurance, workers' welfare, youth welfare, women's welfare, children's welfare, farmers' welfare, rehabilitation and welfare on specific grounds, recreation, welfare of the aged, and administration and cooperation.

The High Council for Social Affairs, in cooperation with the Plan and Budget Organization, is responsible for all welfare services, for the establishment of terms of reference for social organizations, for the perusal and submission of its views concerning bills and regulations relating to social welfare, and for raising the standards of welfare services.

Financing

Government financing of the welfare program comes largely from oil revenues which are channeled by the Plan and Budget Organization into various sectors of the economy. Additional revenue comes from taxes, the social insurance scheme, the land distribution program, and levies for visas to leave the country.

Staffing and Manpower Patterns

Within government ministries, administrative positions traditionally have been filled by political appointment. Attempts are now being made to introduce uniform standards for selection based on educational qualifications and experience. Present standards include a master's degree and a certain number of years of experience for a managerial position, and a bachelor's degree and some previous experience in direct service provision for a supervisory position. Preference is given to those with some training abroad. A shortage of trained manpower, in addition to resistance within ministries, has made the transition slow.

Direct service can be provided by high school graduates who have received additional in-service or short-course training, or by undergraduate social work and psychology students under faculty supervision. In rural areas, where a high school diploma is rare, those with an eighth-grade education are trained to provide direct service.

The country's only social work school, the Teheran School of Social Work, by 1973 had graduated 580 social workers, persons who are now engaged in supervisory as well as direct-service positions. The school offers a two-year diploma and a four-year B.A. degree and, in 1972, it instituted a master's degree program to provide specialists, supervisors, researchers, and educators for the country's growing social services. The school has also fought to gain acceptance for the profession of social work at the government level. In private organizations, the school has tried to introduce social-work intervention in family and juvenile court cases, and to improve facilities and service provisions.

Additional private agencies run training programs, many of them for the purpose of creating their own manpower. The Iranian Women's Organization runs a Village Social Worker's Institute to train rural workers to help village women improve their living standard; a Family Guidance Training Center to train people in nutrition, health, family planning and child care; and various short-term courses throughout the country for instructors in the fields of nutrition, family planning, mother and child health, and mental health. The Farah Pahlavi Charitable Society has established a child-aid center to train staff for its orphanages and child-care centers. The Red Lion and Sun Society trains youth workers.

It has been very difficult to induce people to work in rural areas because of poor housing and the lack of amenities in villages. Therefore, both government and private agencies are attempting to train villagers, particularly young girls, to work with the women in their own villages in areas such as nutrition, hygiene, sanitation, family planning, health, child care, and so on. Social workers are in charge of training.

Undergraduates at the Teheran School of Social Work, during field assignments in rural villages, undertake projects in community organization and engage in group work with teen-agers and village women. In order to encourage development work in rural areas and also to familiarize urban youth with rural problems, the government has established three revolutionary corps. Service in either the Health, Education, or Extension and Development Corps can fulfill the country's mandatory military duty. Conscriptees in the revolutionary corps must be either high school or university graduates. They receive a four-month training program before being sent to the provinces for the remainder of their two-year service. Fully trained engineers, doctors, nurses, and midwives are also enlisted, since these professionals are rarely found in rural areas. Members of the Health Corps help staff clinics and mobile units of the Ministry of Health, as well as clinics run by the Imperial Organization for Social Services, the Red Lion and Sun Society, and the Rural Cooperatives. Extension and Development Corps members help local communities improve environmental facilities. Education Corps members give literacy instruction to children and adults.

The Plan and Budget Organization sets national goals for manpower training and assigns specific training objectives to various private institutions which receive government funding. During the Fifth Plan, it is envisaged that expansion of manpower in the social welfare field will be achieved by establishing additional training courses for child instructors and assistant child instructors; by creating in-service and pre-service training programs for the existing staff of social and public welfare organizations, as well as for new recruits; and by training the executives of public welfare organizations. In addition, the Plan Organization has stated that experts in various categories of welfare services can be trained at the university level by changing the curricula of related fields such as sociology, psychology, and educational sciences.

Assessment of Outcome

Evaluative research is sponsored by the Plan and Budget Organization to determine policy and program needs. Studies are conducted by the Institute for Social Studies and Research at the University of Teheran. Undergraduate and graduate students at the Teheran School of Social Work undertake evaluative studies on the effectiveness of various programs as well as studies to determine community needs.

Development data and statistics are compiled under the auspices of the Iranian Statistical Center of the Plan Organization. National studies are required since self-evaluative procedures are not built into the system. Without such evaluative studies, it would be difficult to determine whether national programs and overall goals are filtering down to local levels.

GOVERNMENT SERVICE PROVISION

Social service provision in Iran is divided among the following six government agencies: the Ministry of Health, the Ministry of Labor and Social Affairs, the Ministry of Education, the Ministry of Cooperatives and Rural Affairs, the Ministry of Justice, and the Ministry of Interior Affairs. Benefits provided by each ministry will be listed below, along with any additional comments on eligibility criteria, duration of services, staffing and manpower requirements, and so forth.

Ministry of Health

Benefits. The Ministry of Health is responsible for providing medical care for the indigent; operating maternal and child health clinics in lower income areas; providing health insurance for civil servants; running family planning clinics and campaigns; operating hospitals for mental diseases and chronic diseases; undertaking public health campaigns; improving environmental sanitation; combating epidemics and providing emergency food and drug supplies; maintaining school health services (in cooperation with the Ministry of Education); administering rehabilitation services for mental patients, drug addicts, and physically handicapped adults; training and administering the Health Corps; training nurses, nursing assistants, sanitary assistants, laboratory technicians, and midwives; and developing local health councils.

Eligibility. Everyone is eligible to receive free services from hospitals and clinics run by the Ministry of Health. Where facilities are insufficient to meet demand, admissions criteria are set by the executive of the particular agency.

Duration of Services. The time limit is determined by the nature of the treatment.

Percentage of Population Requiring and Receiving Services. No figures are available for urban areas. In 1968 it was estimated that about 50 percent of the rural population was covered by outpatient services, although private organizations, such as the Red Lion and Sun Society and the Imperial Organization for Social Services, were supplementing Ministry of Health services. The Ministry of Cooperatives and Rural Affairs also runs clinics in conjunction with rural cooperatives.

Administration. At the local level, health councils are responsible for public health and medical care—such as the maintenance of general and maternity hospitals—for maternal and child health, and for the supervision of family planning activities. Campaigns against major epidemics and the maintenance of training hospitals and establishments for treatment of tuberculosis, leprosy, and mental disorders are the responsibility of the national government.

A medical care planning council representing all agencies responsible for medical care has been set up. The council, which is informed of the programs of every agency, is able to direct medical affairs in various regions and is able to bring about a more equitable distribution of medical services.

Staffing and Manpower. Because of the uneven distribution of health facilities and medical personnel in the country, various means are being used to bring manpower to rural areas. Among these is the establishment of the country's Health Corps, composed both of trained and semi-trained medical personnel who fulfill their mandatory military conscription by two years of service in a rural area. Clinics are set up by local officials in larger villages, and mobile teams travel from these fixed bases to the surrounding villages.

Ministry of Health personnel include licensed physicians (seven-year M.D. program), nurses (three-year certificate and four-year B.A. program), nurses' aides (two-year certificate program), midwives (one- and two-year courses for nurses and nurses' aides), and sanitarians (short-course and in-service training).

Ministry of Labor and Social Affairs

Benefits. The Ministry of Labor and Social Affairs has responsibility for the welfare of laborers and their families, including the provision of health facilities and the establishment of workers' consumer cooperatives and sports and recreation clubs. It is also in charge of social insurance for laborers, profit-sharing schemes in industry, and the vocational rehabilitation of physically and mentally handicapped adults. Social insurance benefits for workers and their families include medical care and treatment (both in hospitals and at outpatient clinics), medical insurance, old-age pensions, disability insurance, and life insurance. Unemployment insurance will be instituted within the current development plan (1973-1978) on a limited basis.

The pressing problems of urban workers include illiteracy, too many children, lack of specialized skills, malnutrition, inadequate environmental sanitation and public health, periods of intermittent unemployment, limitations in the expansion of trade unions, and lack of suitable housing. To combat these conditions, the following efforts were designed to be implemented during the Fourth Plan (1968-1973): extension of literacy classes in major centers of labor concentration; establishment of first-aid courses; organization of on-the-job classes for raising the skill levels of employed workers; establishment of employment referral centers; creation of two pilot social education centers for the training of literate workers, with a view to preparing them for social and trade union responsibilities; establishment of cultural and sports centers for workers in five industrial regions of the country; establishment of four workers' rest homes in pleasant climates for workers and their families to use during holidays; assistance to the private sector in building 10,000 workers' houses; expansion of workers' consumer cooperatives; establishment of six social service centers which provide day-care facilities, health services, literacy classes, nutrition services, family planning services, and sewing and cooking classes; extending safety and labor inspection services; encouraging employers to establish day nurseries where the number of female workers has reached a certain level; and provision, through two banks, of facilities to extend housing loans to workers.

Eligibility. Some benefits extend to workers in private and state-owned industries; others extend only to workers in state-owned industries such as oil, steel, and railways. Social insurance extends by law to all industrial workers and also to civil servants.

Percentage of Population Requiring and Receiving Services. The total number of laborers at the start of the Fifth Plan (1973) was estimated to be 1.5 million, of which more than 600,000 were working for companies covered by the Ministry of Labor and Social Insurance. It was also estimated that 13 percent of the laborers would benefit from welfare services during the Fifth Plan. At the end of the Fourth Plan, it was estimated that some 30 percent of those for whom premiums had been paid could not use the services since facilities were inadequate.

Of the entire urban population in 1972, 28 percent was covered by medical insurance and 35 percent by life, disability, and retirement insurance. Long-term goals are to provide medical, life, disability, and retirement insurance to 90 percent of the urban population in the next 15 years and, during the current development plan (until 1978), to provide medical coverage and services to 45 percent of the various urban groups and old-age pensions to 72 percent of the urban population.

Goals of the Fifth Plan also include extending coverage to 80 percent of civil servants (university professors and school teachers are presently outside the system, and each ministry insures its own staff), as well as to salaried staff in the private sector and to self-employed persons. At present, civil servants are covered, but medical insurance does not extend to retired civil servants or to their survivors, and social insurance has not extended to workers in the private sector or to self-employed persons. The white-collar workers, the tradesmen, and the rising middle class are still excluded from the system. Accident coverage will also be provided to all urban students.

Administration. Within the Ministry of Labor and Social Affairs there is an Undersecretary for Social Affairs, as well as an Undersecretary for Social Insurance. The High Council on Social Insurance under the ministry coordinates the various government social insurance programs, including the Social Insurance Organization, covering salary and wage-earners in the services, industry, and mining sectors; the Civil Servants' Pension Fund, affiliated with the State Organization for Administrative and Employment Affairs; the Civil Servants' Insurance Organization, affiliated with the Ministry of Health, and responsible for the medical care of civil servants; and the Bimeh Iran Insurance Company, which, in cooperation with the Central Organization for Rural Cooperatives of the Ministry of Agriculture, is responsible for insuring the rural population.

Financing. Social insurance is determined by the employer and employee. Funds for training programs come from a tax on employers. Factories which operate their own training programs are exempt from this tax.

Ministry of Education

Benefits. The Ministry of Education is in charge of child welfare, teachers, and the education of handicapped youth. The Department of Special Education within the Ministry is responsible for exceptional children, including mentally retarded, hard of hearing, deaf, speech impaired, visually handicapped, emotionally disturbed, delinquent, physically handicapped, and gifted children. Formerly, there were only private residential schools, run free of charge, for the blind, deaf, and mentally retarded. While private agencies (including the Red Lion and Sun Society, the National Society for the Protection of Children, and the Episcopal Church of Iran) continue to run special schools, institutes, rehabilitation centers, and technical and vocational training centers for exceptional children, the goal of the Department of Special Education is to integrate handicapped children into classrooms with normal children by using specially trained teachers. Exceptional children are also being taught at present in special classes in the public schools.

Eligibility. All Iranian children, including handicapped children, are entitled to free education through the eighth grade. Eligibility criteria for integrated classes for exceptional children are set by the Department of Special Education.

Staffing and Manpower. Consultants from UNESCO and the American Foundation for Overseas Blind are training counterparts in special education.

Ministry of Cooperatives and Rural Affairs

Benefits. The Ministry of Cooperatives and Rural Affairs is responsible for the welfare of villagers and for their social insurance schemes. The ministry grew out of the Land Reform Act of 1962, an Act sponsored by the Shah, who thought that, in addition to land distribution, various supportive measures were required to improve the living conditions of rural inhabitants. Rural cooperatives have been formed to educate farmers to manage their own affairs and to provide them with loans for equipment and materials. Rural cultural houses have also been established to perform, in rural areas, a function similar to that of family welfare centers in urban areas. Government agencies operate out of these cultural houses, offering services such as outpatient clinical facilities; aid to villagers in improvement of health, sanitation, and water facilities; instruction in the basic principles of hygiene, sanitation, child care, health, and nutrition; literacy classes; and technical and vocational training in cottage industries and handicrafts. The social insurance scheme offers free medical service in its own clinics, sick pay, and transportation costs to patients who must travel to receive treatment.

Eligibility. Ideally these services would be available to all villagers. However, the average Iranian village has a population of 250 to 300 persons, and many villages are extremely isolated. The distribution of these facilities has, therefore, been determined on the basis of population concentration. Social insurance is only available to rural residents who are members of rural cooperatives, in order to facilitate administration of the program. Medical treatment in social insurance clinics is available at a nominal cost to non-members of cooperatives.

Percentage of Population Requiring and Receiving Services. At the beginning of 1973, 1,000 rural cultural houses existed for the country's 18 million rural inhabitants. About 50 percent of the rural areas is covered by medical services provided by the Ministry of Health, the Social Insurance Organization, and private organizations such as the Imperial Organization for Social Services. Five percent of the rural population is covered by medical insurance. Long-term goals of the Social Insurance Organization include extending medical, life, and disability insurance to 80 percent of the rural population over the next 20 years and providing medical coverage and services to 21 percent of the rural population by 1978.

Staffing. It has been extremely difficult to recruit manpower for direct service in rural areas because of inadequate housing and facilities in villages. Members of the Health, Education, and Extension and Development Corps who are serving their two-year military duty receive four months of training before being sent to rural areas. In addition, Home Economics Extension Agents provide instruction in nutrition, health, hygiene, sanitation, and child care for rural women. Efforts are also being made by private organizations, such as the Teheran School of Social Work and the Iranian Women's Organization, to train village residents to improve village life.

Ministry of Justice

Benefits. The Ministry of Justice has responsibility for the welfare of unwanted children, juvenile delinquents, and prisoners. It supervises orphanages and runs training and reform centers for juvenile delinquents. The Prisoners' Aid Society, affiliated with the ministry, provides financial aid to families of prisoners and runs literacy and vocational training programs for prisoners and a manufacturing workshop for unemployed ex-convicts.

Eligibility. The public prosecutor at the municipal level is responsible for accepting, placing, supervising, and determining the status of orphans. Juvenile delinquents are recommended to rehabilitation programs by the court.

Duration of Services. Orphans are entitled to government services until age 18.

Administration. Day-care and boarding services for temporarily deprived and orphaned children are administered by the government at the municipal level and by private organizations. The semi-private organization, the Prisoners' Aid Society, administers its own program.

Staffing. There are no special requirements for providing direct service in orphanages. In-service training is provided. The Prisoners' Aid Society is a voluntary organization with paid social workers.

Ministry of Interior Affairs

The Ministry of Interior Affairs is responsible for the welfare of unwanted children, the aged, and beggars. Responsibility for service provision in these areas lies with the municipalities whose administration is under the Ministry of Interior Affairs. In addition to homes for the aged and work camps for beggars, the municipalities operate hospitals for the indigent and day-care facilities and orphanages for neglected and unwanted children. Each municipality is also responsible for maintaining public health and sanitation and for providing medical care for the indigent. Municipal agencies operate with their own boards of trustees. The Mayor serves as chairman.

Semi-Private and Private Organizations

Because government intervention in social welfare delivery has occurred only recently, and because facilities and trained manpower are still insufficient to meet national needs, semi-private and private organizations continue to provide important services and to supplement government service delivery. Most of these agencies receive government funding; others are funded by private and by religious endowments. All operate independently with their own boards of trustees and their own budgets, and they set their own eligibility criteria and staff requirements.

Representatives of the larger agencies sit on the High Council on Social Affairs along with representatives of the government ministries listed above. This High Council coordinates the activities of public and private bodies and submits recommendations to the Plan and Budget Organization. The Plan Organization includes many of these private bodies in setting target goals for expanding services and facilities and for the training of staff. Along with government funding goes the responsibility to help implement national development goals. The larger and more important agencies are listed below.

Red Lion and Sun Society. The Iranian affiliate of the International Red Cross, the Red Lion and Sun Society, is the oldest social agency in Iran and is administered by Her Imperial Highness Princess Shams Pahlavi. The Red Lion and Sun Society provides emergency relief to disaster victims. It also runs a center for the prevention and treatment of tuberculosis; hospitals and clinics in Teheran and in provincial towns and cities; a polio hospital for children; orphanages, nursing schools, and a youth club; and a workshop for the manufacture of artificial limbs.

Imperial Organization for Social Services. Founded in 1946 and largely administered by Her Imperial Highness Princess Ashraf Pahlavi, the Imperial Organization for Social Services is the pioneer body in mass social welfare in Iran. Its goals include the promotion of both improved health standards in rural areas and aid to the indigent for child care, family planning, and education. IOSS operates hospitals, clinics, and nursing schools and runs campaigns against endemic diseases. Family guidance centers have been established throughout Iran to assist families in the areas of nutrition for mothers and small children, hygiene, infant care, and family planning. Dried milk, vitamins, and other nutriments are distributed by these centers. IOSS has established its own pharmaceutical factory to fill the needs of its own hospitals and clinics as well as those of other charitable organizations. In education, it has established a printing house to provide the necessary materials for the national literacy campaign. It supplies elementary education free of charge to the Literacy Corps and the Ministry of Education. IOSS has created two vocational training schools and funds several others. In addition to free tuition, students are provided with free lunches, traveling expenses, and two sets of clothes per year. IOSS also provides lunches, clothing, shoes, school supplies, and medical care for needy school children. Other services include providing disaster relief, paying debts and securing the release of jailed debtors, supplying artificial limbs and other aids to the handicapped, and providing travel expenses for medical treatment abroad for cases which cannot be cured in Iran.

Farah Pahlavi Charitable Society. The Farah Pahlavi Charitable Society was established to educate both temporarily deprived and orphaned children and youth. The society runs nurseries, day-care centers, boarding houses, vocational and industrial schools, and camps, and provides relief aid and scholarships. It has also established lodging centers for youth between the ages of 18 and 25 who are too old to reside in boarding houses but have not yet established themselves. To train staff, the society has founded a child-aid center for students who have completed the first three years of secondary school and who can pass an entrance examination. Upon completion of the three-year program, they receive the equivalent of a high school diploma.

Society for the Protection of Mothers and Infants. The Society for the Protection of Mothers and Infants operates maternity hospitals and offers pre- and post-natal services. It also provides family planning services, free milk to mothers, and medical care and treatment for indigent women.

National Society for Child Protection. The National Society for Child Protection runs feeding programs and distributes milk and vitamins to nursing mothers, pregnant women, and small children. In addition, it operates a child guidance center and an observation center for emotionally disturbed children.

Community Welfare Center of Iran. The Community Welfare Center operates multi-purpose community centers in overcrowded lower-income urban communities. These centers try to raise the levels of health, education, and welfare, and try to strengthen the family unit through family planning services, day-care facilities for the children of working mothers, group educational and recreational programs for teen-agers, handicrafts and literacy classes for young girls and migrant women, educational programs for young mothers, and individual and family casework. Special centers are run in areas of Teheran with high rates of drug addiction and prostitution. Students and graduates of the Teheran School of Social Work help staff and program the centers. Additional centers are to be developed during the Fifth Plan period.

Family Planning Association of Iran. The Family Planning Association of Iran, founded in 1958, initiated family planning efforts through provision of the first clinical facilities and through educational and motivational campaigns. Provision of family planning services became the responsibility of the Ministry of Health in 1967; since then, the FPA has given priority to education and motivation, although it continues to operate clinics in all community welfare centers. The FPA provides free gynecological examinations and contraceptive devices and offers educational sessions for participants in the family planning program. With the aid of the United Nations Fund for Population Activities, it is pioneering sex education classes for teen-age boys and a rural population education program in villages outside Teheran.

Iranian Women's Organization. The Iranian Women's Organization, dedicated to improving the status of women in Iran, runs vocational training classes and educational programs with a special emphasis on literacy training. It also offers a variety of counseling and guidance services to women, including marriage couunseling, career counseling, and legal advice and guidance. Its affiliates, many of them drawn from religious minorities, provide aid to indigent families and run day-care centers and educational programs for members of their own communities.

National Society for the Rehabilitation of the Disabled. The Society for the Rehabilitation of the Disabled runs a hospital vocational assessment center, a sheltered workshop, and a vocational placement office.

Other Societies and International Agencies

Other national societies have been organized to treat and prevent particular diseases and disabilities and to provide rehabilitation programs, such as the National Society for Aid to Lepers, the Anti-Tuberculosis Association, and the National Society for Liberation from Drug Addiction. Many private charitable institutions exist for unwanted children. The Prisoners' Aid Society was discussed under the Ministry of Justice. Financial and technical assistance are provided by international agencies such as UNTAO, UNESCO, UNICEF, WHO, FAO, and the American Joint Distribution Committee.

RECENT CHANGES AND NEW PLANS

On April 27, 1974, a number of cabinet changes were announced, including the creation of a Ministry of Social Welfare. The administrative organization of this ministry has not yet been announced, but long-range welfare goals have been announced by the

Director of the Plan and Budget Organization, who is responsible for coordinating planning and policy in the welfare field.

In an interview, he explained that welfare is a vital instrument in closing the gap in incomes during this transitional period in Iran's economic development. Thus, welfare programs in Iran will include not only the traditional concerns of health and education, but also housing, job opportunities, pricing policy and subsidies, and other factors that help determine standards of living.

The welfare program, which is closely linked with the general economic development of the country, is concerned with closing the gap not only between social classes, but also between different regions of the country. Decentralization will be standard policy, with more authority being given to provincial governments to ensure the proper implementation of local projects, the spread of welfare services, and the creation of employment in less privileged parts of the country.

In the field of health, the government is moving increasingly toward the idea of a multi-tiered health network providing coverage for the entire country. The plan involves creating a graded system of health services, beginning with basically simple facilities at the village level and building up to more sophisticated clinics, hospitals, and other facilities in towns, provincial centers, and large cities. Such a system would be run by various types of medical staff, with fully qualified physicians and specialists at the top, and with more general practitioners, nurses, doctors' aides, and other personnel working on the lower levels. All members of the staff would work under professional supervision.

The emphasis in planning welfare systems will be on flexibility rather than commitment to a single, all-encompassing approach. A number of different schemes will be applied in the fields of housing, health, and education.

The Minister of Social Welfare, in a recent speech, announced that the first priority of the new ministry will be the extension of health services and medical coverage. Previously, workers covered by social insurance have had to receive medical treatment from social insurance hospitals. In the future, workers will be able to take advantage of services provided by other institutions. Plans are now being drawn up to integrate the services of 700 existing welfare and medical organizations. The ministry will also provide coverage for groups not presently included in the social insurance scheme, such as the aged and employees of private institutions.

NOTE

1. The Fourth Development Plan covered the years 1968 to 1973. The Fifth, and current, Development Plan began in 1973 and will continue to 1978.

5

ISRAEL'S SOCIAL SERVICES: HISTORICAL ROOTS AND CURRENT SITUATION

DAVID MACAROV

Israel's social service system has been shaped by a number of factors. Four of the most influential are the pre-history of the State, the events after independence, the structure of the country, and the special relationship which exists between Israel and Jews abroad. Some understanding of each of these is necessary for a compre-hension of Israel's social service system and its unique features.

PRE-STATE INFLUENCES

In most countries it is possible to identify historico-religious influences in the development of welfare systems. Unique to Israel, however, is the fact that Biblical references are confined to the Old Testament, and their meanings are based upon the Hebrew text. Thus, for example, the word *tzaddakah,* commonly used to designate charity, is actually translatable only as "righteousness." There is no Hebrew word for charity as such.[1]

Furthermore, Old Testament texts were subject to hundreds of years of discussion and interpretation and were codified in a comprehensive guide to conduct, the Talmud, which defines the amount of help due to a needy person as that which enables him to continue his previous style of life.[2] Specifically, if a man accustomed to riding a horse with an attendant preceding him can no longer afford to do so, it is the duty of the community to provide him with a horse and an attendant. Inherent in this interpretation is the idea that stigmatization may be worse than poverty itself, and that cosmetic and psychological measures are as necessary as economic ones. Flowing from this interpretation, and obviously arising from the agricultural economy and simple society of those days, is the idea that poverty is a transient, recurring phenomenon due to chance elements—wind, rain, natural disasters—which affect everyone periodically. Consequently, it will be necessary to furnish the horse and attendant mentioned only for a short time, since luck will change and the temporarily poor will again be self-sustaining. From this philosophy there is a strong thrust toward residual and temporary, rather than structural and permanent, social welfare arrangements.

During the Diaspora, Talmudic and post-Talmudic discussions were concerned mainly with explanations of past conditions in Palestine and with re-interpretations of the new conditions under which Jews then lived. Little thought was given to how the Bible and its commentaries would be interpreted in the event of a return to the ancient homeland under conditions of industrialization, urbanization, and emancipation.

Some Jews had always remained in Palestine, however, and immigration had never completely ceased. By the end of the Middle Ages, there was a small but continuous return to Palestine, mostly by elderly people for religious reasons. In a land notorious for its poverty, these returnees lived on remittances from Jews abroad.[3] These were generally collected and distributed on a communal basis according to a system called *chalukah* ("division" of the funds received). Money collected from one place abroad went only to the Jews from that place living in Palestine. As a consequence, almost all communal services, including synagogues, schools, help for the sick, and poor relief were administered by each Jewish community in Palestine for its own members, based on place of origin. From this system grew both a tradition of mutual aid through immigrants' associations *(Landsmannschaften)* and a certain amount of dependence on outside aid.

Near the turn of the present century, however, young Jews, modern in outlook and vigorous in physique, began to immigrate to Israel. They left countries of intolerance and persecution, mainly in Eastern Europe, to make a new life for themselves and their people in their historic homeland. In their own words, they came to Palestine, "to build and to be rebuilt." The product of nineteenth-century revolutionary Europe, these young pioneers saw the cause and the cure of human ills as primarily rooted in economics. They intended to build a society free of poverty and therefore free of the social ills which flow from or are associated with it, naively believing that all other social problems would be non-existent in such a model society. Emphasizing productive labor, mutual interdependence, and egalitarianism, they established cooperatives, collectives, and labor unions. They rejected, and sometimes clashed with, the concept of chalukah, which they thought inherently degrading. To the pioneers, poverty was not inevitable and recurring, but a result of personal laziness or a failure to participate in cooperative or collective systems.

The continued influx of newcomers, including religious Jews and Zionist pioneers *(chalutzim),* led to a growing Jewish community. Under the aegis of the Ottoman Empire, each religious community organized its own affairs, including courts, schools, hospitals, and economic structures. No help was provided by the government for these purposes; on the contrary, each step required multifarious permissions, tax payments, and often bribes. When British rule replaced Turkish rule after World War I, the system of recognized religious communities with large, self-governing areas continued.[4] Thus, it was not only permitted, but became necessary, for the Jewish community to establish all the appurtenances of a state, but without the ultimate ability to enforce its laws or collect its taxes, which right was reserved to the governing power.

With some help from individuals and organizations abroad, the Jewish community in Palestine organized itself through voluntary action and self-imposed taxation and discipline. Its elected body, the *Vaad Leumi* (National Committee), established in 1920, undertook functions which elsewhere would have been those of a sovereign government, including the provision of all necessary socioeducational and health services.

Efforts such as these succeeded in building up a school system which served 95 percent of the Jewish community's school children, medical services covering 70 percent of Jewish workers, a network of local welfare offices, homes for children, unemployment relief, and a number of emergency relief schemes. During this period, 95 percent of the mandatory government's contributions for such services went to the non-Jewish communities on the basis that they were not capable of aiding themselves.[5]

The two attitudes toward social welfare—the "Old Yishuv" living

on chalukah and the young pioneers espousing personal revolution—
were adopted and modified by other groups of immigrants who
arrived during the thirties and forties. Immigrants from Germany had
a more modern philosophy of social welfare, and emphasized the use
of institutions for various social needs. The small number of
Americans who arrived had a broader view of social welfare than
dependence on chalukah or on collectives. For example, Baltimore-
born Henrietta Szold, who became the first head of the Vaad
Leumi's social service department in 1931, attempted to bridge the
gap between the two philosophies by instituting services which
covered persons who were members of neither group. She pressed for
legislation which made provision of services the responsibility of the
entire Jewish community, and placed social services in the hands of
trained professionals.[6]

On the eve of independence, then, a community of 650,000 Jews
existed in Palestine. Organized into a voluntary quasi-government, it
conducted most of the services normally associated with a state. The
social welfare component of this community included elements—not
always compatible—drawn from Biblical and post-Biblical teachings;
attitudes basically rooted in an agricultural economy; an interpretation of social justice flowing from economic determinism; and
some concern that private, mutual-aid, and collective efforts be
supplemented by trained professionals at a governmental level.

THE EFFECTS OF STATEHOOD AND THE LAW OF RETURN

The emergence of the State of Israel in May, 1948 brought about
fundamental changes in the social welfare situation. The newly
created Ministry of Social Welfare took over the former functions of
the Vaad Leumi. Although strengthened by tax support and
legislative sanction, it was simultaneously called upon to include in
its activities all the other religious and ethnic communities in the
country: Arabs, Druze, Circassians, Bedouin, Roman Catholics,
Greek Orthodox, Protestants, Moslems, and others. It was also
required to decide which of the activities of local and overseas
voluntary organizations should more properly become government
functions, which should remain with their former sponsors, and
which new services needed to be created. These massive economic,
philosophic, and administrative problems were further complicated
by Israel's defensive war to maintain its newly won independence

and the additional social welfare problems resulting from army service: deaths, invalidism, and economic dislocation.

Of greater importance than all of these, however, were the consequences of the Law of Return, passed immediately after the proclamation of the State, which opened the country to every Jew wishing to enter. The result was a tidal wave of immigrants. The Jewish population of 650,000 increased by 50 percent in the 18 months following, doubled in the first three years, and has grown to over two and a half million since then. The total population has topped three million.

The effect of this mass—though voluntary—uprooting is visible everywhere in Israel. Urban people attempted to become farmers, since the future of Israel was visualized and planned as primarily agricultural. People who had previously lived in caves and had never seen beds, tables, or kitchen sinks collided abruptly with movies, machines, and free, universal, compulsory education. Others who had grown up in large houses with servants and labor-saving devices found themselves in cramped quarters with only the most functional furniture. Some of the problems experienced by recent immigrants from Russia may serve as examples: the independent craftsman —tailor, barber, plumber—waits in his newly opened shop for the government to direct customers to him; the idea of competing with others to attract customers is simply unknown to him. The Russian mother who wants to visit her daughter in another city cannot believe that she does not need a permit to travel; when finally convinced she is critical of such lack of governmental control. Israeli social welfare rights, regulations, and processes are a mystery to many such immigrants, who come from very different systems. Within this Russian culture, there are sizable subcultures of Georgians and Bukharians who have their own distinctive languages, institutions, life-styles, and problems.[7]

Further, the Six-Day War in 1967 left Israel in control of large territories inhabited by over a million people, including Bedouins, Samaritans, Armenians, Christian Arabs, Moslems, and others. In addition to undertaking various development plans for these areas and their inhabitants, all the regular services of the State such as mail, sanitation, education, and health services, had to be extended. The social welfare services of the State were offered sometimes through the agency and machinery of the United Nations Relief and Works Agency (UNRWA), sometimes directly by the Ministry of Social Welfare, and sometimes through local bodies. At the same time, the activities of various existing voluntary bodies, including many church groups, were continued and encouraged. Existing institutions dealing with beggars, the blind, and the neglected were supported and new ones were established, employing over a hundred local social workers.

For new immigrants, and to a lesser extent for the minorities with a new status, there were changes in economic and social positions, role expectancy, and role performance; in family structures and self-images; and in norms, values, and aspirations. These changes make up the second background factor against which all social welfare activities in Israel must be viewed.

THE STRUCTURE OF ISRAEL

Because Israel is a small country with no political subdivisions or regional units, there are no intervening structures—states, counties, boroughs, provinces, or territories—between the national government and localities. Services are offered by local authorities, the national government, voluntary bodies, or through cooperative arrangements among them.

Politically, Israel enjoys universal franchise from age 18, with national parties elected under a proportional representation system. Since from the beginning of the State no party has ever commanded an absolute majority in the one-chamber legislature, government is invariably by coalition. The three major parties are the left-wing Labour Party, the more right-wing Consolidated Party, and the National Religious Party; the first has always been the senior partner in every coalition.

This structure affects social welfare policies and activities, since government ministries are apportioned to coalition partners in accordance with their strength. In this manner, the Ministry of Social Welfare has almost always been controlled by the minority Religious Party. As a junior party in the coalition, the Ministry of Social Welfare has not often been able to wield enough power to assure itself of the budget or the laws which it desires. Another powerful agent in the social welfare field is the National Insurance Institute. Since this agency is part of the Ministry of Labour, and thus under the control of the majority Labour Party, a certain amount of competition between it and the Ministry of Social Welfare is almost inevitable.

Elections are by party lists, and therefore representatives are neither nominated nor elected locally, nor do they represent geographic areas. Instead, they are part of a national slate which may or may not include people from any given area. Hence, specific groups within the population, such as the aged or the poor, have no machinery for electing someone to represent them specifically, short of organizing a new political party. Occasionally there are attempts to organize parties representing ethnic groups, immigrant groups, or specific strata of society, but none of these has met with much success.

The economic structure also affects social welfare services. Because of the egalitarian ideology of the pioneers, most salaries take into consideration the marital status of the wage earner, with increments for non-working wives and the first two children. Similarly, the law establishes conditions of tenure in many jobs, and prescribes severance pay at the rate of one month's pay for every year worked. There are also increments for academic attainments in some positions. Finally, salaries in Israel are usually linked to a cost-of-living index and change automatically with changes in the economy. These arrangements govern the amount of need which exists, and consequently social welfare policies and payments.

It would be incomplete to leave the structure of Israeli society without describing the General Federation of Labor *(Histadruth)*. Established as an inclusive labor union, at the end of 1972 it had 1,161,036 members (including 300,000 housewives), which is 57 percent of the labor force, or, including family members and some smaller affiliated unions, 85 percent of the employed population.[8] Because of its numerical strength and the fact that many of its early and present leaders are also governmental figures, the policies of the Histadruth have strongly affected the policies of the government in a number of fields. Some of the provisions of the Histadruth have been incorporated into law, so that the benefits flow to the entire population and not just to union members. On the other hand, the Histadruth has fought to preserve some services as its exclusive domain, since such prerogatives result in membership. A case in point is the inability of the country to provide a universal health insurance or service, since the health service of the Histadruth is one of its strongest elements in drawing and maintaining membership. Thus, because of the strength of the Histadruth and the intermingling of labor union and government leadership, there is a constant dynamic interchange between the two regarding social welfare services such as housing, health, and pensions.

The Histadruth, as a labor union, makes its benefits available almost exclusively to the employed, and governmental measures, guided by the ideology of the "productive citizen," also pay out many benefits through employers. This leaves at an obvious disadvantage those citizens who cannot or should not work: youngsters, mothers of small children, the disabled, the aged, and those who cannot find suitable employment.

CONTRIBUTIONS FROM ABROAD

Since the inception of Zionism, individuals and groups abroad have made substantial, sometimes massive, contributions to Israel. The amount of such contributions and the conditions under which they were made have invariably affected not only the relative strength of different services but also the methods by which the services are rendered.

Despite their obvious advantages, these contributions have created certain problems. In the early days of the State, for example, when the population was comparatively young, one investigator found a heavier emphasis on care of the aged than their proportion of the population would warrant, and at the expense of other more necessary services, such as family welfare.[9] It has been held that this was true, in part, because the aged had been discovered as a problem in America, and experts from the United States operating in Israel were projecting onto the latter the problem with which they felt best qualified to deal.

Help from abroad was often offered with the positive intention of changing the type or quality of services in Israel, or to "influence the development of a whole chain of social services in the broadest sense of the term."[10] On the other hand, the shape of help was sometimes dictated more by the needs of the contributing organization than by the situation in Israel, as in the case of a needed youth hostel's conversion into a less necessary youth center so that visiting members of the sponsoring organization would not see an empty building. Help from abroad also sometimes leads to a loss of accountability; although local organizations receiving most of their funds from abroad may not maintain desirable standards, they assure their contributors that the service is good, needed, and effective.

With the four background factors outlined above in mind, it is possible to view the present situation of social services in Israel.

THE STRUCTURE OF SERVICES

The Ministry of Social Welfare

Given a reasonably wide definition of social welfare, at least eight ministries offer direct social services of one sort or another: the Ministries of Social Welfare, Labour, Absorption, Housing, Education, Health, Defense (veterans' benefits), and Justice. The basic responsibility, however, rests with the Ministry of Social Welfare, which establishes policy, supervises the work, and supplements the budgets of local welfare bureaus. The ministry has divisions of Family and Community Services, Child and Youth Welfare, Rehabilitation, and Care of the Aged, the Retarded, and the Blind. It also includes Probation Services for Juvenile and Adult Offenders, the Youth Protection Authority, and the Division for the Supervision of Public Institutions.

In each of the large cities there are municipal social welfare departments. In over 180 smaller communities there are local welfare offices, including 45 run by Arab and Druze communities and eight run directly by the Ministry of Social Welfare. Every local authority is required by law to establish a welfare office, with part of its budget coming from the Ministry of Social Welfare and part from local taxes. Only in those cases where municipal status is still lacking does the ministry administer aid directly. However, almost 80 percent of the local communities have at various times required allocations, and even the largest municipalities require subventions of 40 percent or more of their budgets.

In carrying out its mandate, the Ministry of Social Welfare is affected by some of the problems, already mentioned, arising from history and structure. For example, although the ministry is charged with supervising public institutions, some of these, such as orphans' homes and institutions for the handicapped, are completely or primarily funded from abroad. In cases where these do not reach the standards required by the ministry, and if the foreign donors are too dispersed or indifferent to take action, then the alternative to allowing them to continue functioning is to provide other, better, institutions or services in their places—a step which the ministry may not be able to take since it does not have access to funds from abroad.

Similarly, where the chalukah tradition was concerned with the division of funds, and the chalutz tradition dealt with more basic remedies, social welfare offices both disperse funds and offer services, functions which are not always compatible and which put tremendous burdens on the workers involved.[11] Some attempts have been made recently to divide payments from services, but the outcome of this division is not yet clear.[12] The activities of the Ministry of Social Welfare are categorical, dealing with specific groups on the basis of need.

The National Insurance Institute

The National Insurance Institute, established in 1954, is perhaps the second most important social welfare agency in Israel. Financed by employers, employees, self-employed persons, the voluntary insured (including housewives), and the government, the National Insurance Institute has been developing and encompassing a number of new services in the last few years. The plan assures pensions for men at age 65 and for women at age 60. Eligible pensioners may postpone retirement and acquire an additional 5 percent for each postponed year up to age 70 for men and 65 for women, at which time they are entitled to full pension regardless of other income.[13] About 70 percent of eligible pensioners do postpone their retirement in this manner. The plan assures pensions for an estimated one million people; 165,000 were receiving pensions in July 1973.[14] Included in the pension plan is survivors' insurance for widows and orphans; in 1973, 44,500 persons were receiving this benefit.[15] A single person's pension is set at 20 percent of the average income from salaries. For a widow with two children, payments amount to 30 percent; a recent amendment covers widowers also. Many persons are members of union or private pension plans in addition to National Insurance, and may legally receive as much as 70 percent of a salary less than I£ 1,500 monthly.

Work injury insurance for employment accidents is also covered by the National Insurance Institute. This includes medical treatment, vocational rehabilitation, 75 percent of pay for up to 26 weeks of treatment, and special grants, including burial expenses.

Maternity benefits available from the National Insurance Institute include birth grants, of which 85,000 were given in 1973, and maternity benefits, which numbered 27,000.[16] These cover the cost of transportation to the hospital, expenses there, and a grant for a layette. Working mothers receive 75 percent of their regular salary for a 12-week period, and at that time may choose to take an unpaid leave for another nine months (with their position assured on return) or return to their jobs and work an hour a day less for the remainder of the year. The repayment of transportation and hospital costs seems to have had a side-effect: the percentage of babies born in hospitals has risen, with a consequent decline in infant mortality. Infant mortality among Israeli Arabs, for example, has dropped 50 percent in the last 20 years.

One of the most widespread of the National Insurance Institute's programs is that of family allowances. Grants are paid to all families with three or more children under the age of 18. These grants are not computed as income for families receiving welfare, but, for reasons discussed below, are taxable. In 1973, 170,000 families with three or more children received such grants; this covered 425,000 children under the age of 18. In recent years there has been a proportionately greater increase in payments to large families (six or more children) than to smaller families. While the latter increased 50 percent, the former more than doubled.

Just as programs of the Ministry of Social Welfare are mostly categorical, so the programs of the National Insurance Institute are generally universal. Family allowances are paid to all families of appropriate size, regardless of financial situation, and the same is true of maternity pay; also old-age pensions are paid to everyone who has contributed the minimum amount. The classical question of widespread smaller payments versus selected larger payments, with the subsidiary questions of stigma, quality of service, and public support, was compromised with the last increase in family allowances by extending them to the entire population but making them taxable in order to recover a large share of the sums going to families in the middle and upper income brackets.

Finally, the National Insurance Institute has been the agency designated to administer Israel's new Unemployment Compensation Law. For many years the pioneer philosophy of the productive man controlled unemployment measures, and work relief was the method used to reduce unemployment. This philosophy was reinforced by Israel's labor shortage of many years, which strengthened the view that anyone who wanted to work could find a job. A slight recession immediately before the Six-Day War in 1967 led to legislation establishing a contributory-insurance type of program which began January 1, 1973, but with the return of labor shortages after the war (unemployment was less than 1 percent in September, 1971), little experience has been gained with this law.[17]

The General Federation of Labor

As mentioned previously, the General Federation of Labor (Histadruth) extends a full program of benefits to its members, with heavy emphasis on health services. However, it also includes a pension plan, life insurance, workman's compensation, maternity grants, sickness benefit insurance, and vacation payments.[18] In addition, in almost every locality there is a Workingman's Council *(Moetzet Hapoalim)* which conducts informal educational activities, civic celebrations, and often sponsors a youth or community center. It is supplemented by Working Women's Councils *(Moetzet Hapoalote)* which conduct day-care centers, housewives' groups and courses, and community organization activities.

Other Ministries

There are several ministries other than Social Welfare which engage in similar activities. The Ministry of Health conducts mental health clinics throughout the country using psychiatric, psychological, and social work personnel. It also has social work departments in government hospitals and in rehabilitation units. Perhaps the most successful public agencies sponsored by this ministry are the well-baby clinics *(Tipat Chalav),* open to all pregnant women and young mothers and heavily patronized by women from all levels of the population. Within this setting there are family counseling and other auxiliary services which fall within, or are closely related to, social welfare services. The ministry also cooperates with other bodies in preventive medical centers for the aged, in which social work plays an important role.

The Ministry of Education employs social workers in schools (a service which is growing) and sponsors a series of youth and community centers throughout the country.[19] Many of the latter employ community organizers as part of their staff. The ministry also has diagnostic centers, guidance centers, and boarding schools, all of which employ social work personnel.

The Ministry of Housing is a partner in a number of government-sponsored housing companies (for example, Amidar), which not only employ community organizers but also cooperate with local authorities or Workingmen's Councils in establishing youth and community centers.

Public Agencies and Services

Because each religious and geographic community took care of its own needs, a wide distribution of public agencies resulted, ranging from free-loan societies (estimated at 500), to support of religious schools *(yeshivot)*, and associations of immigrants from various countries with a variety of services for members.[20] The Association of Immigrants from Central Europe, for example, has a network of exemplary homes for the aged. There are also agencies for polio victims and crippled children, for the retarded, for the blind, and for cancer and tuberculosis patients, as well as the Red Mogen Dovid (the Israeli equivalent of the Red Cross), the Soldiers' Welfare Committee, and many others.

On the other hand, the ideology of a model state which would solve all problems has led to a centralization of services by the government, or has at least militated against wide-scale voluntary fund-raising by social welfare councils, community federations, or community chests. Each public agency conducts its own fund-raising in its own manner, although it is common for government ministries to participate in the budgets of such institutions. There have been some attempts to organize and coordinate the various public agencies, but these efforts are still in the beginning stages.

Overseas Agencies and Services

As noted above, Israel enjoys a long tradition of help received from individuals, institutions, and organizations abroad. These include church groups, such as the Quakers, Lutherans, and Mennonites; service organizations, such as B'nai B'rith; philanthropic bodies like the Joint Distribution Committee; and organizations designed primarily to aid Israel, such as Hadassah, the Women's International Zionist Organization, and others. In some cases these agencies undertook specific projects in Israel, such as scholarships for social workers and educators; in other cases, they undertook complete responsibility for an area of service. Thus, at one time Hadassah was primarily responsible for health services, while the Jewish Agency for Palestine was responsible for all phases of the absorption of new immigrants. Most widespread, however, was a cooperative arrangement between overseas and local agencies, and many of the exclusive arrangements eventually moved in this direction. Thus, the American Joint Distribution Committee, the

Jewish Agency for Palestine, and the Government of Israel formed a body (Malben) which was responsible for the care of hard core cases among immigrants. In the same way, the Red Mogen Dovid established a fund-raising arm abroad but retained control over local operations. Similarly, Hadassah turned over some of its operations and institutions to the Ministry of Health and sought government funding for its remaining Israeli operations.

The flow of money, manpower, and expertise which is represented by both local and overseas organizations is considerable. Hadassah spent $20 million in Israel in 1971, and the Joint Distribution Committee spent $4 million. It has been estimated that 35 percent of all welfare expenditures in the country come from such philanthropic sources.[21]

The Jewish Agency

The Jewish Agency of Israel is the executive body of the World Zionist Organization, which a number of non-Zionist organizations have joined in order to participate in its philanthropic, health, and educational activities. Perhaps the most extensive and best known activity of the Jewish Agency is its absorption of immigrants. This begins with preparation in the immigrant's original country, help with transportation if necessary, and responsibility for the immigrant in Israel until he or she becomes self-supporting. Since the latter phase involves temporary accommodations, Hebrew lessons, permanent housing, and employment, all of which involve governmental measures, a Ministry of Absorption undertakes those matters. Cooperation between the Jewish Agency and the Ministry of Absorption is necessarily close.

The Jewish Agency has a social services department which deals with new immigrants. In 1972 this department employed 160 people, most of whom worked at the port of entry, the transitional absorption center, or the permanent residence. In the same year, the department assisted over 8,000 families in permanent residences, and of these, only 455 were unable to achieve independence and were referred to the sociaal welfare authorities. Ninety-three percent of the families which receive assistance are able to support themselves after one year.[22] Special departments of the Jewish Agency deal with immigrants in agricultural settlements, collectives, and cooperatives. Expenditures by the Jewish Agency for health and welfare services were over $100 million in 1971.

Fields of Service

Family and Community Services. The most extensive section of the Ministry of Social Welfare is the division of family and community services, which is in charge of public assistance programs and policies. These are carried out, as indicated, by local authorities. Although much of the work, and many of the payments, go to individual, the name of the division is an indication of the attempt to move toward wider concepts of social welfare, dealing with families as units and their community settings.

Since there are no private family agencies in Israel, the ministry is ultimately responsible for family casework. Social welfare offices, as noted above, combine both financial assistance and other aspects of casework service. In the public mind, however, public welfare offices are generally considered to be for financial aid only, despite the fact that a study of the activities of workers in social welfare offices indicates that only 28 percent dealt with finances as such.[23] Over 10 percent of their activities dealt with general support, family and personal problems, education, housing, and health.[24] In 1972, about 135,000 families, 17 percent of the families in Israel, received help through social welfare offices; 28,000 received regular or occasional financial help, 66,000 received other kinds of material help, and 40,000 received services only. The average welfare income of a family with four children is about 60 percent of the average income of all employed persons in Israel; a family with two children receives about 40 percent.[25]

Child Welfare. Emphasizing family care, there are attempts to keep children at home by dealing with their problems within the family. To this end there has been a large increase recently in day-care services for young children, many of which are sponsored by voluntary organizations and subsidized by the Ministry of Social Welfare. The average age of children benefiting from this service has consistently moved downwards and now includes six-month-old infants. There are also attempts to use such services to involve parents in family-life education activities. Although many of the centers are for working mothers, there are others open to the entire population. Pre-kindergartens are also a growing service; kindergarten is part of compulsory education. There are also settings for casework treatment for children and their parents, separate from the welfare offices, and, as mentioned previously, there are school social workers.

As a result of the correlation between large families and social problems, both universal and categorical schemes have been adopted to aid children by aiding their families.[26] There are therefore measures such as those which add rooms to the houses of large families, give supplementary income, and give a priority for services such as day-care programs. The largest single budget item in the Ministry of Social Welfare is for child welfare (40 percent). There are many indirect services as well.

Nevertheless, there are occasions where out-of-family arrangements are necessary. These arrangements may be more necessary in Israel than in other countries because of the housing and economic pressure on new immigrants, because of a culture which leads some of them to see in institutions a step up for their children on the economic and social scale, and because of the remnants of the previously mentioned European tradition which holds institutional care in high esteem.

Highest priority is given to foster care, and there are many efforts to use this resource.[27] This is inhibited, however, by the small size of the average Israeli house, by the social and economic instability of the homes of new immigrants, and sometimes by the desire of service organizations to establish buildings and children's villages, the latter two being services which can be seen and visited, as compared to amorphous services like foster homes. Yet there are many cases in which foster care is neither possible nor desirable. Some children are away from their homes, for example, not because of special needs, deficiencies, or family problems, but for socioeconomic reasons; a child may be sent to live in a Yeshiva (religious school) or an agricultural or vocational boarding school. Others are in institutions because of placement by social agencies or by court order. The bulk of institutionalized children are in agencies run by voluntary organizations, such as WIZO, the Council of Women Workers, Mizrachi Women, and B'nai B'rith.

Adoption, on the other hand, is not widespread in Israel. There are about 200 adoptions a year, and 40 percent of these are by relatives.[28]

Youth Services. A great deal of attention has always been turned to youth problems in Israel. As a result of social tensions which arose before the Yom Kippur War from so-called disadvantaged youth, a special committee was established by the prime minister to study the problem and make recommendations. The committee concluded that approximately 20,000 young people between the ages of 14 and

17—about 9 percent of the total—were neither employed nor studying. Recommendations included intensification of existing programs, institution of new services, and creation of a youth authority to coordinate all activities.

Existing services include a number of youth movements which stress outdoor life, patriotism, and good citizenship.[29] It is estimated that about 60 percent of youth between the ages of 11 and 17 belong to such movements at one time or another, although the high intellectual content and the lack of leaders from their own backgrounds have kept new immigrant youth from joining these movements. There is also an extensive network of youth centers. Mainly handled by the Ministry of Education, this network includes school-based and building-based activities. There are also multi-purpose youth centers which offer basic education, occupational training, income-producing employment, and sociocultural activities for youngsters from 14 to 18 who are not in school.

In addition to institutions for children with behavioral problems, homes for deaf children, institutions for the mentally retarded and autistic, and orphanages for Arab children, the Ministry of Social Welfare maintains 14 institutions for convicted delinquents, with about 600 youths in residence. An additional 450 are in foster homes or in institutions maintained by voluntary organizations.

For non-delinquents there are over a hundred institutions, including boarding schools, supported by overseas bodies or local public or private groups. About 12,000 children are in such institutions as a result of placement by welfare departments, while about 8,000 are there at the request of their families or because no suitable schools exist in their home areas. Some parents specifically want religious or non-religious schools for their children.

Concern for disadvantaged youth has led to a recent increase in the number of street-corner or detached workers who attempt to help youngsters in their environment. More than 35 localities now use this approach, and in addition to the workers who are trained by the Ministry of Social Welfare, male and female soldiers, as well as para-professionals and volunteers, have been used for this work.

Finally, youth services include the juvenile court system, which is part of the Ministry of Justice and has been moving toward a social welfare rather than a criminal court approach, and a juvenile probation service, which is part of the Ministry of Social Welfare, employing social workers as probation officers.[30] Although about 18,000 young people were dealt with by the police in 1972, with about one-half of them brought into the juvenile court system, the rate of juvenile delinquency has been decreasing: from 19.5 per thousand in 1964, to 18.3 in 1970, to 16.3 in 1972.

Services for the Aged. Until statehood, Israel had practically no old-age problems. The proportion of the population aged 65 or over was less than 4 percent. This situation changed drastically with the onset of unselective mass immigration. In addition, life expectancy has been rising at a constant rate. Consequently, by 1970 the aged made up 7.2 percent of the population. The agreement mentioned previously, whereby Malben undertook the care of all hard core cases among immigrants, included almost all of the aged immigrants. As a result more than a quarter million immigrants have benefited from cash grants, rental or purchase of apartments, housekeeping help, clubs and day centers, meals on wheels, and counseling and guidance activities.

The question of income for the aged has been dealt with in a number of ways. In addition to the pensions sponsored by the Histadruth and other bodies and the old-age payments made by the National Insurance Institute, there is an old-age assistance program for the aged (including those who arrived in Israel at age 65 or close to it) who would not be sufficiently covered otherwise; their contributions to the fund were not enough to make them eligible for payments at a decent level, if at all. Although this is a means-tested program, it is administered by the National Insurance Institute and serves about 27,000 recipients. There are also sheltered workshops for the aged. Social clubs exist in most localities, sometimes within other institutions such as community centers.

Rehabilitation. Rehabilitation of the handicapped is an important part of Israel's social welfare system. The Ministry of Defense connducts a network of services for wounded soldiers, including hospitalization, training, and business loans. In addition, there are a number of institutions and services for the 6,000 blind, including centers in Beersheba and Haifa, a home for the aged blind, a live-in institution in Jerusalem, a training center for seeing eye dogs, a Braille library, and several church-supported schools and institutions. Sign language has been modified for Hebrew, and interesting work is being done in teaching the blind to find their way using audible and tactile cues.

There are three schools for deaf-mutes, two of them with hostels to allow children from outlying districts to attend. The 2,500 deaf-mutes sponsor an autonomous association with its own building, workshops, and social and cultural activities, including a newspaper.

There are two associations for crippled children, an Anti-Tuberculosis League, a Cancer Society, associations for invalids of various
kinds, sheltered workshops, an employment agency for the disabled,
a cooperative warehouse, furnished apartments for invalids, and a
fund to help aged and handicapped farmers until their children can
take over. This latter arrests both the abandonment of farms and the
drift to the cities. There are seven training centers under government
auspices and seven conducted by voluntary groups; in all, there are
350 places.

The Ministry of Social Welfare has a special section dealing with
the mentally retarded, of whom there are estimated to be about
12,000 with I.Q.s of 65 or less. About one-third of these are in
institutions or foster homes, others are waiting for such placement,
and the remainder are helped in their own family homes. As in many
other countries, care for mentally retarded adults is more problem-
atic than for children.

Other mental health activities include community mental health
centers (some with branches in community centers) and separate
guidance clinics for adults and children in the main towns, with
stations for all ages in some smaller localities. A rehabilitation fund
helps persons discharged from mental hospital. There are halfway
houses for patients on their way back into the community, and
resocialization attempts through group sessions and activities are
being made.

Community Work. The Ministry of Social Welfare has a community organization section. The government housing authority uses
community organizers as part of its staff. There is also a growing
number of community centers being established by the Ministry of
Education. Activities range from coordination of services to volunteer clean-up campaigns and from adult literacy classes to the
organization of protest actions. Community organization plays an
important role in Israel, partly because entire communities have been
built on vacant land to accommodate newcomers from many
countries. Difficult questions concerning segregation and integration,
clashes of cultures, values, and language complicate the job of the
community organizer.

Unique Aspects of Social Welfare in Israel

Problem-Free Areas. Despite the many social welfare problems
unique to Israel, there are some areas which are relatively free of
problems in comparison with other countries. Alcoholism, for

example, is not a widespread problem. Wine, locally produced liquor, and beer are relatively cheap. There are cases in which welfare payments are reputedly used to purchase liquor, but public drunkenness, crime resulting from drunkenness, and even drunk driving are rare in Israel. Hence, there is no equivalent of Alcoholics Anonymous, and few social workers need to be aware of alcoholism as a syndrome. Similarly, the number of unwed mothers is small, possibly due in part to the easy availability of abortions (despite their technical illegality) and to sections of the population with very strong mores about family purity and honor. Most drug use is at the hashish level (which is illegal), and addiction to hard drugs has not become a problem of any dimension. The spread of the hashish culture is attributed by some to the influx of young volunteers from abroad and to the opening of borders to Moslem areas; it is thus indirectly associated with bordering countries. It should be noted, however, that in the Moslem culture smoking hashish is usually limited to mature adults. It is the combination of ease of access and Western youngsters which has magnified the problem in Israel.

Prostitution has become more of a problem since the Six-Day War. It is seen as a social problem rather than a criminal one, since prostitution as such is not illegal, although solicitation is. There is little evidence in Israel of organized prostitution as it exists in other countries.[31]

Perhaps the smallness of the country and the inability to cross its borders are responsible for the low incidence of runaway children in Israel. Social workers are not often called upon to deal with other aspects of a counter-culture. For example, there is no widespread activity concerned with evading Israel's nearly universal draft or aiding army deserters. On the contrary, many informal educational and youth center activities are designed to help youngsters pass the army entrance tests and raise their "profiles" so they can undertake more responsible jobs once in the service.

The Kibbutz. Kibbutzim (voluntary agricultural collectives) are socioeconomic forms unique to Israel.[32] Over 80,000 Israelis, or 3-4 percent of the population, live in some 250 such settlements and need few of the social welfare services described above. Kibbutzim provide complete economic, social and cultural services for their members, including universal education through high school and in some cases university education; all needed medical services; leisure activities, hobbies, and vacations; and care for survivors. Consequently, no financial welfare services are needed except when absorbing new immigrants. However, since there are family, marital, psychological, and educational problems, associations of kibbutzim have established their own child guidance clinics and trained their own special educators in accordance with kibbutz philosophy. Kibbutzim do not have policemen, a probation or prison service, or a need for relief payments. Groups of disadvantaged or pre-delinquent youth are often invited to live in a kibbutz. There is also a trend toward introducing individual immigrant children into kibbutz schools and adopting older children into kibbutz families.

Youth Aliyah. Founded in 1932, Youth Aliyah began as a plan to rescue Jewish youth from threatened Europe, bringing them in organized groups to collective settlements in Palestine. It was originally limited to selected groups of volunteers. Later it included any youngsters rescued from Nazism and survivors of concentration camps. During the years of mass immigration, children from Mid-Eastern and North African countries were accepted. Recently, children in need of special frameworks have been included. After being interviewed and tested, children are assigned to children's villages run mostly by the youngsters themselves under professional guidance. More than 150,000 youngsters have passed through the organization since its inception.[33]

Immigrant Absorption. As indicated in a number of places above, the absorption of new immigrants is a continuing and conscious part of the social welfare system, with many agencies and institutions established primarily for that purpose, and others influenced by that goal in various ways. It is worth emphasizing, however, that the integration of immigrants is an enunciated and established policy for social welfare services as well as for others, and social workers and social welfare programs are expected to further this aim. It is not always clear, however, whether the aim is to assimilate new immigrants into the existing culture, to create a melting pot from which a new culture will arise, or to promote cultural pluralism.[34]

The Defense Army of Israel. In times of peace, the army plays an important social welfare role. In addition to extensive educational opportunities as well as vocational training, the army has social welfare officers who deal with problems arising from military service. Female soldiers with the proper background are often assigned as teachers or teaching aides, usually in areas where it is difficult to find enough teachers. In some cases they are assigned to youth or community centers for informal educational purposes. There are instances in which soldiers have been used as community organizers, identifying problems by visiting families in their homes and offering help to large families in difficult circumstances by baby-sitting, shopping, helping with laundry, and so on.

Training for Social Work

There are four university-based schools of social work in Israel, and a training institute which has no academic connection. Most practice training is given on a bachelor's degree level, while master's degree programs emphasize research, administration, and supervision. There is also a diploma program to train senior staff members for the growing network of community centers.

Coverage

Despite the widespread, and often innovative, social welfare services in Israel, there are charges that the socioeconomic gap is not being reduced.[35] Before the outbreak of the Yom Kippur War, increasing attention was being turned to the gap issue and ways to deal with it, including interest in a reverse income tax. The results of the Yom Kippur War, including its costs, the dislocations entailed, and the post-war situation, will undoubtedly have a profound impact on the shape of social services in Israel in the years to come. One projection suggests there will be an increased emphasis on mental health activities, help for war widows, and rehabilitation of the disabled.[36] There will probably be continued movement in the direction of universal as opposed to selective payments, and separation of payments from services. Although financial difficulties may decrease social welfare help, there will be increasing demands for the reduction of the socioeconomic gap.

NOTES

1. K. Kohler, "Charity," in I. Singer (ed.) *The Jewish Encyclopedia, Vol. III* (New York: Funk and Wagnalls, 1903), p. 667.

2. *Babylonian Talmud,* "Ktuvim," Samech Zion, p. 2; Maimonedes, *Mishna Torah,* VII (Seeds) "Giving to the Poor," Chap. VII, Part 3.

3. Mark Twain's description of Palestine is illustrative: "Of all the lands there are for dismal scenery, I think Palestine must be the prince. The hills are barren, they are dull of color, they are unpicturesque in shape. The valleys are unsightly deserts fringed with a feeble vegetation that has an expression about it of being sorrowful and despondent. It is a hopeless, dreary, heartbroken land. . . . Palestine sits in sackcloth and ashes. Over it broods

the spell of a curse that has withered its fields and fettered its energies. . . . Renowned Jerusalem itself, the stateliest name in history, has lost its ancient grandeur, and is become a pauper village. . . . Bethsaida and Chorazin have vanished from the earth, and the desert places round about them . . . sleep in the hush of a solitude that is inhabited only by birds of prey and skulking foxes. Palestine is desolate and unlovely." Samuel L. Clemens (Mark Twain), *The Innocents Abroad* (London: Chatto and Windus, 1881), p. 565.

4. S. C. Leslie, *The Rift in Israel* (London: Routledge and Kegan Paul, 1971).

5. D. Macarov, *Social Welfare* (Jerusalem: Ministry for Foreign Affairs, 1970).

6. J. Neipris, *Social Services in Israel* (Jerusalem: American Jewish Committee, 1972); also in P. Glikson and S. Ketko (eds.) *Jewish Communal Services* (Jerusalem: International Conference of Jewish Communal Service, 1967).

7. One social service department specifically lists "Preparation for 'free world'," in its activities, with over a thousand participants. H. Avidor, *Activities of the Social Service Department: Jan-Dec., 1972* (Jerusalem: Jewish Agency, 1973).

8. *Facts About Israel 1973* (Jerusalem: Ministry for Foreign Affairs, 1973), p. 115.

9. P. Klein, *Social Services in Israel* (Jerusalem: Ministry of Social Welfare, 1958).

10. J. Neipris, "Some Origins of Social Policy in a New State" (Ph.D. dissertation, University of California, Berkeley, 1966).

11. D. Macarov and N. Golan, "Goals in Social Work Practice: A Longitudinal Study," *International Social Work* 26 (1973): 213.

12. E. D. Jaffe, "Separation in Jerusalem," *Public Welfare* 31 (1973): 33.

13. G. Lotan, *National Insurance in Israel* (Jerusalem: National Insurance Institute, 1969).

14. *Statistical Abstract of Israel* (Jerusalem: Central Bureau of Statistics, 1973), p. 671.

15. Ibid.

16. *Statistical Abstract of Israel*, p. 672.

17. Neipris, *Social Services in Israel*, p. 38.

18. M. Zinamon, *The Trade Union Social Insurance System in Israel* (Jerusalem: Histadruth, n.d.).

19. D. Macarov and U. Yannai, *An Exploratory Study of 76 Community Centers in Israel* (Jerusalem: The Joseph J. Schwartz Graduate Program for Training Community Center Directors and Senior Personnel, 1973).

20. Neipris, *Social Services in Israel*.

21. Bank of Israel, "Development of Non-Profit Institutions," *Bulletin* 25.

22. Avidor, *Activities of Social Service Department*.

23. *Survey Results* (Jerusalem: Institute for Applied Social Science, 1970).

24. D. Macarov and N. Golan, "Congruence Between Social Workers' Purposes and Activities," mimeographed (Jerusalem: Paul Baerwald School of Social Work, Hebrew University, 1972).

25. Rates in Israeli pounds are not given here, since the official rate of 7.0 pounds per dollar gives a distorted picture. The actual worth of payments should be expressed in terms of purchasing power, but this is very complex because of extremely heavy customs and luxury taxes on some items, subsidies on others, and supply and demand variations on others. Hence, the percentage of average salaries is given.

26. J. M. Rosenfeld and E. Morris, "Socially Deprived Jewish Families in Israel," in A. Jarus et al. (eds.) *Children and Families in Israel* (London: Gordon and Breach, 1970).

27. E. Jaffe, "Child Welfare in a Developing Country: Dimensions of Foster Care in Israel," *International Child Welfare Review* 22 (1969).

28. E. Jaffee, "Adoptions in Israel," *The Jewish Journal of Sociology* 12 (1970): 135.

29. J. Eaton, *Influencing the Youth Culture* (Beverly Hills: Sage, 1970).

30. State of Israel, *The Prevention of Crime and the Treatment of Offenders in Israel* (Jerusalem: Government Printer, 1965).

31. Neipris, *Social Services in Israel*.

32. See, for example, M. Weingarten, *Life in a Kibbutz* (New York: Reconstructionist Press, 1955); Y. Talmon, *Family and Community in the Kibbutz* (Cambridge: Harvard, 1972); S. Shur, *Kibbutz Bibliography* (Tel-Aviv: Federation of Kibbutz Movements, 1972); A. I. Rabin, *Kibbutz Studies* (East Lansing: Michigan State University Press, 1971).

33. *Youth Aliyah,* Israel Today Series Number 34 (Jerusalem: Ministry for Foreign Affairs, 1970).

34. E. J. Markus and B. Einav-Weiner, "Managing Group Interface," mimeographed (Jerusalem: The Joseph J. Schwartz Graduate Program for Training Community Center Directors and Senior Personnel, 1973).

35. Y. Liron, *Deprivation and the Socio-Economic Gap in Israel* (Jerusalem: Israel Economist Press, 1973).

36. D. Macarov, *The Israel Community Center at War: and Some Implications for the Future* (Jerusalem: The Joseph J. Schwartz Graduate Program for Training Community Center Directors and Senior Personnel, 1973).

6

THE COMPLEX ORGANIZATION OF
ITALIAN SOCIAL SERVICES

ELLEN B. HILL
MARIO CORSINI

INTRODUCTION

The organization of social services in Italy cannot be usefully described without informing the reader about the historical background of the present complex situation. That situation is based on much more than the purely social and economic factors that led up to the present social service arrangements in most other industrial nations.

To begin with, Italy is a relative newcomer among the Western nations. Only Germany, now divided again, was founded after the unification of Italy. Italian unification took place in 1869 when, under the leadership of a northern dynasty, the country obtained a national government located in Rome that covered 700 miles from the Alps to Sicily and consisted of regions of unequal levels of living, very different histories, different dialects, and different aspirations. All these small geographic and political units had lived a long time with their own forms of administration that were now to be, in great part, replaced by a highly centralized government. Furthermore, large parts of Italy, and particularly Rome, had been under papal administration for many years.

AUTHORS' NOTE: *The authors wish to express their appreciation to Rosanna Brichetti for research assistance and to Ernesta Rogers for advice in regard to the interpretation of some of the data.*

Until the unification of Italy, social services were undertaken by the Church with some local government financing. The first national interest in social services dated from 1880 and was mainly concerned with the organization of institutions for children, the aged and the ill, as well as for indigents. Systematic assistance outside institutions had to await the Fascist era, when, to increase population and thus achieve greater political power, Mussolini's government began to organize national agencies to assist needy mothers and children. In spite of the gradual establishment of national agencies for specific clients such as war orphans and invalids, and legislation in favor of no fewer than 60 categories of underprivileged persons, social services today—defined as benefits outside of the social security system, thus not directly linked to compulsory social insurance programs for workers and employees—are in the hands of an estimated 16,000 organizations. They generally receive some public financing but are not effectively controlled with regard to their activities and their expenditures.

Overlapping, lack of service in many areas, and discrimination concerning eligibility and amount of assistance are not caused by purposeful inattention to social problems or by powerful political institutions opposing aid to the weakest members of Italian society. While both inattention and adverse political pressures are producing part of the chaotic situation, the social and cultural heritage must share the blame. In spite of twenty years' discussion of social reforms in the fields of health, education, and welfare, change has been minimal and can be expected to remain equally slow in the foreseeable future. Posttraditional societies, as we have learned by experience, change at different rates, depending on underlying cultural characteristics. It should be pointed out that generalizations with regard to Italy as a single entity are more doubtful than most. The attitudes in the north are closer to the Western European concepts of social responsibility, while the farther south one goes, the more traditional features prevail. This means that assistance is still seen as charity. The family is still conceived of as extended, while industrialization, urbanization, and migration have in fact created much smaller family units that are approaching the nuclear model of technological societies.

Another technical aspect of the social service delivery problem derives from the highly legalistic nature of public and private administration in the country. This tradition goes back as far as the Roman Empire and means, in practice, that administration adheres narrowly to laws conceived under totally different circumstances. While in all bureaucracies it is safer to remain inactive than to take responsibility, this is particularly true in civil services where staff is often hired for political reasons, and at the middle and upper levels where persons are hired on the basis of a law degree. Given the permanent threat of unemployment that has pervaded Italy for generations, very few individuals run risks. Thus, the machinery of state is ossified, although over 20 years ago a special Ministry for Administrative Reform was created to rejuvenate government departments and to adapt their structures to the spirit of the times. So far, no Ministry of Social Affairs exists, and many different ministries are responsible for different programs, and frequently for the same programs. Most services ultimately depend on the Ministry of the Interior, concerned with law and order, which formerly institutionalized the poor by force.

Recently, a valiant attempt was made to codify the 262 laws regulating social service activities from 1944 to 1971. Cataldi and Zucconi have devised a classification system which divided these laws into (a) regulations organizing agencies, and (b) stipulations regarding types of assistance. Laws concerning organization involve 20 important national agencies and an indefinite number of lesser ones, four types of local agencies at the provincial and community level, individual schools, and institutions for the chronically ill. Legislation with regard to welfare programs has concerned itself with 14 separate categories of need. By now even Parliament feels that the legislative output has been excessive and that it hinders the efficient administration of services that were envisaged. Some legislation was passed to keep existing agencies alive when their usefulness had long disappeared. Private agencies, generally under religious auspices, are not likely to be closed as long as the Italian government and the Catholic Church consider each other sovereign states. At the same time the unfinished establishment of regional government (for purposes of decentralization and to guarantee citizen participation) leads to overlapping responsibilities, since new organizations are created while old ones still exist.

Presently Italy ranks tenth among the world's most industrialized nations. Distribution of industry over the country, however, is quite uneven, and traditional social and economic differences between geographic areas have been maintained to a large extent. Immigration from less developed parts of the country has been intense, with resulting problems. All social services have suffered from population

Table 1: Public Expenditures for Social Services 1969-1971 (in billions of lira)

Organization	1969	1970	1971
National government	196.3	232.8	268.1
Parastatal Pension System			
(old age assistance)	47.6	135.5	119.4
Other parastatal assistance agencies	32.5	43.0	38.3
Local government	292.8	308.0	330.0
Provincial governments	202.4	222.5	250.0
School social services	27.2	32.0	34.5
TOTAL	798.8	973.8	1,040.3

density in particular areas. The demographic equilibrium of agricultural areas has been seriously disturbed by the migration of families, and even more so by the numbers of women, children, and old persons who were left behind by the economic migrants.

In the last decade, employment in agriculture has diminished by approximately 13 percent while industrial workers have increased 5 percent and those in service industries by 8 percent. The concentration in areas promising increased earnings has created enormous ghettos surrounding the cities. The ghetto inhabitants have little opportunity, due to cultural reasons, to integrate into urban society. They live in dormitory towns consisting of either high-rise public housing without infrastructures or self-made shelters of poor hygienic character. Their youth and children present severe cases of deviation and delinquency. This pattern is prevalent in all developing countries but appears more striking in a country that is highly stratified and basically feudal. A generation ago Italy impressed its visitors with graciousness in human relations and great natural and man-made beauty. Rapid social change has produced a flood of private expenditures and great reluctance to finance social investments. Expenditures for social services have doubled from 1961 to 1970, although the buying power of the lira decreased considerably during that period. In 1961 social services represented 1.2 percent of the GNP, in 1965 1.4 percent, and in 1970 1.5 percent. Where these funds were employed can be seen in Table 1.

BASIC PRINCIPLES CONCERNING THE SOCIAL SERVICE SYSTEM

According to the Italian Constitution of 1948, social services are part of an overall welfare system under government auspices. Social services are meant for indigent persons or persons incapable of working, while the members of the work force are potential beneficiaries of social security if they meet certain eligibility requirements, such as accidents on the job or work-related illnesses, permanent physical handicaps, old age, unemployment, contamination, or a large number of dependents.

The strict separation of social services (as defined above) from work-connected social security provisions has, however, changed significantly since the foundation of the Republic in 1945. Consequently, some aspects of this division, particularly those regarding public health matters, are slowly becoming obsolete. Amounts allotted in social security provisions and social assistance have become less differentiated. Although individual payments depend on past employment, today's income transfers are no longer totally based on the principle of insurance against specific risks but rather on the guarantee of a minimum living standard related to that achieved during times of employment. The worker's income does not drop below a minimum line. Benefits are provided by insurance funds as well as by general taxation. The same basic right is now accorded to other categories, including persons over 65 years of age without means of support, and the physically handicapped. In short, while the treatment of those who have accumulated social insurance benefits during their working life is still preferential, there is a growing tendency to favor one system of financial assistance for all, one that would guarantee every individual a minimum income, continuously revised according to the cost-of-living index.

Aside from these developments, traditional social services are undergoing changes also. Up to 1969, social assistance was geared to the special problems of certain individuals (children and the aged) who for various reasons could not obtain help from their families. As a result, children's institutions and homes for the chronically ill and the aged were filled with persons who had to rely on help from society. Services had to be extended considerably, and programs had to be restructured. This is particularly true of day-care centers originally meant to take care of preschool children of working mothers, and underprivileged children. Lately, in accordance with the development of regional governments, the philosophy of day-care centers has evolved from custodial to educational goals, to help members of socially deprived families to become integrated into the general school system.

Originally, educational social services consisted of the free distribution of school books and other school equipment to deprived children, who were also eligible for free meals after hours. Now school books are free for all children during the compulsory school years, and school meals have evolved from social assistance programs to educational tools upporting the full-time school.

These examples show a lessening of the traditional separation of social services from social security. Social and medical services will eventually become available to all citizens.

ADMINISTRATIVE ORGANIZATION

The organizational arrangements of social services are extremely complicated. A number of ministries are involved at the national level. At the level of the regions, local administrations, towns and older provincial structures all work together with private welfare organizations, which are legally recognized and are normally under contract to one or several public bodies.

The main administrative problem derives from an inconsistent relationship between national government and regional government concerning public assistance. According to the Constitution, the regions are responsible for legislation on public welfare, medical care, hospitalization, and school social services. At the time of the transition from national government to regions, 25 years after the Constitution had been enacted, the legislative responsibilities of the regions had to be clarified. The Constitution assigns all continuing assistance to the handicapped and indigent persons to the national government. Assistance is defined as the right of every citizen in need. Charity remains a discretionary activity. Charitable activities were transferred to those regions which are expected to administer privately run institutions and the very few private social service agencies. The regions, which constitute an added organization with welfare functions, have been so hamstrung from the start that they cannot be expected to reorganize programs and services. Presently, a parliamentary committee is studying legislation to enlarge the responsibility of the regions.

The ministries involved are the Presidency of the Council of Ministers, concerned with social service planning and control of several national agencies; the Ministry of the Interior, which provides ongoing financial assisstance to the blind, the deaf, and other physically handicapped; the Ministry of Health, which finances and controls mother and child welfare services and administers medical assistance to the physically handicapped through the offices of the regions; the Ministry of Justice, which supplies social services for juvenile delinquents; and the Ministry of Labor, which supervises a program of pensions for aged workers and another for dependents of deceased workers.

Lately, the regions have become directly responsible for local public assistance cases and private institutions in their territory, and for the maintenance of youths and the aged in institutions. The provinces take responsibility for psychiatric care, for illegitimate children (with contributions from their home communities), and for the training of the blind and the deaf. Cities and townships must finance medical assistance to their indigent residents, assist and contribute to traditional services for poor school children, and maintain a variety of services for the tubercular, and needy mothers and children.

The existence of so many specialized agencies (one, for instance, takes care of war orphans, and yet another specializes in war orphans with psychiatric problems) explains the high cost of administration and the little money left for direct services to clients. Apart from the financial drawback, efficient planning is impossible. Solutions are often duplicated. Public assistance at the local level is meant to be an emergency measure, but many persons must be helped permanently because they are ineligible for other programs. These persons tend to remain in closed institutions, the mainstay of welfare under laws dating from the nineteenth century. Because these institutions depend for their financing on several public agencies with different administrations, they are often overfinanced because of organizational overlap.

Depending on the method employed, different estimates have been made of expenditures for specific social services. This is in part due to the fact that funds are channeled through practically all ministries of the central government as well as through regional and local public agencies, about 1,000 in number, not counting regional and local administration channels.

Old-age pensions and assistance to the handicapped have been improved. Regional and local governments have enlarged their programs. The increase in expenditures does not mean an improvement in social services. Some of the funds have been spent by agencies to guarantee their own survival. These agencies transfer funds for services rendered among themselves and, as a result, administrative costs increase. At the same time, it is impossible to check service costs.

CLIENT GROUPS

Statistics concerning clients and services are unavailable. The following information is indicative rather than precise and cannot be compared because it was collected at different times. What is known concerns the following groups: families and children, the aged in and outside of institutions, the physically and mentally handicapped, the unemployed, and public assistance cases receiving aid to round out insuffient income from other sources.

Families and Children

Family and children's services comprise a network of over 1,900 maternal health centers and more than 6,000 pediatric clinics run by a national agency (ONMI) dating from the Fascist era. However, only one-fourth of the pregnancy cases obtain prenatal care from these centers. The others are seen by general practitioners and gynecologists in the clinics of the social insurance system to which they have access as dependents of workers. The same proportion holds true for patients seen in the pediatric clinics.

Children who do not have families able to care for them come under the responsibility of the provincial administrations. At the end of 1971 these children were raised in nearly 100 orphanages under public auspices, institutions which contained approximately 5,500 beds. Approximately 53,000 children were placed in some type of foster care, now the preferred solution for homeless children. So far only a few have been adopted. There is still resistance against the trend toward foster care, in part because legislation is unclear, in part because the orphanages—particularly the private ones—do not wish to release their charges. As of this writing there are approximately 2,500 institutions for normal children, and about 400 for the retarded and mentally ill, for both adults and children. Today such children comprise an estimated 150,000 institutionalized minors in all of Italy, despite their dwindling number due to recent foster-care placement and increased financial family assistance. A positive case is the national agency for aid to orphans of workers (ENAOLI) which assists 140,000 children in their own homes, as compared with 22,000 still in institutions.

Delinquent youth are mainly relegated to other institutions, and receive different degrees of treatment severity, as decided upon by the juvenile courts. In 1971 approximately 28,000 minors came before the courts and 24,000 were adjudicated. Long-term cases, usually placed in reeducation centers, numbered 4,300 while another 10,000 spent some time in penal institutions, and another 5,300 were on probation in the community under the supervision of social workers.

Other children's services emanate from the continuing overhaul of the educational system. There are about 800 day-care centers for children up to the age of three years. Six hundred of these are financed by a national agency, and the remainder by local and private resources. In all, there are places for 37,000 children in day-care centers, which means that there is room for 10 percent of the total age group. A law enacted in 1971 foresees the establishment of at least 3,800 new day-care centers to be run by the local communities and financed by state, regional, and local government funds.

In view of the constitutional rights of every citizen to education, the regions have passed several laws so that potential school dropouts from poor economic backgrounds would be encouraged to complete their basic education. For this purpose the Ministry of Education has assisted school children with meals, books, summer camps, after-school activities, and transportation to and from school. As of 1973, the regions have taken over in these areas, and criteria for assistance are being reviewed for type of aid as well as for eligibility. The trend is toward a full day of schooling, but so far only 15 percent of elementary school children and 20 percent of those in high school can spend their after-class hours in these programs; these limits are due to a shortage of premises, particularly in the big cities where two and three shifts of classes are necessary.

Family counseling services are for the most part in private hands. Family planning has been undertaken by two pioneering organizations, one with 16, another with 30, counseling centers. The numbers of clients are not known because provision of information on birth-control methods was illegal until a short time ago. The publicly financed ONMI runs a total of 16 premarriage and marriage counseling offices dealing with family problems.

The Aged

It is estimated that about 130,000 aged people live in institutions. About 1,700 institutions are reserved for the elderly, while 200 others are mixed with other age groups. The national agency

Table 2: Old Age Pensions and Aged Population 1969-1971

Year	Male	Female	Total	Male Percent of Population	Female Percent of Population	Total Percent of Population
1969	54.013	416.843	470.856	2.21	12.61	8.20
1970	94.567	671.460	766.027	3.79	19.89	13.04
1971	101.272	718.500	819.772	3.96	20.86	13.66

responsible for old-age pensioners (INPS) cares permanently for approximately 7,000 persons in institutions, a number completely insufficient given the needs of the nonambulatory aged. The same organization admits another 4,300 persons every year for two months' care. With the overall aging of the population at large, the problem has come to the attention of the general public, and efforts are now being made to increase community services to permit more of the aged to remain longer in their own homes. Pensions of persons over 65 years of age who have no other income amount to less than one-third of the average earnings in industry. Financial assistance presently goes to approximately 14 percent of the population over 65 years of age or about 800,000 persons. Table 2 demonstrates that the percentage increase in aged population is accompanied by an increase of persons who receive a pension.

The Physically and Mentally Handicapped

A relatively large number of people who are unable to provide for themselves for physical reasons receive modest pensions for an unlimited period of time. Table 3 presents the 1973 descriptions of these persons.

Persons in the Partial Invalid category have a legal right to a certain number of jobs and thus find employment more easily than others with disabilities. They therefore make every effort to be recognized in this category.

Besides pension payments, social services for the handicapped mainly take the form of institutionalization: it is estimated that about 40,000 handicapped live in approximately 650 institutions. Of these, 300 take in all kinds of persons in need of shelter, while about 230 care for the physically handicapped exclusively. The remainder care for psychiatric patients and retarded persons. Problem children of all types have access to mental health centers run by two national agencies in 200 clinics. However, diagnostic centers

Table 3: Physically Handicapped Persons Receiving Pensions in 1973

Category	Number
Invalids (not work connected)	14,504
Deaf mutes	8,350
Blind	37,925
Relatives of invalids under 18 years of age	570
Relatives of blind	4,885
Partial invalids	149,161
Partial blind	47,446

generally are unable to refer their cases for treatment because of the small number of therapeutic facilities.

On the other hand, there are a number of voluntary associations of the handicapped (for example, the subnormal and persons with muscular dystrophy), all of which have medical clinics and special training centers distributed over the country. It is not possible to estimate the number of cases covered in relation to total need in each category as there is no systematic case reporting. In general, the tendency of the associations is to integrate the handicapped into normal community life, including schools, whenever possible. Special classes in elementary and high schools are now being abolished, setting hopes for handicapped students' progress on treatment by psychological school staff rather than on separation from their peers.

The Unemployed and the Unemployable

The unemployed are mostly agricultural workers. In 1971 approximately one million of them received unemployment benefits at the rate of $1.30 a day for an average of 159 days. This means that approximately one-third of the agricultural work force was unemployed at some time during that year. In the same year, 200,000 industrial workers became eligible for unemployment benefits for an average of 125 days. They represented about 0.5 percent of industrial labor. Their benefits are pegged to their earnings.

Public welfare offices at the local level represent the last resource of the needy who do not qualify for any other assistance. The settlement of an application can take years. In 1970 about 1,600,000 persons were on the welfare rolls. Since that time, old-age pensions have come into effect and have provided for about half of them. It is estimated that about 800,000 persons remain the charge of local welfare offices. Payments vary as they depend on financial resources of a particular locality.

STAFFING AND MANPOWER PATTERNS

Civil servants have to comply with general regulations governed by the hierarchical and technical level of the position. A university education, especially in law—and more recently in the fields of political science, education, and psychology—is the condition sine qua non for a professional career in all public social services.

On the other hand, thousands of persons are estimated to be employed in semi-clerical jobs dealing directly with the client population concerning social security and social assistance programs. For these positions there are no specific educational requirements. Social professions received a definite impetus with the influence of reconstruction efforts after World War II and the influx of Fulbright scholars in social work education. By the late sixties there were 54 schools of social work, 87 for nursery teachers, eight for vocational counselors, and nine for community workers and others. Most social work schools are private, some are church sponsored, and some are connected to labor unions. Four are part of universities.

The levels of the social work schools are by no means equal, and only about 30 of them are recognized by the government. Their graduates have a chance to participate in competitions for job openings in publicly supported agencies. In theory, the schools of social work have similar programs, all more or less patterned after American professional schools. They have a three-year curriculum following completion of a high school education. The university connected schools demand, in addition to classwork, a written thesis and acceptable performance in supervised fieldwork.

Scholarships are available largely from public sources. Students at university connected schools have the same right to financial assistance as do other university students, based on need. As in many countries, social work increasingly has become a field of study for the children of the working class. The dominance of socially minded upper-class women is no longer in evidence. In fact, faculty are greatly preoccupied with overcoming the cultural gap between home and school.

It is expected that another year of training will be added in the near future, which would bring social work education to the four-year basic university education required in the established professions. Obtaining a social work degree would then allow for a civil service career. There are about 4,500 persons with diplomas in social work presently working. They are located in psychiatric hospitals, probation departments of juvenile courts, and other settings with a casework emphasis. There is also a sprinkling of group workers in social centers similar to settlement houses, and in community organization and development programs, particularly in the south of Italy.

Most social workers are female, a fact that can be ascribed to a relatively short and less expensive education in a country where educational expenditures go mostly to the males in a family. The wage scale for social workers is inadequate to raise a family. Lately, the reformist goals of social work have come under attack from radicals and, consequently, more politically conscious individuals —usually men—have left the profession, and recruitment has been curtailed.

The image of the social worker in Italian society is vague, has low status, and professional education is not yet firmly established. Many important positions are filled through political influence. As a result, social policy is definitely linked to the political fortunes of parties, labor unions, and other pressure groups. Social workers do not yet represent a genuine professional group, although professionalization has been attempted and an association of social workers has been formed. The association has not been able to influence either social work education or employment practices, social policy, or even minor aspects of the lives of social workers.

ASSESSMENT AND OUTCOME

Systematic research in social services and social policy is not highly developed in Italy. There is scarcely a tradition of research activities in the modern sense, although a National Research Council was established in the postwar years and a Ministry of Science guides the national effort in this direction.

Research in the behavioral sciences takes place in university institutes, greatly hampered by lack of funds, and in some national planning organizations. None of these activities is coordinated and, as we have seen, the simplest descriptive data are hard to obtain. The Central Statistical Office (ISTAT) is charged with collecting and publishing all government statistics. However, statistical data are incomplete with regard to social services, and are nonexistent concerning the results obtained. Valid extrapolation thus is not feasible since even demographic data are limited.

There has been no official attempt to evaluate social service programs, although some steps have been made in the direction of evaluative research in the field of education where the Ministry of Education has established a planning office. Studies in education have been intermittent, depending on the personal interests of the minister in charge, whose time in office generally lasts one year. Public health research has been more successful because of a growing interest in reforming medical services delivery, although most research has been confined to epidemiological studies, control of pharmacological prescriptions, and the like. There exists a special medical research institute attached to the Ministry of Health. The Institute for Economic Research, which is part of the Ministry of the Treasury, does evaluative research on economic programs, but unfortunately its findings are not made public.

National welfare agencies do have perfunctory research departments which deal with administrative aspects rather than with substantive matters or the needs of prospective clients. Few institutions have used case material for research purposes. This contrasts with the schools of social work which, in accordance with their curriculum, demand fieldwork reports and generally prepare their students for professional research activities at a modest level. Applied social research was undertaken in schools of social work before it became part of teaching methods in university courses, and the increasing number of theses written in the professional schools must be regarded as the main contribution to the development of theory and practice.

The university research institutes have only recently considered social services and their results as the object of study. Applied social sciences in the universities date from the last decade, and they have been pushed by a belated recognition of the lack of significant connection between the political power system and welfare services, thus keeping back both the social sciences and the social services.

Some private organizations and foundations have now begun to investigate social policy and social services. A yearly report on the social situation is prepared by the Study Center on Social Investments (CENSIS) for the National Council of Economics and Labor which has consultative status with the government. Two large industrial firms, Fiat and Olivetti, have established foundations which hold conferences and support ongoing social research projects. Another foundation, Zancan, collaborates in welfare research and training with the School of Social Work and the Economics

Department of the University of Padua. Its main contribution, apart from summer courses for practicing social workers (in which research techniques are figured), has been the publication of teaching material and studies in local community development programs. Rome has an Institute for Research in Social Work (ISTISS) with a small staff. It is enlarged whenever contributions from public sources are available to investigate the possibilities of new programs. These have been described in monographs or reported in a quarterly which the Institute founded in 1961.

OUTLOOK

The structure of social services in Italy is undergoing significant change in all its details. The institution of regionalization, when completed, will make practical the application of newer views. All political parties, after many reciprocal concessions, agreed in principle on a number of points. Of these the following have a good chance of being eventually implemented: the administration of social security provisions and social services is to be separated, and social services in turn are to be divided into ongoing and crisis assistance; social welfare services are to become part of public services available to all citizens so that the importance of the means tests is reduced; community participation is to be encouraged in direct services and is to have a say in the control of program execution.

At the national level, social and health services are to come under one combined ministry which will set policy and coordinate the activities of all regions. As a result, the national government would limit its activities to policy-making in the field of health and welfare. The regions would undertake programming services and their control, and train welfare personnel. Local governments would administer actual services, and would fund and control private institutions in their local areas, enforcing standards the regions have set. Basically, the aim is to provide for a system that assists individuals and families with problems to live under normal conditions and to avoid their becoming outsiders because they receive services. Ultimately, social services are to be therapeutic, continuous as long as the need persists, and—in the final analysis—rehabilitative.

7

POLAND'S NEW PRIORITY: HUMAN WELFARE

SOPHIE WOJCIECHOWSKI

In 1974 the Polish People's Republic will celebrate its thirtieth anniversary. Within this period, Poland has rebuilt its devastated economy, caught up with and, in some cases, surpassed pre-war standards, and made the results of its economic growth available to a much larger portion of its population.

The pre-war welfare system in Poland had many progressive features, but war changed it completely. Over six million Poles (about 22 percent of the population) perished, and another 600,000 were partially or totally disabled. Six years of exploitation of the country's resources left Poland the most impoverished country in Europe. Its industry was destroyed, agricultural resources decimated, the countryside deforested, and transportation destroyed. The capital, Warsaw, was 60 percent demolished. Many schools, hospitals, and other social institutions were mined. Large population transfers

AUTHOR'S NOTE: *Among the many persons who have helped me to understand the Polish welfare system during my recent visit to Poland, I particularly would like to thank the following: Professor Cecylia Hibel of the State School of Social Workers, Warsaw; Dr. Aleksander Kaminski, Professor, Lodz University; Mr. Mieczyslaw Karczewski, Director of the Department of Social Welfare, Ministry of Health and Social Welfare, Warsaw; Dr. Irena Kryczynska, Assistant at the Institute for Teachers Education, Warsaw; Dr. Jerzy Mikulski, Director, State School of Social Workers, Warsaw; Ms. Aleksandra Oleszynska, Chief of the Section in the Ministry of Health and Social Welfare, Warsaw; Dr. Jerzy Piotrowski, Professor, Academy of Social and Economic Planning; Professor Tadusz Pudelko, State School of Social Workers, Warsaw; and Dr. Jan Rosner, Professor, Academy of Social and Economic Planning. I also wish to express my gratitude for the time, information, and hospitality extended to me on my visits to various institutions.*

in a relatively short time resulted from the shift of Poland's boundaries. Immediate rescue operations, in which foreign aid played a major role, were required. Poland, a fairly advanced country before the war, suddenly found itself in the category of "underdeveloped" countries, in need of rebuilding its entire economy.

Today the Polish economy provides its 33 million persons with a fairly decent, if modest, living characterized by "a rapid rise in real earnings and total money incomes backed by the maintenance of a full employment" (Chelstowski, 1973; Karczewski, 1973). This is not to say that the Polish economy is not confronted with many challenges. An expansion of consumer goods production and services, as well as housing, is urgently needed. However, there is ample evidence that these needs are now given high priority, far higher than ever before. Polish society has shifted from an exclusive preoccupation with basic industrial growth to much broader concerns with human resources and general standards of human existence. As in any transition period, traces of past struggles and achievement remain. One of these is the multiplicity of approaches in the welfare system.[1]

Multiplicity of Approaches

When faced with misfortune or a sudden problem, where does a Polish family or single person turn for help? The avenues of social assistance are many and remarkably varied.

In an economy of full employment, where most persons work in the "socialized sector," the place of employment (called in Poland, work establishment) is the most natural route for those who seek help. Within industrial plants and most other places of employment, all kinds of social services are made available to the worker and his or her family. Financial assistance or loans can be obtained through a special management committee or the trade union. There is often a competently handled referral service. There are recreation and vacation arrangements, as well as facilities for children and youth. To be sure, such social services are not uniformly available in all places of employment. There is a vast difference, in this respect, between large work establishments and small ones. Services offered also vary in different parts of the country.

If the work-related approach cannot be used, the man in need of help can get in touch with a so-called "social counselor," a public officer in charge of his district. There are over 65,000 such volunteer counselors in Poland, each serving his or her community. In a city the social counselor is most likely an older, retired woman; in a rural community, an older man. Such an indigenous worker, dedicated and usually well acquainted with existing resources, can be of real help in locating and organizing assistance.

A man looking for help has other options if he lives in a city. He can apply directly to a number of private social agencies. The Friends of Children Society has offices scattered all over the country, all providing volunteer services. There is the Polish Red Cross, the Polish Committee for Social Services (P.L.P.S.), and many other smaller organizations. There are also sectarian organizations, mostly Catholic, such as Caritas and PAX, offering extensive social services. Most of these organizations raise their own funds through membership fees and voluntary contributions, but they also rely on state subsidies for providing special services of all kinds.

A cursory investigation leaves the impression that the social welfare system in Poland is extremely complex and might benefit from a better coordination of resources and efforts. Yet this complexity makes possible the citizen involvement which is so characteristic of the Polish social welfare system. Voluntary participation is found at every level, ranging from actually dispensing social services to long-term planning.

SOCIAL WELFARE AND SOCIALISM

Since the advent of the new leadership in December 1970, national priorities have shifted. In the preceding years economic progress was stressed, based on industrial and technological developments and advances in transportation. Today social progress seems to have become the overriding concern.

This has not always been the case. Attitudes toward social welfare have undergone various changes during the entire 30-year period since the end of the war. At first the most widely held point of view was that socialism would eliminate unemployment and poverty and thus almost automatically eliminate any need to develop complex systems of social services and assistance. Social work would be no longer necessary.

This view proved erroneous. It is true, of course, that as the building of socialism advanced, the particular social groups—the unemployed and the poor—for whose protection pre-war social welfare was devised have been gradually shrinking; yet as they disappeared, new needs for all kinds of social services developed. Working mothers need all sorts of assistance to bring up a healthier generation of children. The handicapped and the retarded who are unable to work have become the responsibility of society.

The initial mistaken assumption that socialism would eliminate the need for social assistance (largely due, as it was, to the confusion of the meaning of pre-war and modern social policy, goals, and terms) hampered the development in this field from 1947 to 1957. Since 1957, there has been a gradual shift to a more modern approach. This change of attitude was reflected in the "Position Paper on Guide Lines for Long-Term Planning," prepared by the Ministry of Health and Welfare in 1966. It clearly states that socialism does not eradicate the need for social assistance. Today, it is universally taken for granted that socialism, while changing the basis for assistance, sets up new tasks, new requirements, and new standards of quality and methods of operation. In short, socialism creates unlimited opportunities for the development of various forms of institutional welfare. The progressive character of this development is expressed in the Constitution of the Polish People's Republic. Article 60 proclaims:

> The citizens of the People's Republic of Poland have the right to the protection of health and to assistance in case of illness or inability to work. To help exercise this right on a constantly broadening scale, extended Social Insurance of physical and mental workers and the expansion of various forms of social assistance will be used.

Today, social policy experts in Poland firmly believe that social development is essential to the full economic growth of the country, and deplore the lag in social advances as compared with the economic progress already achieved.

In social development, as in economic growth, ordering priorities is essential. The infrastructure of economic and technological progress requires a previous development of transportation, communications, power and energy resources, and agricultural improvements. In the same way, the infrastructure of social development rests on institutions concerned with health, national education, law, and accessibility of culture and individual advancement to all citizens. According to Kazimierz Secomski (1974), "Neglect and obvious delays in the rate of expansion of the social infrastructure are now surfacing as factors hampering the general economic progress."

Social Services Tailored to Special Needs

The ideology upon which socialism is being built in Poland considers the family, not the individual, as the basic social unit. The Polish Code of Family Law holds the family legally required to support its children, and adult children are responsible for the support of their parents. Even siblings are mutually responsible for each other's support, and in this respect the Polish Code of Family Law is unique. In a society fast becoming industrialized—in 1946, 68 percent of Poland's population was engaged in agriculture, in 1972 it was only 46 percent—and the family needs a great deal of help from various social institutions to fulfill its responsibilities.

The situation is further complicated by demographic trends.[2] Poland's demographic policy aims to create a steady and healthy growth of population in harmony with the economic growth of the country. The post-war period, however, was marked by wide demographic fluctuations. First came a population explosion. Between 1946 and 1960, about 10 million young persons reached school age and employment age. Now the pendulum is swinging the other way, and the proportion of elderly persons to total population is rising steeply.

As a result, an average Polish family is faced at this point with many problems. The following are probably the most crucial: families with many children, despite a system of family allowances, are faced with the problem of substandard living conditions; the expansion of child day-care facilities is lagging behind the growing number of mothers seeking employment; a growing number of the elderly, many of them bedridden and completely helpless, must be cared for by their families, because the growth of institutional resources is not keeping pace with the present demographic trend.

Families with Marginal Incomes

There are signs of growing prosperity in Poland. The Gross National Product has been increasing impressively, reaching 334 zlotys per capita in 1972. This figure was only 76 zlotys in 1947 and 246 zlotys in 1968. Individuals are beginning to put some portions of their earnings into savings. The average annual savings were 544 zlotys per capita in 1960, and in 1971, savings reached 4,057 zlotys.

Under a socialist, full-employment system, there is not much room to become really affluent, but neither is there extreme poverty. The scale of earnings is fairly equalized on a very modest level, ranging from 2,000 to 3,500 zlotys a month. According to statistics, the average Polish family consists of 3.2 members and has an income of 4,300 zlotys per month with 1.6 members working. More than 87 percent of its income derives from employment; the rest comes from various social sources such as family allowances, free meals, and vegetable garden allotments.

The Polish press mentions 10 percent of families "living in deprivation." The term means families whose income is less than 1,000 zlotys per person per month—the accepted social minimum. (For those living singly the minimum is 1,500 zlotys.) Almost 17 percent of these families have an income below 800 zlotys per person, and 3 percent less than 600 zlotys. The size of the family seems to be the main factor causing this level of deprivation. Alcoholism could be another. As a rule the breadwinner in such a deprived family is a physical worker with only grammar school education and many dependents. In most cases he is supporting more than three persons.

To alleviate the plight of deprived families (in effect, the Polish equivalent of the American working poor), various remedies are advocated. The two most often mentioned are improving the family allowance system and reforming taxation. Family allowances are, indeed, much too low—only 8 percent of average wages per dependent—and out of step with the current cost of living. However, the problem is only part of the general picture now drawing attention.

At the end of 1973, a debate on family life in Poland was initiated and widely promoted. Many aspects of family life are being discussed by prominent sociologists and public scientists in academic publications, in the press, and in various committees. This new outburst of interest is obviously encouraged by high government circles, and it is hoped that it will be reflected in the debates of the Polish legislative body in the near future. There is hope that out of these deliberations will emerge new social legislation aimed at long-term social policy projects. In the meantime, families and individuals in poverty situations are provided with supplementary financial assistance and assistance in kind (free meals, coal, and clothing) by various social agencies.

One of the most difficult problems is the acute housing shortage.

Despite continuous and intensive building of public housing, the increase in available units cannot keep up with demographic trends. The number of persons per room has been decreasing rather slowly, from 1.7 in 1950 to 1.4 in 1970, and more slowly in the urban communities than in the rural ones.[3] There are only 200 apartments available for each 300 new marriages. Newlyweds have to wait long periods, often years, for an apartment of their own, doubling up with their families in the meantime. Population shifts from rural to urban areas further aggravate the situation in the cities. Rents, on the other hand, present no particular problem. Since all new housing is government controlled, either directly or through housing cooperatives, rents are reasonable—about 10 percent of a family's earnings.

Food is the biggest and most important item in the budget of a low-income family. Any rise or drop in the prices of food registers very strongly. The government has been able to stabilize the prices of basic food items, but it is still not successful in controlling the distribution system. Unpredictable distribution of food supplies affects most low-income families which cannot afford to buy more expensive food items as a substitute for the missing, less expensive ones. Long hours spent in lines, especially waiting for meat, are a Polish housewife's nightmare. Although conditions have improved in the last few years, shopping for food is still more like hunting, and one never knows what one will bring home from the market. It must be emphasized, however, that there is no hunger in Poland, not even among the most deprived, because people in such conditions have access to free or low-cost meals. There are no beggars on city streets.

Child Welfare

The Polish People's Republic has introduced new models of child care more comprehensive than those of pre-war years. Under the present social security system, the state assumes the responsibility for complete development of children and youth, including their health, education, and access to recreational facilities. The state is assisted in meeting this responsibility by many social agencies and various volunteer committees. As much as possible, services and help are provided within the child's environment—family, school, and community. Early detection of problems is considered essential. Institutional placement is looked upon as a last resort for cases involving children whose families are not capable of fulfilling their basic obligations or those whose problems call for special forms of intervention.

Services for Children of Working Mothers

Women are granted 16-week maternity leaves at the birth of the first child, and 18 weeks for subsequent children. A working mother has the right to a 3-year leave without pay to take care of her children without losing her job. Numerous nurseries for children under three years of age have been organized under the sponsorship of the state and various work establishments. Their number is increasing, though not fast enough to keep up with the growing demand. Some figures from the most recent *Statistical Yearbook* (1973) are shown in Table 1.

The shortage of nursery facilities is particularly acute in rural areas. Here a substitute form of child care is now planned, with special training being given to young girls to prepare them for the task of running rural nursery centers.

Kindergarten facilities for children from three to six years of age have doubled in number between 1960 and 1972 and serve twice as many children. The 1972 figure shows about 26,000 schools serving about 900,000 children. This represents 40 percent of all children in this age group and 85 percent of the children of working mothers. Here again, rural facilities are trailing behind urban ones. In 1970, 385 of every 1,000 Polish children were in pre-school facilities, compared to 582 in Czechoslovakia and 766 in Belgium.

Many organizations, in addition to state and work establishments, are now involved in expanding pre-school facilities. Different models have been developed to meet particular urban and rural needs. The pattern of child day care is changing due to the now prevalent belief that a young child is better off when placed close to home rather than exposed twice a day to the long, often arduous trip many mothers must make to reach their place of employment.

School-age children of working mothers can frequently use school facilities which are extended to offer after-school programs. Special

Table 1

	Number of Day Nurseries	Number of Children Served
1960	948	51,509
1968	1,012	61,887
1972	1,084	69,914

teachers are assigned to work with pupils staying after school hours. The children are given hot meals, helped with their homework, and provided with recreational leadership. Teenagers have often a choice between school facilities and a recreational club organized by the local parish. The question of helping working mothers seems mostly to be a matter of developing more facilities to meet growing needs. The proper concern is already there, and the groundwork done.

Services for Children Living at Home

In 1971, about 177,000 children afflicted by special problems —such as parental illness or natural disaster—were given financial assistance from various sources. About 1.4 million children are getting free meals at school. The widely publicized slogan, "A glass of milk for every child," is scrupulously observed. More than 12 percent of all school children take advantage of supervised afternoon school activities.

During summer and winter vacations, children are offered a vast range of camps and camping activities, all well supervised and generally well equipped. More than 50 percent of children in Poland use these facilities regularly. In addition, many social agencies organize and supervise recreational facilities for children living in a particular neighborhood. Such day-camp activities are often held in the backyards of apartment houses in urban communities.

Orphans and "Social Orphans"

For children and youth without parents, there are various forms of institutional care. For very small children (under three years of age), there are about 70 special homes accommodating over 5,000 infants and toddlers. Children aged three to eighteen are placed in one of 400 special homes, with a current population of about 26,000 youngsters. These homes provide a high degree of individualized educational supervision and strive to make the children's surroundings as similar as possible to those of family life. The cottage parents concept is still in an experimental stage. Foster care is gaining recognition, especially for children with frail constitutions for whom institutional placement is not recommended. There are, at present, about 16,000 children in foster care paid for by the state.

Children in Need of Special Care

According to a national survey, about 3 percent of children in Poland are mentally impaired or physically handicapped to a degree requiring special care and a special educational system. The number of special schools has been vastly expanded. All blind, deaf, and severely handicapped children are placed in specialized institutions, some of which have attained an international reputation. Over 100 trade schools for the handicapped are helping more than 12,000 physically and mentally impaired children to learn a trade. There are 88 kindergartens for retarded and emotionally disturbed children. In general, the Polish system of child welfare is fairly well prepared to take care of the physically handicapped and the retarded. It is less well prepared to help children with problems of maladjustment, learning difficulties, or similar problems. There are some child guidance clinics organized by the Friends of Children Society, located mostly in large urban communities. Some vocational guidance facilities are also being developed in schools, but most of these fairly recent developments are primarily diagnostic and not treatment-oriented.

Juvenile Delinquency

Delinquency among the young is being closely scrutinized and widely discussed in the Polish professional literature. The general approach to youthful offenders is not so much punishment as reeducation and rehabilitation. Juvenile courts were established in 1949, and along with them the institution of parole officers, entrusted with the rehabilitation of youthful offenders up to the age of 17. There are about 240 paid professional officers attached to 96 juvenile courts. In addition, almost 25,000 volunteer youth custodians work directly with young persons in trouble. Currently juvenile delinquency cases are on the decline, having dropped from 29,730 in 1965 to 26,816 in 1972.

THE PROBLEM OF THE ELDERLY

According to international demographic standards, by the middle of 1966 Poland had already reached the classification of an elderly population structure, with 7 percent of the total population 65 years or older. This, of course, is the result of general progress, especially better health care, but it poses a problem. And the problem is more acute because, according to statistical forecasts, while the total population will increase by 25.5 percent between 1966 and 1985, the number of persons aged 60 and over will grow by 47.5 percent—almost twice as fast—and the number of people 70 and over four times faster.

Worse yet, recent studies have shown that 17.2 percent of persons over age 60 (about 600,000) are becoming progressively more senile. Various infirmities compel them to seek outside help or admittance to a social welfare residential establishment. About 140,000 persons are permanently bedridden.

Even those whose health resists the encroachment of old age have a hard time. Although it seems that persons live longer in Poland, they are aging much less comfortably than in other European countries. As Professor J. Piotrowski points out in a 1973 study, the prospects of advancing age are full of pitfalls occasioned by poor housing, poor family relationships (one out of every six elderly persons lives alone), small pensions, and the poor image the elderly have of themselves.

There is a growing awareness of the plight of the aging in Poland, and as a result, the current Polish program for the development of social assistance and welfare from now until 1985 calls for the expansion of existing facilities and services for the aged. The program also includes establishment of new forms of assistance, including money allowances, aid in kind, and modern institutional care.

Institutional Care

The government is promoting a radical reorganization of institutional care facilities. Old-fashioned homes for the aged are being replaced by modern institutions with private rooms and recreational facilities, most of which are located in big cities. For example, the "House of Peaceful Old Age" in Cracow, well-run and built on an exceptionally handsome site, serves as a residence for 100 senior citizens on retirement pay. Across the road there is an equally well-organized nursing home for the chronically ill. In 1972, more than 8,000 senior citizens were living in government-sponsored retirement homes, and about 19,000 were living in institutions for the chronically ill—twice as many as before. Plans are being made for expanding home-care facilities and household help for the sick in cooperation with the Red Cross and the trade unions. There are also Catholic homes for the aged with nuns in charge. They enjoy a very good reputation, especially among elderly intellectuals.

Homemakers

So far, in spite of all efforts, institutional-care facilities fall far short of demand. Increasing numbers of the chronically ill and handicapped are completely dependent on help in kind, organized by various social agencies, which provide them with fuel, free meals, and homemaking services.

Many young persons are involved in helping the old. Such involvement is looked upon as a very positive educational experience for the young. Girl Scouts and Boy Scouts are particularly active in this field, and to encourage them, special prizes are awarded to particularly helpful teenagers. At one such prize-giving ceremony an elderly client was overheard complaining, "My girl is just as good as that one that got First Prize. It's too bad I didn't know how to tell them."

Day-Care Centers

For the elderly able to move about, day-care centers for senior citizens are of great help, and many such centers are being organized, primarily in urban areas. Early in the morning, old folks from a given neighborhood come to spend the day at the center, which provides hot meals, companionship, and organized activities. The only drawback is that they must attend the center daily in order to take advantage of its facilities. Trade unions and various local agencies are organizing clubs for senior citizens that operate on a less rigid basis and where occasional attendance is possible.

These facilities exemplify growing concern to improve the circumstances of the unavoidable process of aging. Trade unions in particular show an enlightened approach to the problem. Employees who retire not only retain membership in their unions, but all of its benefits as well: the right to financial assistance, loans, lunchroom privileges, participation in vacation plans, sanatorium facilities, and recreation activities. At the same time the management at their former establishments takes advantage of their experience: retired workers are invited to participate in production conferences, contests, and field trips. This not only assists retirees financially, but also boosts morale. It helps to fill the social and professional void produced by retirement and gives a sense of usefulness and importance.

A series of articles which have appeared recently in the Polish press discuss the role the aging should play in society and the urgent need to create a social climate which would not exclude them from participation. Professor Piotrowski (1973) says:

> The elderly ought to live in the midst of all of us, not somewhere on the periphery of life, between the milk bar, the bench in the square, and the prospect of ending in an old people's home. . . . It is imperative that an elderly person have a choice between living among members of his own generation, or participating in the life of multi-generation society. A man without a choice is slighted even by those who love him.

ADMINISTRATIVE ORGANIZATION OF PROGRAMS

The state assumes the responsibility for providing the necessary services in the fields of health, education, and welfare in order to assure everyone's constitutional rights. Poland never had a separate Ministry of Welfare (such as exists in Israel, for instance). The Ministry of Health and Welfare took over as chief coordinator of welfare from the Ministry of Labor and Social Welfare; it has been a policy-making body since its establishment in 1960. The Department of Welfare has direct jurisdiction over services for the aged, the unemployable, the mentally disturbed (especially retarded children), the chronically ill, alcoholics, and victims of natural disasters. However, the complexity of tasks in the field of social assistance demands the involvement of more than one central administrative unit. Thus, maternity services and infant services (up to the age of three) are the responsibility of the Health Department. Services to children and youth between three and seventeen are the concern of the Ministry of Education. The problem of juvenile delinquency falls under the jurisdiction of the Ministry of Justice, where a special department was created to deal with it. Finally, the Ministry of Labor, Wages and Social Affairs, which controls employment and wages, is also in charge of social services provided to all employees of the socialized sector of the Polish economy. Moreover, its jurisdiction extends over the Office of Social Security (Z.U.S.), the unit responsible for the system of retirement payments, pensions, and various other benefits. All these executive organs are, of course, responsible to the Sejm, the legislative branch of the Polish political system.

For administrative purposes, Poland is divided into 17 provinces plus five self-contained large cities. The 17 provinces are composed of 314 administrative districts which are subdivided into 2,367 small municipalities.

On all these administrative levels, a new policy, inaugurated in 1973, attempts to weld the various aspects of social development into a cohesive, interrelated whole. On the district level, for instance, health and welfare services are to be integrated, and local centers are to be staffed with social workers, a public health nurse, and a district physician, who will have access to specialized tubercular and psychiatric clinics.

Instead of the small township (wies), the small municipality (gmina) is to become the basic administrative level on which most services are to be discharged. Each small municipality serves an average of 7,000 people, and has, or will soon have, a Health and Welfare Center staffed with both professional and volunteer personnel. It is here that volunteer counselors, working in the field as government agents, can report and refer cases which they are unable to assist locally. It is hoped that this pooling of resources will improve the effectiveness of services rendered to the people.

On all administrative levels Health and Welfare Centers are headed by a manager (administrator) who is assisted by People's Councils representing local groups. In fact, since the advent of the present government in 1970, much of the local administration is being reorganized with the object of bringing more people with professional training into the government. While workers and peasants still predominate in legislative and advisory bodies such as People's Councils, executives are becoming specialists. The new stress is on efficiency.

The Role of Industrial Plants and Trade Unions

The contribution of industrial plants and trade unions to the Polish welfare system is impressively large. In a full employment economy, with a majority of workers working in its public sector, many social problems reveal themselves at work. Thus, the job site provides excellent case finding grounds. As a result, industrial plants and trade unions have become major contributors to the country's welfare system. The services they provide assume many forms. Most workers take advantage of free or heavily subsidized meals offered in the plant. A worker in temporary difficulties can get financial assistance or a loan. At vacation time the worker can participate in vacation plans which allow him and his family to spend his leave at a well run and often luxurious resort hotel, boarding house, or camp—places once accessible only to the wealthy. Prices are nominal. Many plants provide various recreational facilities for children and youth, and have clubs for retired workers. Some make small garden plots available to their employees.

Funds spent on such activities have more than doubled from 1965 to 1972, and amount now to about 15 billion zlotys. All these services, which contribute substantially to a worker's wages over and above the take-home pay, are provided on the basis of individual requests which are then evaluated by the appropriate factory committees. Some progressive trade unions, such as the Miners' Union and the Foundry Workers' Union, now go out of their way to reach members with special social needs and to provide them with preventive services. For example, one union recently conducted interviews with all workers earning less than 400 zlotys per family member. Subsequently, in each case where possible a plan was developed in order to increase the earning power of the family as a whole by giving additional training or employment to another member besides the principal breadwinner. There is a growing tendency in industrial plants and trade unions to use trained social work personnel to assist in the task of various workers' committees.

Not all work establishments and trade unions are equipped to offer a vast range of services to their employees. Indeed, the disparities are often glaring. Only recently a lively campaign in the press was calling for a pool of all existing vacation facilities in order to assure a more efficient and more equitable allocation of these facilities among all Polish workers.

Although they contribute greatly to the country's welfare system, work establishments and trade unions confine their services to workers and their families, and, to some extent, to retired workers and their families. Those outside the work force of the public sector—and they include a large share of the rural population—have to rely on services provided by the state and various social organizations.

The Role of Social Agencies

Many of the social agencies which contribute to the present welfare system have a long tradition of service reaching far back into the country's past. Four are national in scope and deserve special mention: the Polish Committee for Social Service (P.K.O.S.); the Polish Red Cross (P.C.K.); the Friends of Children Society (T.P.D.); and Caritas and PAX. Each of these organizations offers specific types of services, conducts fund-raising drives, and provides an opportunity for social involvement to a large number of civic-minded individuals.

The Polish Committee for Social Service was formed in 1958 as a social agency supplementing the welfare activities of the state. It has about 8,000 local branches (3,600 of them in rural communities) which offer help to people who are unable to support themselves or whoo cannot rely on their families for support. More than 65 percent of the Committee's clients are elderly persons without financial means or with very small pensions. Another group of the Committee's clients consists of families too large to be supported by a single breadwinner. The Committee provides, in addition to some financial assistance, fuel, free meals, and clothing, as well as laundry and homemaking services. It also sponsors local Senior Citizen's Clubs, and the number of such clubs is constantly growing.

The Polish Red Cross, originally established in 1919, was reactivated in 1964 as an organization devoted to helping both the sick living alone and victims of natural disasters. It dispenses help in Red Cross Centers or at the clients' homes, free of charge or for a nominal fee on the basis of referrals. As in many other countries, the Red Cross in Poland is also very active in training service personnel, especially nurses.

The Friends of Children Society, founded in 1949 as the result of a merger of two pre-war organizations, is Poland's principal advocate of children's well-being, and to this end organizes special events, such as International Children's Day. Where pre-school facilities are inadequate, the Friends of Children Society supplements the program with its own special child activities conducted in the vicinity of a child's home. These informal nursery schools or playgrounds, which the society runs in both urban and rural areas, emphasize educational components and imaginative leadership. The Society has also established a network of special guidance centers for parents in many urban communities. It has also created a special committee devoted exclusively to the care of socially maladjusted and retarded children. Since working with children requires special skills and training, the Society puts great stress on its training activities.

Caritas and *PAX* are lay Catholic organizations. Caritas has a long tradition of service to the poor in a country deeply attached to Catholicism. Caritas's main contributions to the present welfare scene are numerous institutions maintained for people who are unfit to live alone, particularly the very old and the very young with serious handicaps. PAX, on the other hand, has no institutional facilities but offers counseling services. In addition to providing other services, its volunteers work on a person-to-person basis with juvenile delinquents.

In addition to these organizations, which are national is scope, there are many local ones, primarily dedicated to the care of orphans and handicapped children, and often staffed by members of religious orders. One of these, Laski (near Warsaw), is a model community for the blind and is internationally famous. It enjoys a striking degree of cooperation between the secular administrators representing the government and the various religious orders which supply the most important ingredient, manpower. After a tour of the very impressive facilities of a large children's institution near Warsaw, the director of the establishment complained that not enough young girls are entering religious orders nowadays, since "Nuns provided such terrific manpower for institutional care." It seems that although the dialogue "at the top" between heads of the Catholic church and the Polish People's Republic has not always been friendly, the cooperation between secular and religious social workers is flourishing.

STAFFING AND MANPOWER PATTERNS

The new emphasis on the need to accelerate the pace of social progress, the recent reorganization of Health and Welfare Centers on all administrative levels, and the growing complexity of social problems, have all combined to reveal the current shortage of properly trained manpower. Lack of qualified personnel to staff social services is a problem confronting many countries, as the UN Hague Conference in 1972 demonstrated. The solution to this problem is considered by the Polish Ministry of Health and Welfare as one of its most urgent tasks.

The proposed solution would combine the existing institution of volunteer social counselors with a new type of professionally trained social workers. It is hoped that a proper division of their respective tasks and the establishment of a new order of authority will result in better use of social work manpower, which will team up with its counterpart in the health service.

A cadre of over 65,000 volunteer social counselors forms the backbone of the present welfare system. The institution of volunteer social welfare manpower was known in Poland before World War II, and was reactivated on a large scale both in urban and rural communities in 1959. Social counselors are nominated by the proper state authorities from a list of candidates selected by local groups. They are usually local persons, often retired, and serve without pay except for reimbursement of traveling expenses. They act on behalf of the government and enjoy semi-official status. There are several different categories of social counselors. Most of them work in their communities, some (usually because of their professional background) serve as specialists in specific welfare problems, and still others, about 10 percent of the total, serve within work establishments. In terms of socialist ideology:

> The local social counselor is an organ of the people's government, ready to help anyone who needs help. He thus becomes a connecting link, bringing closer together the citizen and the state organization. He represents the essentially humanitarian aspect of the state, and thus helps form the proper relationship between citizens and the people's government and its organs. At the same time the local social counselor is that particular representative of the national council to whom a citizen in need of assistance has the easiest and quickest access [Rajkiewicz, 1972].

Who are these people? They represent many professions and many educational levels, since there are no clear-cut requirements for candidates to the post. Dedication and willingness to serve are essential. There are many highly motivated persons, most of them retired, who feel obligated to help their fellow men. War conditions fostered a spirit of mutual help among the Polish population, and the present social counselors who belong to the war generation reflect that spirit. But recruiting new, younger candidates for a post involving such heavy responsibilities is now more difficult.

The scope of activities of a social counselor goes far beyond counseling. The establishment of a large staff of these voluntary social workers has allowed the government to pursue a more assertive policy of social welfare. The reaching out in local communities to people living in deprivation or having various special needs has become a major case finding part of a counselor's job. Serving an area with an average of 800 people, he has to know all the community resources, be able to make accurate diagnostic judgments, and often has to act fast. He must also know how to work in cooperation with other organizations in the community and how to be his clients' advocate.

The training of social counselors is a continuous process. The Ministry of Health and Welfare, with the cooperation of prominent educators and community work experts, has set up training facilities and publishes a steady stream of handbooks and booklets designed to make the work of social counselors more effective by improving both skills and understanding. These publications are enthusiastically received by the volunteer counselors who need all the help they can get to cope with the mounting load of social problems. The constantly growing complexity of family life in a country shifting from agriculture to industry, combined with the various problems caused by demographic trends, make it absolutely necessary to reinforce the institution of volunteer counselors with fully trained professionals.

Social work as a profession did not exist in the Polish People's Republic during its first 20 years. However, there is a tradition of professional social workers dating back to pre-war years. Their education consisted at first of two years of college-level courses, which were later extended to four years. A school of social work headed by a well-known and highly respected social worker, Professor Helena Redlinska, enjoyed wide recognition and esteem in pre-war Poland. It was not until 1966 that the first school for professional social workers opened in Warsaw. By 1973, there were six, plus two special work-study programs, designed to reach those already working in the field.

Although these schools accept graduates of Polish secondary schools and thus represent the equivalent of the junior college education, they do not have academic status. The goal of the two-year program with a curriculum combining theory and social work practice (fieldwork) is to prepare competent personnel able to supervise volunteer counselors and to provide direct services in other branches of the welfare system. Up to September, 1973, a total of 1,343 persons graduated from these schools. There is a plan to establish a school of social work in every province (wojewodztwo), thus bringing their total to 17. This is part of a general plan which would develop a new educational system especially designed to supply qualified manpower to all segments of the Polish economy and society. Schools of social work are under jurisdiction of the Department of Medical Education in the Ministry of Health and Welfare, and not under the jurisdiction of the Ministry of Higher Education. As a result, their graduates earn no credits transferable to institutions of higher learning such as universities.

The curriculum stresses the connection between health and welfare. The subjects taught, in addition to those designed to broaden the student's liberal arts background, acquaint him with social work methodology and skills, and include public health concepts and services, hygiene, anatomy, and physiology. Placing students in fieldwork presents a major problem because there is an acute shortage of qualified instructors. Plans are being made to unify the curriculum in all six schools. New syllabi are being prepared for faculty discussions. The task is difficult because a unified curriculum aims at a completely new image of a professional social worker.

The urgent need for professional social workers has emerged so recently that the tasks they are to perform are not yet clearly defined or classified. As a result, some graduates cannot find jobs and most of those who are employed are very poorly paid. Fortunately, planners at the Ministry of Health and Welfare are drafting an organizational chart of professional social work jobs and their allocation at all administrative levels. They estimate that in the next five years about 8,000 social workers will be needed to fill positions in the government sector, work establishments, and trade unions. There is also a plan for considerable expansion of work-study programs for workers in the field seeking further education. Because of the new demand for highly qualified personnel in leadership positions in social welfare, social research, and training, the Ministry of Higher Education has been approached with the suggestion that universities offer courses leading to a Master's degree in social work.

In-service training of volunteers is offered by many social agencies, notably the Red Cross, Caritas and the Friends of Children Society.

FINANCING

Social benefits are financed in Poland through four different channels:

(1) By the government through the social security system. The total amount funnelled in this way in 1970 was about 44 billion zlotys and is on the increase (Rocznik Statystyczny, 1973).

(2) By the government through the Department of Welfare in the Ministtry of Health and Welfare. The total in 1970 was between 2.3 and 2.5 billion zlotys, and does not seem to be expanding rapidly, reflecting the general principle that improvement in social security coverage diminishes the need for public assistance expenditures.

(3) By work establishments and trade unions. Their combined contribution is estimated at close to 15 billion zlotys per annum.

(4) By social agencies. Their contribution is difficult to assess but known to be substantial.

On the average, social benefits tend to add about 19 percent to the basic earnings from work. Of this, 8 percent is in the form of monetary assistance. It is interesting to note that social benefits are increasing slightly faster than work-related average income (Rosner, 1972).

Social Security

The principal function of social security, in socialist Poland as in other industrial countries, is to protect individuals and families against various risks such as the death of a breadwinner, illness, accident, and other contingencies which reduce income derived from work. Since the state employs about 80 percent of the work force, the whole system is a branch of government known as the Social Insurance Institution (Zaklad Ubezpieczen Spoleczny). Before World War II, there was a fairly well developed social security system in Poland, but only 15 percent of the total population was fully covered. During the war, social security reserve funds were wiped out so that it was necessary to start from scratch. Nevertheless, by 1972, 82 percent of the population was covered by various social security benefits. The principal categories of benefits are: health insurance and maternity benefits; family allowances; retirement and pensions; workers' compensation; and benefits for farmers, artisans and the self-employed. The system makes no provision for the risk of unemployment. This is because every citizen has the right to employment, and work is regarded as the normal contribution of every member of society to the aggregate national product.

Top priority among risks covered by the Polish system goes to

Table 2

Type of Payment	Amount (in 1,000 zl.)
Illness benefits	5,310
Maternity benefits	465
Funeral benefits	502
Retirement	33,710[a]
Pensions for war veterans	10,463[a]
Family pensions	6,488[a]
Family benefits	8,367[a]

a. In 1971 the average monthly pension was 1,265 zl. (for miners, 2,173 zl.); retirement pay was 1,600 zl.; disabled veterans' pay was 1,035 zl.; and the family allowance was 971 zl.

health, because illness or disability of a citizen endangers the national economy. Health insurance and maternity benefits are based exclusively on employers' contributions. The coverage is very broad, with substantial benefits. For example, maternity benefits amount to 100 percent of earnings, and benefits because of illness amount to 70 percent.

Retirement benefits and pensions, which are very modest, are being constantly re-evaluated and improved, especially for certain categories of workers—such as miners, railroad workers, war veterans, military personnel—and for their families. Old age protection for farmers is a sore point. A farmer can get retirement pay only if he agrees to socialize his farm, in which case the amount of his retirement pay depends on the size of his farm. Otherwise, old farmers must depend on their children's support. Table 2 shows some of the principal types of social security benefits, and the amounts paid in 1970. The present Polish Social Security system does not include an automatic adjustment of benefits to the increase in the cost of living, but the subject is frequently introduced for consideration.

Government-Financed Welfare

There are various special categories of clients receiving support from the government. Some examples from the 1971 budget are shown in Table 3. Most of these disbursements are channeled through various levels of welfare administration, and some are disbursed through voluntary social agencies which are also contributing financially.

Table 3

Categories	Amount (in million zl.)
Persons suffering from tuberculosis	42
Families of the temporarily unemployed	20[a]
Families of alcoholics	24
Families of prisoners or those released from prison	16
Families in need because of natural disasters	4

a. Recently reassigned to the Ministry of Labor, Wages and Social Matters, this item is now excluded from the Department of Welfare budget.

Service Fees

Payments by parents for day-care facilities or for institutional help for emotionally disturbed or handicapped children are based on a sliding scale adjusted to the parents' earnings, and usually cover only a small part of the cost of such facilities.

In the homes for the aged, those receiving pensions or retirement pay contribute financially to the cost of such facilities. However, they are entitled to retain a small sum (200 zlotys) for personal expenses.

Most services to various disadvantaged groups are free, with the government paying the cost. It must be kept in mind, however, that government funds reserved for social services are primarily to help those in the pre- and post-productive stages of life. Such funds are expended according to current priorities which might not always satisfy the felt needs of various groups.

PLANNING AND RESEARCH

Human needs are universal. The ways societies attempt to meet them and to solve human dilemmas differ greatly. In many parts of the world, the belief in the self-regulating qualities of the economic system hold strong. Some economists, pursuing the laissez-faire doctrine in the capitalistic free-enterprise system, are convinced that increasing national wealth will automatically reduce poverty. But Poland is a country strongly committed to the concept of governmental intervention through planning. Like the U.S.S.R. and other Eastern European Bloc countries, Poland's economic and social policies are carefully laid out in advance. The famous five-year plans, the bases of economic and political strategy, call for constantly taking stock of progress, as well as for frequently re-evaluating basic assumptions.

The methodology of economic and industrial planning has a long and well-documented history in various socialist countries. On the other hand, long-term planning in the field of social progress—a fresh objective—seems to call for new innovative approaches.

The Polish People's Republic devoted the first few years of its existence almost exclusively to rescue work, in order to salvage as much as possible after the war. Assistance to war orphans and to disabled war veterans and the reunification of broken families were the primary objectives of social welfare. Later on, too great a reliance on the ability of the socialist system to do away with poverty hampered new approaches to social needs and goals. Not until the late sixties did some coherent planning of welfare services begin in earnest.

Poland is now through most of its latest five-year plan, 1971-1975. The primary aim of this plan is "rapid and tangible progress in the standard of consumption to be achieved by higher earnings, full employment of the whole working-age population, rises in farm incomes, and more and bigger welfare benefits." The current years are also a test period for the new strategy adopted at the beginning of 1971, calling for a substantial increase in independence and responsibility. The strategy requires the modernization of planning and management, not as an end in itself but subordinate to the overriding objectives of social development and economic advance. The new strategy is markedly people-directed; rising wages and consumption are seen as a reward for better performance. The increase in real wages was to come to 18 percent over the entire five-year period. In fact, it looks as though this target will be reached in three years. A dynamic expansion of employment leaves employment offices with far more vacancies than applicants. These are achievements which count most from the social point of view.

By and large, it is quite evident that social progress has been substantial with respect to the segment of population currently in the labor force. There is, however, a need for more forceful planning of a coherent system of services for the segment of Polish population of non-productive age or in special life situations requiring help. At present, such services are dispersed among too many units of government and various social agencies. The situation calls for a well-coordinated social plan projecting social needs and social services into the 1980s.

The Welfare Department of the Ministry of Health and Welfare seems to be moving in this direction. The department has been researching various social needs and assessing the numbers of prospective clients. The department is studying demographic trends made available by the Central Statistical Office, which permit it to project fairly accurately the future social needs of special groups.

There are many agencies and institutions in Poland engaged in many kinds of research. Experts in the field are numerous and there is a tradition of scholarship. But, as in some other areas, there seems to be a lack of coordination among various research endeavors.

Most recently, a very impressive investigation has been launched in Poland as part of an international project sponsored by the U.S. Department of Health, Education and Welfare. This research study will last three years and will cover the following areas of welfare programs: child welfare services in Poland; the role and function of day-care centers for the aged in Poland; and investigations of social workers, their skills, effectiveness, and method of training. Teams of competent researchers have already been selected, including prominent academicians, experienced educators, and representatives of appropriate governmental units. The results of such investigation will undoubtedly provide valuable data for the long-term planning of welfare services in Poland.

NOTES

1. The Statute enacted on August 6, 1923, still provides the basis for some welfare programs.
2. The population of Poland increased from 23.6 million in 1946 to 33.2 million in 1972.
3. Kitchens and bathrooms are not counted as rooms.

REFERENCES

CHELSTOWSKI, S. (1973) "Yesterday, Today, Tomorrow." Polish Perspectives (December). Warsaw.

Conference of European Ministers Responsible for Social Welfare (August 1972) United Nations Economic and Social Council. The Hague, Netherlands.

Family, Child and Youth Welfare Services. (1965) United Nations Department of Economic and Social Affairs. New York.

HULEK, A. (1972) Teoria i Praktyka Rehabilitacji Invalidow [Theory and Practice of Rehabilitation of Disabled Veterans]. Warsaw.

KAMINSKI, A. (1972) Funkcje Pedagogiki Spotecznej [Social Goals of Extra Curriculum Education]. Warsaw.

KARCZEWSKI, M. (1973) Opieka Spoteczna [Social Services]. Warsaw.
KRYCZYNSKA, I. (n.d.) Wskazowki Metodyczne dla Opiekunow Spotecznych [Guidelines for Social Counselors]. Warsaw.
Kungres F.I.C.E. [XXIV Congress of International Federation of Societies of Friends of Children]. (1973) Warsaw.
LALLY, D. (1970) National Social Service Systems: A Comparative Study and Analysis of Selected Countries. Washington, D.C.: U.S. Department of Health, Education and Welfare.
LAUCZMANSKI, Z. (1967) "Tezy programowe w sprawie dziatania pomocy spotecznej [Program Outline of Social Services]." Praca i Labespieczenie Spoteczne 2 and 3. Warsaw.
MIKULSKI, J. (1972) "Rola i Zadania Panstwowych Szkot Pracownikow Socjalnych w Procesie Realizacji Nowej Politik: Socjalnej [Role of Governmental Schools for Social Workers in the Realization of New Social Policies]." Opiekun Spoteczny 3. Warsaw: Ministry of Health and Social Welfare.
OLESZCZYNSKA, A. (1973) Dzienne Osrodki Pobytu dla Ludzi Starszych–Ich Funckje Rehabilitacyjne w Srodowisku [Day Care Centers for the Elderly–Rehabilitation in the Community]. Warsaw.
Opiekun Spoteczny [Social Counselor]. (various dates) Nr. 1 (50) ROK XIV, No. 2 (47) ROK XIV, Nr. 2 (51) ROK XIV, No. 3 (52) ROK XIV. Warsaw.
Pamietniki Opiekunow Spotecznych [Memoirs of Social Counselors] (1971). Warsaw: Ministry of Health and Social Welfare.
PIOTROWSKI, J. (1973) Miejsca CzYowieka Starego w Rodzinie i Spoteczenstwie [Place of the Elderly in the Family and Society]. Warsaw: P.W.N.
––– (1966) Zabespieczenie Spoteczne–Problematyka i Metody [Social Security–Its Problems and Methods]. Warsaw: Ksiazka i Wiedza.
Polityka Gospodarcza a Polity ka Spoteczna [Economic Policy versus Social Policy] (1971). Warsaw: WiedzaPowszechna.
Pomoc Spoteczna w P.R.L. [Social Services in Poland] (1970). Warsaw: Ministry of Health and Social Welfare.
Poradnik Pracownika Socjalnego [Handbook for Social Workers] (1973). Warsaw: Ministry of Health and Social Welfare.
Proceedings of the International Conference of Ministers Responsible for Social Welfare, United Nation's Headquarters, September 3-12, 1968 (1969) New York: United Nations.
PUDELKO, T. (1968) "Przyklady Osiedlonych Dzialan Spoteczno–Wychowawczych T.P.D. [Examples of Social and Educational Activities of the Society of Friends of Children]." P.P.K.O. Nr. 9/10. Warsaw.
PUSIN, E. (1964) "The Role of Social Services in Different Stages of National . Development." International Social Work 7 (January).
RAJKIEWICZ, A. (1973) Polityka Spoteczna [Social Policy]. Warsaw: P.W.E.
––– (1972) "Social Policy and Tomorrow." Polish Perspective, Monthly Review 15, Nr. 6 (June). Warsaw.
Rocznik Statystyczny [Statistical Yearbook] (1973). Warsaw: Central Statistical Office.
ROSNER, J. (1973) "Przedewszytkiem Sluzby Spoteczne [First of All, Social Services]." Trybuna Ludu Nr. 310 (December 29). Warsaw.
SECOMSKI, K. (1974) "Ekspansje Gospodarki Polskiej i Mechanizm Jej Wzrostu [Expansion of the Polish Economy and the Mechanism of its Growth]." Trybuna Ludu (January). Warsaw.
––– (1967) "Wzrost Gospodavczy a Postep Spoteczny [Economic Expansion and Social Progress]." Nowe Drogi 10. Warsaw.
Socjalne i Prawne Srodki Ochrony Macierczynstwa i Rodziny [Social and Legal Protection of Motherhood and Family] (1973). Warsaw: Instytut Praci i Spraw Socjalnych, Sympozjum, April 9, 1973.

Sprawozdanie z Dziatalnosci Towarzystwa Przyjaciot Dzieci w Latach 1969-1971 [Report of the Society of Friends of Children] (1972). Warsaw.

SZCZEPANSKI, J. (1973) Reflekcje Nad Oswiata [Reflections Concerning Education]. Warsaw: P.Z.W.

SZEJNERT, M. (n.d.) "Dwanascie lat ala Superdorostych [Twelve years of Superadulthood]." Literatura 10 and 18 (October). Warsaw.

TITMUS, R. (1966) "Social Policy and Economic Progress." Social Welfare Forum. New York: Columbia University Press.

Training for Social Welfare—Fifth International Survey: New Approaches in Meeting Manpower Needs (1971). New York: UN Department of Economic and Social Affairs.

8

SWEDEN'S MODEL SYSTEM OF
SOCIAL SERVICES ADMINISTRATION

ÅKE ELMER

Sweden is a country of eight million inhabitants in an area the size of the state of California. The population is unusually homogeneous in terms of race, language, religion, and education. In recent years the number of immigrants has increased, but they still constitute a relatively small part of the population.

The political system is based on the principle of representative government on three levels, national, county, and community. The Swedish Parliament (the Riksdag), chosen in direct elections, has decisive power. The government is dependent upon the relative strength of the political parties in Parliament. Under the government's authority, there is a public administration with central boards and agencies in Stockholm and subunits in the 24 counties. However, in each county there is also a directly elected representative body, mainly responsible for medical services and related tasks. This body, the county council, then elects executive bodies which in turn appoint officials. In addition, there is a directly elected representative body, the commune council, in each of the 278 local districts. Local authorities are in charge of social services, schools, public utilities, and local planning. They have their own agencies for different branches of administration. These are under the control of citizen's committees elected by the commune council, but they also have many salaried employees. In Sweden there are no officials directly elected by the people with the exception of members of the Riksdag, county councils, and commune councils.

Apart from official public agencies, there are social insurance offices that are formally private but in fact are state controlled. These offices administer social insurance with the exception of unemployment insurance, which has its own offices associated with the trade unions.

The Riksdag, county councils, and commune councils each have the power to tax. The counties and the local authorities collect a proportional income tax. The state collects a progressive income tax and a property tax as well as indirect taxes—a general sales tax on goods and special taxes on gasoline, alcoholic beverages, and so on. The state supervises the collection of all taxes and social insurance fees, including the taxes and fees decided on by county councils, commune councils, and social insurance offices.

Practically all social services are financed with public taxes. Church and private efforts play an insignificant role. There are both national and local fund-raising campaigns, organized by the Red Cross for example, but these are of negligible importance. Nursing homes, children's homes, and other institutions are almost entirely run by public agencies.

The fact that church and private charities play such a small part in social services in Sweden has, partly, a historical explanation. In the beginning of the sixteenth century, all Swedes were Roman Catholics. But King Gustav converted the Catholic Church into a Lutheran Church and made himself head of the church, replacing the Pope. The state took over the property of the church and at the same time its duties toward the poor and sick. For 450 years Sweden has had a Lutheran State Church and state responsibility for medical and social services.

The state's dominance in the service sector is not matched by an equally great dominance with regard to production. About 8 percent of the Swedish people work for private companies, which are, however, firmly controlled by the state. In addition, companies and employees both pay a larger share of their income in taxes than in most other countries.

DIVISION OF RESPONSIBILITIES AMONG PUBLIC AGENCIES

The main principle in Swedish social services is that state agencies legislate about, control, and partly finance the different activities, while the agencies of the county councils and the local authorities have direct contact with the citizens. However, there are exceptions to this rule. The state is directly in charge of employment exchange and parts of vocational education, as well as the police, the judiciary, and the penal system. The most important task of the county councils is, as mentioned previously, medical service—hospitals as well as out-patient departments. There are also doctors with private practices, but in relatively smaller numbers than in most other Western countries. A majority of dentists have private practices. Thus, local authorities are in charge of most social services, with the exception of employment exchange and medical services.

SERVICES FOR "THE NORMAL COURSE OF LIFE"

It is commonly said that "the welfare state" takes care of its citizens "from the cradle to the grave." This is true in Sweden insofar as the state offers a number of services that citizens can utilize. This does not mean that everyone in fact has access to all services to which, in principle, he is entitled. Nor does it mean, of course, that everyone cares to take advantage of all available services.

Social services can conveniently be divided into those concerning "the normal course of life" and those available in case of need. The dividing line between the two categories is not clear-cut but changes among different people. What is normal for one person can be unusual for someone else. I shall further divide the normal services into the following categories: maternity welfare, welfare for infants, welfare for pre-school-age children, child-care facilities, pre-schools, home-help service, social services in the schools, leisure-time services, employment exchange and vocational guidance, sex counseling, abortion, home furnishing assistance and consumer advice, housing assistance, services to immigrants, dental services, medical services, services to the elderly, homes for the aged, and funeral services.

Maternity Welfare. Services for children begin during the mother's pregnancy. All mothers-to-be have access to free medical examinations and regular health control during pregnancy. They also get free prophylactic medicines. In large towns there are special maternity centers. Otherwise, the service is given at ordinary medical centers or out-patient treatment centers which exist in every local district. Over 90 percent of mothers make use of these services. The services are paid for by county councils and thus are financed from proportional income taxes from all income-earners.

Maternity hospitals are connected with ordinary public hospitals. Approximately 99 percent of all deliveries take place there. The confinement is free of charge and travelling back home is paid if it exceeds six kroner. Administration and financing is the same as for maternity welfare. In cases of delivery in the home, which is very rare, midwife services are free, while 75 percent of the costs of medical care are paid for by insurance. There are also private maternity hospitals, but very few children are delivered there.

Welfare for Infants. At the maternity hospital the new mother is told of a child welfare center or medical center where the child may receive free health service. There, also, the obligatory vaccination against smallpox is given, and voluntary vaccinations are offered (almost all of which are taken) against polio, tuberculosis, diphtheria, and other diseases. Prophylactic medicines such as vitamins are free. Nurses give advice about the care of the child and, as a rule, also visit the mother and child in the home. Practically all children come to the child welfare center at some time and over 90 percent come regularly during the first year of life. If someone does not come, the home is visited by a nurse who reminds the mother of the possibilities of help. The nurse can also report to the social authorities if the child seems obviously neglected or maltreated in the home.

Welfare for Pre-School-Age Children. Child welfare centers are available to all children up to the age of seven or when the child starts school. But after the first year, the frequency of visits decreases drastically. In most counties a special examination is made of four-year-olds in order to discover conditions such as hearing defects and mental retardation. The examination is voluntary, but the majority of children come. Since all children are registered, a visit may be paid to those who fail to come. Children who have special needs usually have priority in day nurseries and kindergarten.

Child-Care Facilities. The number of pre-school children whose parents both work or who have a single parent has increased considerably in recent years. The local districts, with state aid, have set up day nurseries and also employ women who receive other people's children in their homes to be looked after. The parents pay for this, as a rule, in proportion to their income, but they never pay the full cost. The number of places in day nurseries and private homes is far from sufficient, and many parents must solve the problem in some other way. During the last ten years the number of places has multiplied, but the demand cannot be satisfied. Social agencies of the local authorities distribute available places among applicants. The economic status of the parents and the child's need for care are the decisive criteria.

Pre-Schools. Kindergartens exist for children four through six years of age. The number of kindergarten places has also increased in recent years. Kindergartens are free in some districts, and in others a fee is charged. As of 1975, however, all local districts will be required by law to provide places for all six-year-olds, either in a day nursery or in a kindergarten. The day nurseries have teachers as well qualified as those at the kindergartens. Officially, day nurseries and kindergartens are both called "pre-schools" in order to stress the fact that the social and intellectual training of the children is to be given as much weight as is their general care. It is probable that it will soon be obligatory for all six-year-olds to go to pre-school and that an increasing number of four- to five-year-olds will also attend. Kindergartens will then be free, but a fee will be charged if the child is to be taken care of all day.

Home-Help Service. When children of gainfully employed parents are ill, they cannot stay in the day nurseries. One of the parents must then stay home from work, unless he or she can turn to home-helpers or child-care aids of the local district. The local districts have people, usually paid by the hour, who step in to assist in such cases. Their numbers are not sufficient during the colds and flu season, when many children are ill at the same time. Then the father or the mother can receive sick benefits from social insurance in order to look after the child.

The local authorities also have home-helpers employed full time who can take care of everything in the home—for example, when a parent who works in the home is ill or in the maternity hospital. In the latter case the father can receive sick benefits in order to look after the older children. The home-helpers also are used when a low-income mother of several children goes away on a holiday, or when the elderly or handicapped persons living alone need help. For all home-help a fee is paid to the local authorities in proportion to the income of the family. Thus, in some cases, the help is free. In this connection it should be mentioned that all parents receive cash family allowances for their children until the children finish school; low-income families receive an additional allowance. There are almost no tax reductions for children.

Social Services in the Schools. Practically all Swedish children between seven and sixteen years of age go to "comprehensive schools" run by the public authorities. Private schools exist but have an insignificant attendance. They do not receive public support except in special cases. There are drop-outs in the highest grades, but not many. For blind, partially sighted, deaf, and mentally retarded children there are special schools, but efforts are made to integrate them as much as possible into the general school system.

In the voluntary high school ("gymnasieskolan") about 75 percent of the students study for an additional two years and 30 percent an additional three years after completion of comprehensive school. The two-year stream gives direct vocational training, while the three-year stream leads to the university. About 20 percent of twenty-year-olds continue their studies past the high school level. There are no colleges in the American sense in Sweden. All education is free of charge (except at a few private schools), both at schools and universities. Besides tuition, the children in comprehensive schools and high schools get free school books, free school supplies, and a free meal every school day.

In the schools there is also free health supervision by the school doctor and school nurse, but not actual medical care. For the higher grades there are social workers to assist with social problems, but not as many as are needed. All children get free dental care at the National Dental Service clinics or with private dentists at the expense of the county council.

For the lower grades especially, there is great need for supervision and leisure-time services after school hours. Since both parents work in many families, this need is partly satisfied by centers run by local districts or by day-care in private homes, but the supply is insufficient. Parents pay for these services in proportion to their income.

Students over the age of 20 are considered independent in relation to their parents' income. They receive scholarships as well as study loans that are forgiven if they do not later reach a certain minimum income. These benefits, intended for living expenses and textbooks, are diminished if the student has an income, but not if he or she receives financial support from his or her parents.

The local authorities administer the comprehensive schools and the high schools, but the state pays the greater part of the costs and is completely in charge of the universities.

Leisure-Time Services. When children are older and no longer need looking after, the need for leisure-time activities still remains. This need is not specific for youth but concerns all ages. However, it is especially relevant to youth before they make a home and start a family.

Leisure-time activities are arranged largely by commercial enterprise or by associations of different kinds. Athletic associations are the most widespread, but boy and girl scout associations as well as religious, social, or political societies also attract many members. State and local authorities support youth organizations through financial assistance for activities as well as for the training of instructors and leaders. In addition, most local authorities themselves organize leisure-time activities in the form of youth centers, sports grounds, swimming areas, and facilities for outdoor activity. These are often in the form of large natural areas owned by the local district and used for skiing and other exercise, or simply for excursions. There is also the so-called "every man's right," a law which permits everyone to enter private land if he does not damage it and which also forbids fencing off beaches and open spaces.

Employment Exchange and Vocational Guidance. In every large population center there is a state employment agency, where everyone can get free service; employment exchanges are forbidden to charge fees. The possibilities of getting a job depend, of course, on supply and whether or not employers report vacancies. A person who is uncertain in choosing a profession or who wants to try a new area of occupation can get vocational guidance, including psychological and technical tests. In schools, students can get systematic vocational guidance (if the system functions, which is not always the case). Special teachers have this responsibility, and in the comprehensive school all students must work two weeks or more in order to get into contact with working life. For the unemployed, the service also includes education in ordinary schools as well as in special courses.

Sex and Birth Control Counseling. Counseling in sexual and birth control matters does not exist in an organized way other than at the maternity centers and at a very small number of sex counseling clinics. Instruction in this area is given in the schools, but is often inadequate. Some advice is given, however, in connection with school health supervision. A private organization (associated with the International Planned Parenthood Federation) is active, and a considerable extension is now planned under public auspices. This extension is primarily connected with an enlarged right to abortion.

Abortion. A circumstance that has led to plans for increased birth-control counseling is the fact that the number of legal abortions has increased rapidly. In principle, abortions are not allowed as a means of birth control, but only in emergency situations. In practice, however, almost all applications for abortions are granted. In 1974, there was a bill pending in the Riksdag which would give women the formal right to abortion before the eighteenth week of pregnancy; after the twelfth week, compulsory consultation with a social worker is proposed. Abortions are done free of charge at hospitals. It is now proposed to make contraceptives, including pills, more easily available, and to emphasize birth control instead of abortions. In 1973 more than 20 percent of all pregnancies ended in legal abortions.

Home Furnishing Assistance and Consumer Advice. When setting up a home, both newly married couples and single parents can get loans and advice from the state. There are domestic advisers at the state regional administration and also in some local districts. They give advice for setting up a home and purchasing expensive consumer goods. This activity, however, is of rather modest proportions.

Of greater importance is the central state consumer office which publishes a paper and distributes information about good consumer products. The state has a special consumer representative (ombudsman) who intervenes against irresponsible advertising of consumer goods and who can also carry through court decisions on prohibitions against misleading advertising and against the sale of dangerous products.

Housing Assistance. In Sweden there is very little housing reserved for people with low incomes. There are, however, special lodgings for students and for old-age pensioners. Instead, the principle is to give economic support for each family to find a suitable place to live, whether as apartment-dwellers or homeowners. Housing construction is, in general, strictly controlled by the state, since 90 percent of the dwellings are built with the aid of state loans.

Through grants and loans, the state has contributed to an increased supply of spacious dwellings for families with children, in blocks of apartments as well as in houses. Apartment dwellings supply a large portion of housing needs in Sweden. The need for children's playgrounds and other collective services is great, but satisfied only in part. Accommodation allowances depend on the number of children, accommodation costs, and income. These allowances are paid by the state but administered by the local authorities.

Services to Immigrants. As already mentioned, the number of immigrants has increased greatly during the last decades, especially the 1960s. Most immigrants come from neighboring Scandinavian countries; among those, the majority of Finnish immigrants have language problems. Considerable groups also come from Italy, Yugoslavia, Greece, and Turkey: these people not only have language problems, but also experience difficulties in adjusting to a totally different culture. Immigrants compose no more than 5 percent of the total population, but since they often settle together, e.g., because some industries employ many immigrants, there are places where more than 25 percent of the school children are of foreign extraction.

There are no "guest workers," in the Western European sense, with limited terms of employment and other contractual limitations. All immigrants have virtually the same rights as Swedish citizens, as soon as they receive their work permit, in employment rules, social services, and so on. It is, for example, forbidden to dismiss an immigrant worker earlier than a later-employed Swede if there is a shortage of work. But when times are bad, many immigrants return home all the same, especially to Finland. And it is, of course, more difficult to get a work permit when there is already unemployment.

An immigrant who is employed in Sweden has a right to be instructed in the Swedish language and taught about Swedish society for at least 240 hours. This teaching must be done during worktime and the employer has to pay full wages for the time used for teaching. The teachers are paid by the state.

In places where there are many immigrants, local authorities usually arrange for information services to immigrants. The information centers are sometimes connected with other agencies—for example, the public library or the social service office—and sometimes they are independent. In addition to information, the immigrants also get help and advice in approaching authorities and organizations. The interpreter service is, of course, of great importance. In some communities there is also an advisory committee for the immigration service. The immigrants' own societies are often represented there, besides the people elected by the commune council. However, the immigrant services are different in different cities. At some places there is no such service at all, in spite of obvious need.

Dental Services. Dental care for children is given at public clinics, while most adults go to dentists in private practice. Since 1974, however, private dentists also fit into the state system. Dentists must follow detailed tariffs. Of the fixed price, the patient pays half and social insurance half. For very expensive treatment, insurance pays more.

Medical Services. For medical consultations the system is somewhat different. For a visit to a doctor in public service, a fixed fee (at present, twelve kroner) is paid regardless of how much treatment the visit requires—x-ray, laboratory tests, and so on. It is now planned to introduce a similar system with private doctors, with a somewhat higher fee. Medical insurance will then pay the rest according to a standard rate. The county councils are in charge of a system of out-patient clinics at hospitals as well as at medical centers with one or more doctors in every local district.

Physician-prescribed medicines are paid for by the patient at pharmacies at a subsidized price, maximum of fifteen kroner regardless of the actual price. Some vital medicines, such as insulin, are completely free.

The benefits above apply to all persons residing in Sweden, including foreigners, but excluding tourists or persons who have come to the country in order to seek medical treatment. The benefits are life long and may be used an unlimited number of times. Costs are divided between the county councils and medical insurance.

It should be added that all persons residing in Sweden who are gainfully employed also have a right to disability benefits for 90 percent of their income, up to a certain maximum, for an unlimited period. If the illness is or becomes incurable, the sickness benefit is replaced by an early retirement pension which, as a rule, is somewhat lower. For the lowest income groups, however, it is higher.

Services for the Elderly. There are services of several kinds for old persons. The local authorities rent small inexpensive apartments, either together in special buildings or separately in ordinary blocks of apartments. Everyone over the age of 67 (this will soon be lowered to 65) has a pension, and those who have no other appreciable income also get a housing allowance to help pay for a good home, regardless of the type of dwelling.

All pensioners who are in need of help with daily chores, but who do not need care in an institution, have a right to such help. The home-help is arranged by the local social agency and is paid in part by the local authorities. The pensioner pays a fee to the local authorities in proportion to his income. Persons with a high income can also get such help. Most of the "home Samaritans" are housewives who work a few hours a day with one or a few elderly persons, but some are students or have other professions. Some work full-time. If the pensioner is ill, he can get an allowance to pay for a nurse. Besides, he has free access to the care of the district nurse and, like other people, to medical services for a standard fee (twelve kroner for a visit to the doctor, twenty kroner for a doctor's visit to the home).

There are also other services for the elderly, depending on the local district. Old persons usually can get cooked food to be fetched or sent home, they have access to inexpensive care of the feet, and other services. So-called day centers are common, where the pensioners may gather to talk, read the papers, play cards, or work with some kind of hobby such as weaving or woodworking, often with competent instruction available.

In some cases such centers are used by different age groups, but mostly by old persons during the day and youth in the evening. The social agencies of the local authorities administer these activities, sometimes with the assistance of the pensioners' own societies. The costs are usually paid with local taxes, but sometimes there is a low "club membership" fee.

Homes for the Aged. For some old persons, especially among those over 80, it is impossible to manage in the home even with daily help. They must then move to some kind of home for the aged, where they can get continuous care.

A sort of middle way is the pensioners' dwelling, where there is a nurse on duty who can be reached by means of a bell in the apartment. About 5 percent of all pensioners live in old-age homes and about the same number are so ill that they are cared for in hospitals, often in special wards or small nursing homes.

The ordinary old-age homes are administered and financed by local authorities. The users pay with part of their pension or, if they have other resources, in proportion to their income. The homes are used by all classes of society. Authorities try to make the homes into something of "holiday hotels," where possible, with separate rooms or apartments for everyone, with their own furniture. However, unavoidably old-age homes often have a gloomy aspect, since they are full of infirm human beings. In spite of all attempts at entertainment and hobby activities, existence becomes quite monotonous. The local authorities therefore try as long as possible to help old persons stay in their own apartments, especially if they have relatives in the neighborhood. As a rule, this also proves to be less expensive for the community.

Funeral Services. Funeral services are usually managed by private firms or by cooperatives. All burial grounds, however, are public. They are administered and financed by the Lutheran State Church, which for this purpose (and for population registration) has the right to tax even non-members. One does not have to pay for a burial place, or for a funeral service, unless one wants special arrangements. However, it is common to pay for a family grave and a gravestone.

INTERVENTIONS IN CASE OF NEED

As previously mentioned, the line between "the normal course of life" and cases of need is not clear-cut. Under the latter category the following topics will be considered: illness, mental illness, disabling conditions, alcoholism and drug dependency, children who need protection, juvenile delinquency, economic need, family crises, need of legal aid, and crime.

Illness. The county councils run hospitals of all kinds, for acute medical treatment as well as for care of chronic invalids, both somatic and psychiatric. The most important specialties are represented in all counties, but rarer specialties are concentrated in the seven regional hospitals, which also serve as institutes of education for doctors.

All acute medical treatment is free, including the trip to the hospital, all costs for doctors, and medicine. For long-term treatment patients pay a low fee from their pensions, either an early retirement pension or an old-age pension. The costs, beyond the fee, are paid from proportional income tax from all income-earners.

In a technical sense, everyone can get acute medical treatment when needed. However, there are waits for certain types of operations—in cases of eye disease and orthopedic diseases, for example. Likewise, there is a shortage of places in long-term nursing homes. Improvements in out-patient services are needed to take care of simple operations and some special examinations in order to free more beds for long-term patients, especially old persons. A more adequate program of home nursing and other services in the home will decrease the pressure on hospitals. The number of doctors educated in recent years has increased greatly. The government decides every year how many students are to be accepted for training. Thus, it has become possible to get a sufficient number of doctors even for hospitals in remote places and for out-patient treatment in sparsely populated areas. As yet, however, all posts are not occupied. In 1971, there were in Sweden 139 doctors, 82 dentists, 420 registered nurses, and 1,700 hospital beds for every 100,000 inhabitants. These figures refer to every kind of hospital and medical care.

Mental Illness. Earlier, mental diseases were treated only at special mental hospitals. Psychiatry is now considered one specialty among others, and there are psychiatric wards at every large hospital. There are still hospitals with only psychiatric departments, however, and it will probably be a long time before they disappear completely. The number of places in the hospitals is actually sufficient; but because of the lack of space for long-term care, some old patients are tended at psychiatric wards although they do not need this kind of treatment. Many patients could also be treated as out-patients, if the out-patient services were sufficiently developed. Plans for such development are now being carried out.

By a special law, mentally ill persons can be committed to a hospital by compulsion under certain conditions, e.g., that the sick person is dangerous to others or that he obviously does not understand in what danger he puts himself by not seeking treatment. Any doctor can write a certificate giving the police the right to intervene at the request of relatives or social authorities. To lessen the consequences of a mistake, the condition of a patient compulsorily committed is examined immediately in the hospital. Patients or their relatives can also appeal to a discharge committee—made up of doctors, lawyers, and laymen—that exists in every hospital where compulsory commitment can occur.

The number of psychiatrists in private practice is very small in Sweden. As mentioned, there has also been a shortage of psychiatrists at the medical centers of the local districts.

For psychiatric services, the same payment rules as for other medical services apply: acute hospital treatment is free, a low fee is charged for long-term care, a visit to the district doctor costs twelve kroner, a visit to a private doctor is paid in part by medical insurance, and travel to and from the hospital and doctor is paid if it costs more than six kroner.

Disabling Conditions. In principle, all handicapped persons (blind, deaf, disabled, and mentally retarded) must receive free education, access to free aids, and access to personal service or care, free or at a low cost. In reality, there are shortcomings in the programs. The possibilities exist, but they must also be distributed actively to those who need them. Some of the programs are not sufficiently well developed, either in quantity or in quality.

Responsibility for services to disabled persons is divided among several authorities: the state is in charge of education and service for the blind and the deaf; the county councils, for education and care of the disabled and the mentally retarded; and the local authorities, for daily service. In education the trend now is to avoid big boarding schools and connect education to the ordinary school system, with special measures of support for the handicapped. Thus, the local authorities play a greater role than they otherwise would.

All handicapped persons who need special aids such as hearing aids (but not glasses), wheelchairs (including motor-driven ones), household aids and other equipment in the home (including elevators for wheelchairs) receive these free—insofar as the need becomes known. They also receive allowances for rebuilding the home and for a specially designed car in order to get to work. In most local districts they also get transportation by taxi or special bus, for the same fare as by public means of transportation. However, the local districts differ greatly in regard to the amount of transportation available. In some places handicapped persons get practically as many trips as they need, while other districts pay for only a couple of trips a month.

There is special legislation for the mentally retarded. Each county council has an elected board especially for their care. Under the authority of this board, there is a principal of special schools, a chief welfare officer, and a chief medical officer. In addition, there is a board with a judge as chairman which settles disputes about compulsory commitment or detention. There is a system of special schools and nursing institutions for the education of the retarded. This arrangement attempts to allow, if possible, for the mentally retarded to live in their own homes or board with a family or in a small boarding house. The intention is to avoid institutionalization and to make life as normal as possible. However, this cannot always be completely realized.

All care and education, of course, is free. The problem is to reach the children before school age. The examinations of the four-year-olds mentioned earlier constitute one means of identification. Compulsory care can be provided in cases where persons are dangerous, grossly disturbed, or helpless. Parents who take care of handicapped children in the home get a special child-care allowance which corresponds to an early retirement pension for an adult. If the child cannot support himself, the pension is transferred from the parents to the child on his sixteenth birthday. Adults with a pension must pay with part of this if they are permanently cared for in an institution.

Alcoholism and Drug Dependency. Sweden, like Finland and Norway, has a special law concerning the treatment of persons with alcohol problems, the Temperance Act. Earlier, there was an elected board in every local district solely for this purpose, but now the local authorities have one common board for administering the care of alcoholics, child care, social assistance, and other social services. This board has social workers and other employees at one or more social welfare offices.

A person with alcohol problems who wants help can turn to the social welfare office to get therapy with a welfare officer, be directed to a doctor, get help in finding accommodations, and so on. Many local districts have special dwellings for these people, either in ordinary apartments or in hostels with certain supervision and service. But it is rare that someone comes on his own initiative. As a rule, it is the police, relatives, neighbors, or employers who report to the social welfare office that a certain person has been arrested for drunkenness, is maltreating a spouse, or is behaving in a disturbed manner. The social welfare office then contacts the person in question and offers help if this is considered necessary. If the alcoholic is considered dangerous to the safety of his or her family or others, grossly neglects the family, or is in a helpless condition because of alcohol abuse, then the social welfare board can turn to an administrative social court that exists in every county and demand that the alcoholic be compulsorily taken into care. He or she is then taken to some institution for alcoholics or put on probation, with the risk of compulsory care in an institution if there is no change in the person's way of life.

There are two kinds of institutions for alcoholics. Those where compulsory commitment can take place are run by the state. There are about 25 such institutions with about 2,000 places. In addition, there are about as many institutions run by local authorities or by private foundations with substantial subsidies from the state. There, only voluntary inmates are received. At the state institutions, also, about half of the inmates are voluntary, at least formally. The length of stay as a rule is only a few months the first time. Then there is discharge on probation, but many come back several times.

Although only a small number of clients are subjected to

compulsory measures, the risk exists and therefore, as previously mentioned, not many seek the assistance of the social welfare office voluntarily. The "voluntary" inmates of the institutions usually have not come to the social welfare authorities on their own initiative. Hence, many local authorities have started special counseling centers where the clients can remain anonymous if they want to, and where they do not get into the records of the social welfare authorities. The county councils also have set up psychiatric out-patient departments that are intended especially for alcoholics and drug addicts. Persons with alcoholic diseases constitute, as in all countries, a large portion of the patients in ordinary hospitals, mostly in the psychiatric wards.

Drug addicts are not subject to the same compulsory measures as are alcoholics. (If addicts are under 20 years of age, they are treated differently—see below.) In many cities there are counseling centers and out-patient departments for voluntary care. However, not infrequently, drug addicts are committed to a psychiatric ward by compulsion because of their mental symptoms.

Children Who Need Protection. The local social welfare board is also concerned with child care. There is a Child Welfare Act that, to some extent, is the counterpart of the Temperance Act. The law prescribes that the local authorities shall give help and service to children and youth who need it. But they are also to intervene to protect children under the age of 18 from physical or mental maltreatment or neglect and to prevent delinquent behavior among children and youth under the age of 20.

In Sweden, children under 15 cannot be brought into court, and youths aged 15-18 only in exceptional cases. Parents who maltreat or neglect their children are also as a rule dealt with by the social welfare authorities; they are brought into court only in very grave cases.

The social welfare board and its personnel must try, first of all, to influence children's living conditions in general. They are to see to it that there are playgrounds, day nurseries, leisure-time activities, and so on. But they are also to try to initiate contact with children who in some way are in some danger. They must see to it, for example, that the paternity is established of all children born to unmarried mothers. All deliveries are reported to the population registration. Unmarried mothers can get help before the child is born. If the mother (or the father) demands it, the board must appoint a person who can be contacted as an adviser in critical situations. Such a child welfare adviser can be appointed for any child if one of the parents demands it, but is intended first of all for unmarried mothers. In these cases, the size of the maintenance allowance must also be determined, and must be paid.

All single parents have a guaranteed income. Apart from the general family allowance, they get a maintenance allowance advanced from the local authorities, who then demand payment from the other parent, if possible. If the other parent is dead, the child's pension is always paid. These benefits are paid out regardless of the parents' income, but there is a supplement for people with a low income.

The social welfare authorities also are informed about children who need protection in reports from the personnel of the child welfare center, from the police, or in connection with the family's need of social assistance or help because of illness, alcoholism, or drug addiction. The social welfare board can then, in consultation with the parents (and the child, if he or she is over 15), arrange for placement in a foster home or other help. If there is serious danger and the parents will not cooperate, the board can demand at the county social court that the child be placed in a foster home or in some kind of children's institution.

Juvenile Delinquency. The social welfare board also helps control youths who are delinquent or in the process of becoming so. It can be a question of habitual criminality, prostitution, or alarming consumption of alcohol or narcotics. The welfare board tries to reach these young persons with assistance of different kinds. It can be a question of therapeutic talks (if possible, together with the family), or help in getting better work or a better living environment, sometimes through placement in a foster home. In big cities the social welfare authorities have field workers who try to make contact with young persons where they gather. In other places they must be content with reports that come from the police, the school, the neighbors, or parents. Youths over the age of 15 who commit crimes are regularly referred to the social welfare board by the prosecutor who, as a rule, does not prosecute if the board believes it can do something. Those under 15 are always referred to the social welfare authorities, if they have been involved in criminal activity.

In serious cases, the board can, as in the case of maltreatment of children or the care of adult alcoholics, have recourse to compulsory commitment, through the county social court. This court can prescribe that the young person be taken in charge for public care. The rules are largely the same as in the case of children taken in charge because they are maltreated or neglected in the home. The first recommendation is placement in a foster home or in a special hostel for young persons; but for more serious cases, there are also special youth welfare (reformatory) schools run by the state.

There are about 20 youth welfare schools with an average of 40 to 50 places in each school. Some receive children under 16 who are still of compulsory school age, but most of the students are between the ages of 16 and 21. They are officially called "vocational schools." In the schools there is some vocational training, but mostly it is a question of therapeutic talks in preparation for placement and work on probation outside the school. The first period of care in the school is six months on the average. But many come back. The total period of care at and outside the school is two to three years.

The results of this treatment are not good. Most of the pupils abuse alcohol or narcotics and have had contact with the social welfare authorities or the judicial system many times. At present, there is a tendency to commit these children less often, not because delinquency is decreasing, but because public care has few desired effects. The same is true for the care of adult alcoholics in special institutions and the placement of criminals in prisons.

Economic Need. In spite of all Sweden's social insurance schemes and public benefits, every year 4 to 6 percent of the population needs economic support from the social welfare authorities (social assistance). In most cases, it is a question of temporary help in an acute situation or while waiting for a decision, e.g., about an early retirement pension. But many families and single persons live in such difficult conditions that they cannot manage the strain of illness or unemployment in spite of social insurance benefits. Besides, these do not cover all situations. There are also families (especially in the large urban areas) with low incomes and high rent who do not manage although they have regular income from work. Of course, there are also a great many with an anti-social way of life, where the income is spent on liquor or drugs, or where the breadwinner is in prison.

All persons who are unfit for work, and all children, are entitled to social assistance. In the case of healthy adults, a grant of social assistance depends on the practice of the social welfare board and, ultimately, on the judgment of the official who handles the case. However, practice in recent years has become more generous than before. It may be said that all who are considered needy by the social welfare authorities get help, but that the judgment of this need is different in different local districts.

Social welfare authorities, according to regulations, also try to help the needy person in other ways. It often turns out that other help and services are needed. It is also the duty of the local authorities to investigate the needs of those who do not themselves seek help, but this does not occur to any considerable extent.

Family Crises. In the different cases of need considered in the preceding sections, there are often conflicts between husband and wife, between children and parents, or between other persons living together. Hospitals or local social welfare authorities offer to deal with these problems, but sometimes they are so serious that more expert help is needed. Besides, there are many family crises that do not give rise to contact with medical services or social welfare authorities.

For various types of family conflicts there are special family guidance centers usually run by the county councils. There are also some local and some private centers. Altogether there are about 50 centers in the country. Family guidance is given by specially trained social workers with the help of psychiatrists and other consultants. The majority of those seeking help do not come from the social welfare authorities or the medical services. At some centers, advice and assistance is also given to women applying for an abortion, but as a rule, the county councils have special welfare officers for this purpose at the county's central hospital. At these hospitals, there are also special guidance clinics for parents who have serious problems in bringing up their children. These clinics work in close connection with the psychiatric clinics for children and are led by psychiatrists with the assistance of psychologists and social workers.

Legal Aid. It has become generally recognized that personal and social rights cannot be utilized by large portions of the population without special help. Many people are ignorant of their rights and cannot make use of them. The authorities combat this ignorance by advertising in the newspapers and sending out brochures by mail to every household. In some cases, they also send out application forms. In many places the local authorities have set up information centers where one can ask about everything. All local and state agencies are obliged to give information when asked.

In order for citizens to be able to take advantage of their rights, the state organized public legal aid in 1973. In large towns there are public legal aid bureaus, but most private lawyers take part also. These lawyers pledge themselves to apply the tariff fixed by the government for advice and assistance. The client, however, does not pay according to this tariff but a fee which depends on income and number of children. Old-age pensioners and persons without means do not pay anything. Those who earn more than a certain (quite high) income pay the full costs. The state pays the lawyer according to the tariff.

Legal aid includes not only advice in different matters, but also assistance in litigation and in bringing a matter before administrative authorities. The lawyer can also make investigations or find witnesses in order to support the client's cause. Legal aid applies only to personal problems, including economic ones, but not, as a rule, those connected with business. In criminal cases, the client usually is ordered to pay the costs if he is found guilty, but otherwise not.

Crime. In Sweden the whole judicial system is under the authority of the government. This is true of the police, the courts, the prosecutors, and the treatment of offenders. There are also, as previously mentioned, legal-aid bureaus run by the state, but the majority of the lawyers are in private practice. In criminal cases and family civil disputes, the court of first instance consists of one judge plus five laymen. The decisions are reached by vote, so that four laymen can outvote the judge. The laymen take part in all decisions—not only, as is the case with the Anglo-Saxon jury, regarding the question of guilt. In the six Courts of Appeal and in the Supreme Court there are judges alone. All professional judges are appointed by the government, while lay judges are appointed by the commune council.

The punishment for criminal acts is a fine in 90 percent of all cases. In the rest, about half are sentences involving prison terms and half different forms of suspended sentence ·or compulsory care from psychiatric services or social welfare authorities. Most terms of imprisonment are one to two months. Those who get terms longer than six months are always released on probation after at least half the time. Those released on probation as well as convicted probationers are under supervision by a special staff of officials with the help of voluntary assistants. The number of convicted persons on probation is about five times the number of actual prisoners. In 1971, about 11,000 persons (171 per 100,000 inhabitants) were sentenced to prison terms.

CURRENT TRENDS

It is the general opinion in Sweden that public services should be enlarged and their quality improved. This applies particularly to child-care facilities, leisure-time services, and care of old persons. Furthermore, it is agreed that more information should be made available to citizens about existing services, and that this information should be actively communicated. At the same time, this information must not be one-sided, but services should be arranged the way the people want them. One restraining factor, of course, is the fact that better services entail higher taxes, but by and large, the people have accepted this when they feel they get back something essential.

As previously mentioned, it is also a widespread opinion that institutional care should be avoided as far as possible. Out-patient care is preferred to hospitals, if they are not absolutely necessary. Assistance in the home with daily chores should be attempted before placement in institutions for disabled persons, the mentally retarded, or old persons. Probation is preferable to prison. It is also generally recognized that this development has not gone far enough. Many hospitals have been built without corresponding improvement in out-patient services. Psychiatric out-patient services and mental health guidance services are particularly neglected. In this case, suggested developments would not be expensive. At the same time, so many shortcomings have been discovered within the already existing institutions that sometimes it has been considered necessary to use available funds to deal with these first.

Compulsory measures in social welfare services constitute a special problem. They result from the desire to keep some categories of people out of the penal system. It has been considered inhuman to let children and youth go through the ordinary court processes and, even more, to put them in prison. To some extent, the same is true for alcoholics, but not as consistently. In both cases, intervention is warranted, it is argued, not because of certain unlawful acts, but rather because of the general life situation that is considered threatening either for the person in question or for his or her environment. Decisions about compulsory public care and treatment are preferably made by other agencies than those of the penal system.

Strong opposition has emerged against this point of view in recent years, above all from professional social workers. They complain that they have difficulties in getting meaningful treatment started as long as the client knows that the social welfare authorities have access to compulsory measures. This in itself is generally recognized, but many maintain that the above reasons for treatment outside the judicial system have more weight. The question was under consideration in 1974 by a special government committee, and a recommendation is expected in the course of the year.

Recruitment of Personnel

It has been an old tradition in Sweden that social services should be attended to by popularly elected laymen without any special remuneration. Doctors constitute an obvious exception. This tradition is still alive, in that the representative councils of local districts and counties appoint committees or boards for different activities.

As long as social activities were limited in scope, the elected laymen could handle them themselves. The chairman or other members of the board distributed social assistance, took care of children and alcoholics, and so on. In some rural districts this has continued up to recent times. Gradually, it has become necessary to engage salaried personnel, without any training required. Nowadays, all local districts have trained personnel, but there are still many older employees without special training.

Doctors, dentists, and pharmacists are trained at universities run by the state. Nurses are trained at special schools, most of which are run by the county councils. There are also some private schools, such as that connected with the Red Cross. Swedish nurses get relatively advanced training and perform many tasks that are done by doctors in other countries. In addition, both high schools and hospitals have training programs for assistant nurses. Some of the assistants thus gain competence which approaches that of the qualified nurses. For all personnel there is a certain, rather limited, possibility of further studies to become a doctor.

Qualified social workers are educated at the six state schools of social work and public administration and one small church school. This education is at an academic level, but the schools of social work are (at least so far) independent of the universities. The degree is most nearly comparable to an American MSW. The trained social workers ("socionomists") work for the most part in the local social welfare service, where they are called "assistants" because they formally assist the elected boards and have no independent authority. In addition, many socionomists work at hospitals and at other institutions such as prisons and youth welfare schools as well as in posts of administration and planning within the public adminis-tration. In administrative posts, socionomists have begun to compete with the lawyers who predominated earlier. Other important groups are those who work in schools, in probation within the penal system, and in personnel departments of state and private enterprises.

Of current interest is the question of delegating routine tasks within social welfare services to less educated personnel. The number of trained socionomists has increased greatly during the 1970s, but it must still be considered inefficient not to use them for more qualified tasks.

Socionomists usually do not work in children's homes, day nurseries, leisure-time centers, old-age homes, or other similar institutions. For these tasks there is special training on a somewhat "lower" level within the hierarchy of education. The same is true for the vast majority of personnel working in prisons, institutions for alcoholics, and youth welfare schools, who are trained mostly through organized in-service training programs.

Assessment of Services

The existing means for assessment of services is most unsatisfac-tory. Investigating committees, set up by the government to submit proposals of reform, sometimes make assessments of the outcome of earlier activities, but this happens only sporadically. The National Central Bureau of Statistics keeps yearly statistics of different activities. These are published in printed form but are not assessed systematically. Selective studies of both official statistics and of data collected especially for this purpose are carried out mainly in the form of examination papers at the schools of social work and the universities.

Since 1973, there has been a state Institute for Social Research, which is connected with the Univeristy of Stockholm, but so far it has had rather modest resources. Here is a possibility, however, for more extensive research in the future.

9

CHANGING PERSPECTIVES ON U.S. SOCIAL SERVICES

NATHAN E. COHEN

The traditional approach to examining social services is to define the differences and similarities among social welfare, social services, and social work within a country and between countries, and to describe their scope, identify their function in relation to economic development, and set up a system of classification. In the United States, for example, social services tend to be viewed more narrowly than in most industrialized and developing nations. As pointed out by Kahn (1973: 27-28) in the United States, social services such as education, public (cash) assistance, medical care, and public housing have become so elaborate and comprehensive as to achieve independent status, and for cultural and philosophical reasons are seldom thought of as social services. The term "social services," as used by Kahn, refers to functions and programs related to socialization and development; therapy, help and rehabilitation (including social protection and substitute care); and access, information, and advice. He sees these as encompassing a field with changing boundaries and including some "freestanding" programs (child welfare or family service agencies) and some located in other institutions (school social work, medical social service, social services in public housing, industrial social welfare programs, and so on). Kahn attributes the American separation of general social services from such broader fields as health, education, and public housing to the fact that early social services had Poor Law derivations, and often implemented the controlling, punitive, or rehabilitative aspects of "last resort" public provision of funds for families in dire economic need. The stigma attached to this early history, he believes, is still part of the general social service legacy.[1]

The United States has pioneered in services related to socialization, development, and therapy involving special emphasis on psychological factors. In recent years, however, there has been a marked shift toward viewing problems as residing not only in the individual, but perhaps even more in the social institutions through which he or she functions. Although there are quality socialization, therapy, and rehabilitation services identifiable in most major communities, their number is not sufficient to meet the needs of a rapidly expanding technological and urban society. Many of these services grew out of the needs of earlier periods and reflect the emphasis on specialization, with its fragmentation of the problems affecting people. The growing realization of the interrelatedness of economic, psychological, and social factors attendant in many problems has led to experimentation through demonstration projects with new patterns of service delivery reflecting more interdisciplinary and integrative approaches. It has also become evident that the separation of general social services from such broader fields as health, education, public housing, and jobs has been more meaningful for purposes of classification than for the solution of individual and social problems.

There may be differences of opinion as to how social services should be classified, but there is general agreement that major reform is essential to meet the problems of people in a highly mobile and rapidly changing society. At the heart of the problem of establishing a new set of objectives are the barriers of money, lack of knowledge, governmental boundaries, resistance of agencies whose programs are institutionalized around an earlier definition of needs, and differences in social philosophy concerning the responsibility of the individual. In a society which in recent years has had to face the impact of the revolt of non-White minorities, youth, and women, questions of values and social philosophy have loomed large. With the earlier emphasis on problems residing primarily in the individual, the core question in socialization, development, and therapy was: "Who am I?" The context of the question was, "How am I relating to societal norms and values, and what intrapsychic changes do I have to go through to accomplish the appropriate adjustment?" With the recent revolt, the ground shifted. The question became group-oriented and took the form of: "Who defined who I am, and by what right did they do it?" The context of the question shifted to, "How were the values and goals that affect my life determined, and what restructuring should they go through to achieve greater equity in the distribution of social roles, resources, and rewards?"

Social services are in a state of flux, as is social work, the gatekeeper of general social services. This is part of a revolt by the people against all the helping professions. The causes and solutions of expanding social problems have become less clear, and the pluralistic structure of America reveals sharp differences of values and goals among its constituent publics. It is perhaps more important, therefore, to analyze the forces at play and what they augur for the future, rather than to describe in detail what now exists. For those seeking such detailed information, there are numerous books and articles already available, as cited in Kahn's (1973) bibliography.

THE HISTORICAL CONTEXT

To understand the evolution and future of social services in the United States, it is necessary to view them historically. The nature of the services, the role of government, the structure of the services, and the groups to be helped have reflected the changing economic, political, and social climate of the nation. In its early history, dominant American traits were being forged in an agricultural economy, in a land sparsely inhabited, with abundant resources yet to be tapped. That all men are created equal, with rights to life, liberty, and the pursuit of happiness was a dominant theme. It was a period when the concept of self-help was strong and when individuals had to do many things for themselves now regarded within the normal province of government. In the America of 1800, says Commager (1951: 315), men were for the most part able to take care of themselves. The country was surpassingly rich, and land was available almost for the taking. There was little poverty and no unemployment. The new nation was wonderfully fortunate. There was no standing army to support, no established church to maintain, and no idle aristocracy to subsidize. There was little for government to do, and much that men individually and collectively could do for themselves, especially men as virtuous and enlightened as the Americans of that generation appeared to be.

It was a period in which the theme of liberty received the greatest emphasis. This fit into the growing individualistic tradition more readily than the concern for equality, which involved a more positive governmental role in furthering the people's welfare. The prototype of the American as the hard-working, practical man, who believed that every man can look after himself, was forged during this period. This philosophy has had a marked effect on the attitude toward those who need help. Even today we find it being enunciated at the highest level.

Events in the first half of the nineteenth century were such that it was not easy for the average American to foresee that the role of government as protector of life, liberty, and property would have to change as society became more complex. Increased population, the closing of frontiers, industrialization and urbanization, new inventions, the discovery of new resources, expanding international relations, and so forth, were to bring new types of problems that fell within the definitions of common danger and common welfare.

During this period, voluntary philanthropy played a major role. The Elizabethan Poor Law was the model for public charity in the United States. It emphasized locating responsibility for the poor in the smallest governmental unit, establishing eligibility not only in terms of need but also in relation to a legally defined period of residence. The underlying philosophy was: "The family shall take care of its own; charitable individuals should help their neighbors; when all else failed, the government of his home community must take care of a needy person" (Pumphrey, 1971: 1449) The Poor Law still remains the core of general assistance programs. As Pumphrey says (p. 1446): "Some major structural changes have occurred during the twentieth century, but today, nearly four centuries later, the 'general assistance' provisions in the laws of many states retain much of the language of the law of 1601."

The role of the federal government in social services during this period was tangential. It dealt primarily with specific target groups such as the Indians and American seamen. A major contribution to the welfare of the nation came through land grant policies. The philosophy of the federal government toward its role in public welfare programs was best expressed in the veto message by President Grover Cleveland in 1887, in response to a bill which would have provided for a distribution of seeds in drought-stricken farm areas:

> I can find no warrant for such an appropriation in the Constitution and I do not believe that the power and duty of the General Government ought to be extended to the relief of individual suffering which is in no manner

properly related to the public service or benefit. A prevalent tendency to disregard the limited mission of this power and duty should, I think, be steadfastly resisted, to the end that the lesson should be constantly enforced that though the people support the government, the government should not support the people.... Federal aid in such cases encourages the expectation of paternal care on the part of the Government and weakens the sturdiness of our national character, while it prevents the indulgence among our people of that kindly sentiment and conduct which strengthens the bonds of a common brotherhood.[2]

It was to take approximately 50 years before the federal government, faced with the Great Depression of the 1930s, would go through a major ideological revolution, redefining its responsibility and role.

A major ideological revolution of such magnitude as the New Deal, with its program of the Three Rs—Relief, Recovery, and Reform—does not develop overnight. It was formed over many decades with many interwoven strands of influence. The magnitude of the economic crash, with one-fourth of the nation unemployed by 1933, and 20 million individuals on relief by 1934, brought the nation face to face with the fact that a highly industrialized urban society with an expanding technology could no longer think in terms of a nineteenth-century welfare role for government. The philosophy that the family should take care of its own was swept aside with the growing recognition of changes that had taken place in the patterns of family living. As pointed out by Clough (1953: 62-64): (1) close ties developed from working on common tasks, as a producer group was absent in the urban pattern of family living; (2) with the family depending completely on wages for meeting the basic economic needs of food, clothing, and shelter, unemployment affected the total fabric of family living; (3) urbanized living, with its demands for more material things and more expensive recreation, and with increased emphasis on installment buying, resulted in the average family living close to the margin and having little savings; (4) urban family living did not provide flexibility in matters of food, clothing, and shelter for absorbing additional dependents as was true in the rural pattern of family living; (5) with the increased unemployability of the aged, the dependent aged were not often welcome in the homes of their relatives.

Voluntary philanthropy was inadequate in providing financial assistance, and attention turned to professional social work services. Public charity could no longer be left to the smaller units of government whose taxing power was limited. The federal government, which had actively entered the economic arena, turned to social welfare. Frederick Lewis Allen (1954: 16) described two new political principles that emerged during this period. One principle is that the fortunes of individual Americans are inextricably inter-locked. We are "all in the same boat" and if any of us fall into deep trouble, it is the job of the rest of us—the federal government—to help. The other principle is that it is the federal government's job to prevent another Great Depression. Most of us want to keep as much economic liberty as possible for ourselves. Most of us hate to see the powers of the federal government extended, but we realize that it is the only instrument on which we can rely, in a severe economic emergency, to provide us with a measure of security.

The new and expanding role of the federal government was legalized in an historic Supreme Court decision in 1937. Responding to a challenge against the old-age provisions in the Social Security Act, the Court in its decision reflected the changing social philos-ophy, and provided a new context for an expansion of federal programs. Justice Cardoza, in this decision, reflected the new mood as follows:

> Nor is the concept of the general welfare static. Needs that were narrow or parochial a century ago may be interwoven in our day with the well-being of the nation. What is critical or urgent changes with the times. . . . The problem is plainly national in area and dimensions. Moreover, laws of the separate states cannot deal with it effectively. . . . Only a power that is national can serve the interests of all.[3]

It was this establishment of the constitutionality of Social Security which "raised the possibility of a nationwide health insurance system," now an important concern in the legislative halls of Washington (Cohen, 1974).

The emphasis in the early periods of the nation's history was on political democracy. The ideological revolution of the 1930s was an attempt to meet the growing demand for an expansion of economic democracy. A new wind was blowing in the 1960s, a growing awareness of the unfinished business of social democracy. As the nation girded itself to deal with a new set of demands, it became clear that political, economic, and social democracy were inter-twined, and that solutions depended upon a greater understanding of their interrelatedness. The times called for a new dialogue and for new patterns in the delivery of services, rearrangement of the distribution of resources, and democratization of the decision-making processes through greater citizen participation at all levels.

TRENDS IN THE 1960s

Even though we were involved in an "ideological revolution" in the 1930s, it revolved primarily around the role and responsibility of the federal government, but did not reflect a basic change in the sacrosanct position of economic individualism. In looking at the strategies utilized in the 1960s, it is important to understand the nature of American society. We have never sought the total reduction of conflict which characterizes a utopian society. We have been basically Hobbesian in our approach, with the struggle for power operating as a continuous process. In fact, this struggle has been viewed as part of the nation's motivational structure. Thus, our social reform efforts have not consisted of doing away with the competitive climate, but rather of making sure that the armaments for battle are more equally distributed. For example, in the 1930s we made it possible for labor to grow in power in order to be able to contend better with the powerful industrial complex, because we regarded it as unfair for a lightweight to be matched against a heavyweight. We do not seek utopian peace, but support a workable ongoing process of competition by attempting to redress the imbalances that tend to interfere with this process.

Such a redress of imbalances does not take place automatically. It is the result of long periods of conflict. The general pattern in American society has been to postpone social change and to permit the problems to fester. Then come periods which look like ideological revolutions because of "the tendency of postponed social changes to pile up as in a dam; and to be released with a rush when the dam breaks" (Ogburn, 1934: 115).

Which problems in the 1960s forced newly launched policies and programs on the federal government? Topping the list were urban decay, poverty, mental health, and delinquency; and pushing them into greater visibility was the growing civil rights movement. The complacency of the 1950s—the feeling that our traditional economic problems had been largely solved—was suddenly shattered by the growing militancy of the Blacks. In spite of the generally improved economic climate, one out of every two Blacks was living in poverty. Poverty in the South was double the national poverty average.

The nature of the urban population had changed because of an unprecedented emigration of Blacks from rural sections of the country between 1940 and 1967. During this period, approximately four million Blacks migrated from predominantly rural areas of the South to the urban centers of the North and West. The 1960 census shows that approximately 45 percent of the Black residents of ten major northern and western cities were born in the South. These migrations have been accompanied by an exodus of Whites to the suburbs. Slums expanded and became more ingrown. The new migrants brought with them the deficits of institutionalized racism: lack of education, inadequate skills, poor health, and mistrust of governmental authorities. The problems loomed even larger in a period when accelerated technological advances were increasingly displacing unskilled human labor, creating unemployment and underemployment, with greater demands on the existing inadequate welfare programs.

The new migrants sought refuge from racism, only to find again that they were faced with differential access to available opportunities. Furthermore, they were entering the urban complex at a time when the humanizing structure of the urban community had broken down. Its basic institutions dealing with religion, health, welfare, education, recreation, and social control had not been able to keep up with the growing demands emerging from the breakdown of the family and neighborhood life. Furthermore, social welfare programs and serrvices were inappropriate to the needs of urban migrants.

The profile in the inner city, where most Blacks settled, revealed a much higher percentage of adult and youth unemployment than in the general population: for adult men it ran as high as 15 percent; and for the school dropout, approximately 50 percent. For those employed, about 7 percent were on part-time jobs, and another 20 percent were working at a salary below the poverty level. With approximately 40 percent of families and unrelated individuals in the slum community earning under $3,000 a year, the numbers on welfare ran high.

The new migrant also found himself a victim of the nation's failure over the past half century to plan adequately for housing for low-income families. Although a decent home in a suitable environment was established as a national goal by Congress in 1949, the gap between the ideal and the actual for the poor was great. Housing for the poor has not been supplied, since it has been left primarily to the private market. Some existing housing, furthermore, has been destroyed to accommodate the growing demands of the automobile for highways and expressways, and by urban renewal programs which have given priority to the construction of commercial buildings and luxury high-rise apartments. These programs have created problems of relocation for the very segment of the population which traditionally has been least able to help itself. These people have received only token assistance in relocation, since there has been very little replacement of low-cost housing.

The exodus of Whites to the suburbs has been accompanied by a growing movement of industry to these areas. This has created two major problems for low-income groups. First, the tax base of the cities has shrunk in a period when the need for education, health, and welfare funds has expanded. Second, the need for transportation to jobs in the suburbs has increased. Again, the group least able to help itself has been given an additional burden—compounded by discriminatory practices in the suburbs which prevent the Blacks from living closer to places of employment and in communities which provide more adequate health, education, and welfare programs.

In the 1960s, a strong reaction erupted from an accumulation of grievances. In the early part of the decade, the reaction was expressed through the civil rights movement, with a special focus on the South. By the middle of the decade, the scene had shifted to other parts of the country and the reaction took more militant forms, resulting in violence and bloodshed. Since seven out of ten poor people were White and were facing many of the same frustrations as the minorities, coalitions formed to fight against inadequate social programs.

The 1960s saw the emergence of a series of demonstration projects stimulated primarily by federal legislation. These included: the Area Redevelopment Act of 1961; the Manpower Development and Training Act of 1962; Amendments to the Social Security Act of 1962 and 1967; the Economic Development Act of 1964; and the Demonstration Cities and Metropolitan Development Act of 1966. Related developments included the President's Committee on Delinquency and Youth Crime (established by executive order, May 1961); and the Comprehensive Mental Health Programs (President Kennedy's message to Congress, 1963).

By the 1960s, it was becoming clear that our approach to social problems was fragmented, with too much focus on the individual as the entrepreneur and as the cause of his own predicament: not enough attention was being given to the part played by our social institutions. A concrete step in this direction was taken through a special conference on social problems called by the National Association of Social Workers and supported by a grant from the Ford Foundation. Out of this conference came a model for viewing social problems from a social work point of view. The model emphasized the following major considerations (Cohen, 1964):

(1) Definitions and etiology of the problem.

(2) Societal norms and values, and assumed social work norms and values affecting the problem.

(3) The current programs (actual), both social work and non-social work, and the consequences of continuing these programs.

(4) The ideal, or the social change objective.

(5) The relationship between the actual and the ideal: identification of the gap between them, sources of resistance to and support of closing this gap, action priorities for social work, and theory and research needs for attaining necessary knowledge and programs.

Social workers began to recognize the comprehensive nature of social problems and the multiple causation involved. In a sense, the profession was finally drawing a distinction between a societal problem and an individual problem. It was attempting to overcome the tendency to utilize treatment and program instruments as diagnostic tools for social problems. It realized that its treatment tools were primarily geared to the individual and his psychologyy. Using these instruments to diagnose social problems could fragment the perception of the problems.

Paralleling this development was the shift in delinquency theory from its heavy emphasis on individual causation and treatment to a sociological approach based on "anomie theory," soon to become known as "opportunity theory." The core premise of the theory stated:

Much delinquent behavior is engendered because opportunities for conformity are limited. Delinquency therefore represents not the lack of motivation to conform but quite the opposite: the desire to meet social expectations itself becomes the source of delinquent behavior if the possibility of doing so is limited or non-existent [Cloward and Ohlin, 1961].

In brief, the majority of delinquents did not have equal access to the opportunity structure. This meant that:

> in order to reduce the incidence of delinquent behavior or to rehabilitate persons who are already enmeshed in delinquent patterns, we must provide the social and psychological resources that make conformity possible.

Consequently, policy and program pushed treatment into a secondary role, and emphasized programs such as job training, job placement, and job counselling. Accompanying this shift was a new set of questions placing the onus on the institution rather than the individual. As pointed out by Kahn (1969),

> When confronted with the problem of disadvantaged and "closed out" youth, the new predilection was to ask what there is about the school, the job placement center, the social agency which closes them out, where once the only question asked was why they did not adjust or how they could be made competent to conform.

Demonstration projects based on opportunity theory were launched under federal grants in 16 major communities. An important criterion was experimentation and innovation for eligibility for these grants. This new approach was to become an important strand in the "War on Poverty."

Another trend was the growing impact of the civil rights movement. Out of it emerged the view that poverty was not merely related to inadequate resources, but perhaps that even more basic was a sense of powerlessness and social isolation. Until this was overcome, the poor would have difficulty in exploiting the opportunities available to them. Viewing the condition of Blacks and other non-White minorities as a form of colonialism, the rationale was to rebuild the culture, that is, to restore the withered roots of ethnicity. Unlike the opportunity theory approach, where change was to be brought about elitist fashion by professionals and research, the civil rights movement began to focus on participation and people power as the instruments for change. The concepts of self-help and participation in overcoming powerlessness were to become other important trends in the War on Poverty. People would be encouraged and aided to help themselves, but "encouragement alone is insufficient if inadequate services are available, and services alone will do no good if people do not choose to use them" (Graham, 1967).

The full rationale behind the War on Poverty was not clear. Some attributed it to concern for the number of people living below the poverty line in the early 1960s—approximately 34 million. Others saw it as a political move to cope with the growing militancy of the civil rights movement. Moynihan (1969: 29) stated that the War on Poverty began not because it was necessary, but because it was politically feasible. The ambiguity of the legislation was greatest in the Community Action Program Title (Section 202), especially in the phrase "maximum feasible participation." It is Moynihan's interpretation that the phrase was an addition by the drafting committee as they discussed their concern about southern Black people not receiving their fair share in the benefits of local programs (Moynihan, 1969: 87-88). He states (p. 95), furthermore, that there was no discussion of this clause in Congress at the time of the enactment of the legislation in August 1964.

What were the options available for a "War on Poverty"? Kahn (1969: ch. 2), in a detailed analysis, refers to such options as: (1) aggregate demand (trickle-down theory); (2) structural strategies (major focus on changing the capacities of poor people, not on institutions); (3) area redevelopment (special help to regions in economic difficulty); (4) redistribution (of wealth, or income redistribution measures to groups like the aged and public assistance recipients); (5) amenities and benefits in kind (improve community resources for everybody); (6) capital funding (low-interest or interest-free loans or grants to the poor to launch them on farms or in businesses); and (7) power (helping to overcome the sense of powerlessness by giving the poor control over the programs and funds earmarked for the slums and ghetto communities). From this set of options, the core approach became structural strategies focused on education and training to help those unable to enter the labor force to retool, and on the creation of special protected jobs (paraprofessionals, for example), to prepare people to enter the regular job market later. In brief, all efforts were to be redirected toward the goal of getting people back to work. As stated by Marris and Rein (1967: 327):

> Thus to partially solve the problem of depressed areas—unemployment, public welfare, delinquency, poverty, and urban decay—we have pursued the goal of promoting economic self-sufficiency by placing our faith in social "investment programs."

The question of expanding the job market was left to "aggregate demand" or chance. The funds allocated for the structural strategy, furthermore, were most inadequate—1.25 percent of the federal budget, or .25 percent of the gross national product.

In the same way that the demonstration projects on delinquency were pushed into the background or absorbed into the War on Poverty, the Demonstration Cities program, renamed "Model Cities," began to take priority.[4] Its conception reflected a recognition of the need for an even more comprehensive effort than the anti-poverty programs, and looked like a move toward a more total social strategy. The stated objective was far-reaching:

> rebuild or revitalize large slums and blighted areas; expand housing, job and income opportunities; reduce dependence on welfare payments; improve educational facilities and programs; combat disease and ill health; reduce the incidence of crime and delinquency; enhance recreational and cultural opportunities; establish better access between homes and jobs; and generally to improve living conditions for the people who live in such areas [Powledge, 1970: 149-150].[5]

The new slogan was "Improve the quality of urban life." The reward system of large federal grants was to be utilized to stimulate comprehensive planning and coordination in the local community with both public and private resources and programs. Under this large umbrella would be placed previous programs such as urban renewal, education, anti-poverty, public housing, public assistance, building inspection, health, and manpower. The guidelines also stressed the importance of "widespread citizen participation in the program." To be eligible for these awards, cities had to come up with a plan which showed a comprehensive effort of "sufficient magnitude" to make "substantial impact," local matching funds, citizen involvement, a viable administrative structure, and a spirit of experimentation and innovation. In the first year there were 193 applications for planning grants submitted, and 75 were approved.

Model Cities faced many of the same barriers which have plagued the poverty program, annd because of the magnitude of its objectives, the problems loomed even larger. Its success depended on a more advanced working relationship between competing federal bureaucracies, and stronger political clout than existed. The funds allocated were totally inadequate to meet the stated purposes and goals. It would have been more realistic if the budget for Vietnam had been the budget for Model Cities, and the Model Cities budget the available expenditures for the Vietnam war. This might have resulted in peace on both fronts at an earlier stage. As stated by Powledge (1970: 149-150):

> Given President Johnson's obvious displeasure with the way the war on poverty was turning out (it had become, as Moynihan pointed out, a war of the Democratic poor against the nation's Democratic mayors), it was not too difficult to imagine that the Model Cities program represented a retreat from the "unconditional" war on poverty that the President had promised. Commented one Democratic mayor . . . Model Cities is baloney. The Johnson Administration, in its last two years, has engaged in delaying tactics. . . . The thing of it is that in order to pay for the war in Vietnam, increasingly the war on poverty and the war to rebuild our cities have been cut back. And so they develop Model Cities, and what is that? All they give you is planning money and now they're even cutting that back. The whole Model Cities program was a farce. It was designed to stretch out the buck and get a greater bang for fewer cents.

In spite of its many shortcomings, the War on Poverty made some progress. Between 1959 and 1969, the number of people in poverty declined from 22 percent to 12 percent, leaving a total of approximately 24 million poor people. The groups remaining in poverty were those least eligible for the work force—the aged, children, single-parent families headed by a female, and non-White minorities. Of those in the working force, approximately one million were earning insufficient income to bring them above the poverty line. About 55 percent of all the poor were receiving some form of welfare by 1970. The expanding rolls began to alarm the nation. The Aid to Families with Dependent Children program was viewed as the core of the problem because of its growth and its large numbers of unmarried mothers. The value stance of being able to forgive acts of God, such as old age and disablement, but not acts of people, such as bearing children out of wedlock, still operated.

DEVELOPMENTS IN THE 1970s

The late 1960s and early 1970s saw a new administration and a new social philosophy, which were to have a marked effect on social services in the United States. There was growing agreement that our social service system, especially as it related to the poor, was not working, and was in need of a basic overhaul. A major breakthrough in the analysis of the problem was the study by the Heineman Commission. The Commission, which was appointed by President Lyndon Johnson in January 1968, undertook a comprehensive study over a period of 22 months.

Several new principles emerged from the study. The first of these principles is, "that more often than not the reason for poverty is not some personal failing, but the accident of being born to the wrong parents, or the lack of opportunity to become non-poor, or some circumstance over which individuals have no control" (Presidential Commission on Income Maintenance Programs, 1967).

A second principle is that "under the welfare system we have clung to the notion that employment and receipt of assistance must be mutually exclusive. This view is untenable in a world in which employable persons may have potential earnings below assistance standards" (Presidential Commission, 1967).

Third, "the three-pronged strategy of the 1930s—employment . . . social insurance . . . and residual aid—has not eliminated poverty, and it cannot . . . and that there must be a larger role for cash grants in fighting poverty than we have acknowleedged in the past" (Presidential Commission, 1967).

The fourth principle is that any person in the society will not be permitted to fall below a minimum income each year, whether he works or not, and that the federal government will guarantee this minimum, and will finance and administer such a program.[6]

Before the Heineman Commission's report was completed, President Nixon created a special office on urban problems with Daniel P. Moynihan as its head. There is no question that some of the findings of the Commission influenced Moynihan. He began to draw a sharp distinction between a service strategy and an income strategy in dealing with the problem of poverty. Moynihan (1970: 21) pointed out that the premises of an income strategy are threefold:

(1) The single most powerful determinant of behavior and well-being in the society is the level of security of an individual's income.

(2) The most efficient role government can play with regard to the social system is that of adjusting inequalities of income, in particular, insuring a minimum income for those most in need.

(3) The provision of adequate income makes unnecessary the elaborate secondary markets wherein the poor are required to obtain the goods and services that other persons obtain in a general market. Thus the segregation of the poor, as well as their deprivation, is avoided.

However, the legislative package, which finally emerged, the Family Assistance Plan (HRI), again held the work ethic as the overriding guiding principle.

President Nixon unveiled his Family Assistance Plan in an address to the nation in August, 1969. He called for change in four areas essential to a comprehensive plan for getting people off welfare, putting more people to work, and protecting family life. The four suggested major reforms comprised, first, a complete overhaul of the welfare program through a new approach to income maintenance, approaching the principle of a guaranteed minimum level of income; second, greater emphasis on job training and placement; third, a reorganization of the Office of Economic Opportunity, with a major redefinition of functions; and finally, federal tax revenue sharing with the states.

The legislative bill which emerged contained over 207 provisions, categorized under Titles as follows: I—provisions relating to old-age, survivors, and disability insurance; II—provisions relating to medicare, medicaid, and maternal and child care health; III—assistance for the aged, blind, and disabled; IV—family programs; and V—miscellaneous.

Most of the controversy centered around Title IV, which reflected the extent to which the nation was prepared to face some basic changes in its value system as against pragmatic patching around outworn concepts.

The major concern about Title IV was its lack of universal coverage. It did not provide for uniform eligibility based on need. Single people and childless couples were excluded. It also separated the employable from the unemployable poor.

Second, the minimum of $2,400 for a family of four was regarded as totally inadequate. Furthermore, there was no guarantee in the legislation that the recipients now receiving a higher level of support in the more progressive states would not have payments reduced. There was also no provision for built-in increases in benefits over a specified period of time to reflect growing inflation and the expanding income of the top 20 percent of the population. The amount recommended was both inadequate and unrelated to the total structure of income distribution in the nation.

Third, although the proposed legislation implied a guarantee of income as a right, it built in a series of social controls that tended to be punitive. Again, the poor were viewed as having a different set of values from the population in general. The rights of the participants were not adequately protected. In fact, the suggested administrative procedures surrounding the obligation to work without choice flew in the face of our traditional concepts concerning the rights and dignity of the individual. For example, the requirement that mothers of children aged six and older must register for work was a threat to individual freedom. By 1974, if the legislation were enacted, it would apply to mothers with children three years of age and older.

Fourth, the proposed legislation obliged a person to accept a job offered under threat of serious penalties, regardless of the suitability or the nature of the tasks involved. This provision included working for substandard wages. The measures seem even harsher when one keeps in mind the small number of welfare recipients without age, physical, and emotional handicaps, and the large number of hard-core unemployables in these ranks. Furthermore, the growing rate of unemployment, now at approximately 9 percent, no longer appears to be temporary but tied to the growing impact of automation.

Fifth, although the legislation had as a major objective strengthening family life and unity, the provisions requiring mothers to work appear to contradict this goal. An interesting insight into the value difference for the poor is contained in President Nixon's veto of day-care legislation. He stated that day care would result in children's exposure to socialist ideas of child-rearing. Yet Title IV included as a major item setting up day-care service for children of the poor. There are two possible interpretations of this concern. One is that the poor really do not count in U.S. society and the other is that it is more important to push poor mothers into jobs for economic reasons than it is to worry about how their children are reared.

Sixth, lack of concern for strengthening family life was reflected by the little attention paid to supportive services in the proposed legislation. There was the implication that, with $2,400 a year, a family of four could purchase such essential services as counselling, family planning, health care, recreation, and legal aid. If the family is to function in today's complex society, these services are a necessity and not a luxury. They are needed by all groups in society and should be made available on the basis of the ability to pay, including free services for those unable to pay.

Finally, the administrative structure as projected in the legislation called for an expanded rather than a simplified bureaucracy. It required two tiers of administration, one on the federal level and the other at the local level. The requirements of family declarations, quarterly estimates, and redetermination of eligibility would result in more red tape, complexity, confusion, and additional costs than exist in the present system.

The administration, in the meantime, began to hedge on its own legislation. In a highly charged presidential election year, it began to regress to the "stick approach," sensing that this is what middle America wanted. As pointed out in an editorial in the *Christian Science Monitor* (1972):

> There is mounting evidence to indicate that President Nixon is beginning to have serious second thoughts about his earlier leftward ventures into welfare reform and minimum incomes for poor families. Instead he appears to be backing off onto safer political grounds with programs aimed at rewarding the middle income majority as the "builders" of the country.

President Nixon made his real position crystal clear in his 1972 Labor Day message. He stated that, "A policy of income distribution would result in many more Americans becoming poor, because it ignores a human value essential to every worker's success—the incentive of reward" (Los Angeles Times, 1972; subsequent quotations are from the same article). He drew a sharp distinction between the work ethic ("there is really no such thing as something for nothing and . . . everything valuable in life requires some striving and some sacrifice") and the welfare ethic, depicted as "suggesting that there is an easier way out, namely, attaining the good life right now through government." President Nixon brought us full circle back to Social Darwinism with the statement that "the welfare ethic breeds weak people."

The Family Assistance Plan was defeated, but the principle of a right to a minimum income from the U.S. Treasury was finally recognized. Legislation establishing the principle of a federal income guarantee was enacted on October 17, 1972, and went into effect on January 1, 1974. Although the legislation excludes children, and deals primarily with the aged, the blind, and the disabled of any age, it establishes for the first time an income guarantee as an absolute right. The money for this Supplemental Security Income (SSI) Program comes from general funds of the U.S. Treasury, and not from the Social Security Trust Fund, whose programs are based upon earlier payments of payroll tax.

Of the four major reforms projected by President Nixon in August 1969, the one receiving the greatest attention by the administration has been federal tax revenue sharing with the states. General revenue sharing legislation was enacted by the Ninety-Second Congress and signed into law on October 20, 1972. President Nixon's special revenue sharing proposals, which are essentially forms of grant consolidations and which will have a marked impact on social services, have met with little interest in Congress.

The rationale for revenue sharing is based on the fiscal plight of state and local governments. Heavy migration into the cities, increased demands for public services, and the rising costs of local public services have placed an inordinate burden on state and local budgets. State and local government expenditures have been increasing more rapidly than those of the federal government, going from $13 billion in 1946 to approximately $152 billion in 1973. The federal government has attempted to deal with the problem through grant-in-aid programs which have expanded from 71, at a cost of $2 billion in 1950, to 530 at a cost of $24 billion in 1973.

Under the General Revenue Sharing Act, $30.2 billion is being distributed to the states over a five-year period. Two-thirds of these allocations are for local governments and one-third for the state. These funds, unlike categorical and matching grants, are to be utilized by state and local governments in accordance with their own priorities within what the statute defines as "high priority expenditures." The list is very broad, however, and includes maintenance and operating expenses for public safety, environmental protection, public transportation, health, recreation, libraries, social services for the poor or aged, financial administration, and "ordinary and necessary capital expenditures authorized by law." Experience to date shows that highest priority is being given to capital expenditures, public safety, and public transportation. Human services have been low on the priority list.

Local governments have been hesitant to utilize the funds for continuing programs as there is no guarantee that the funds will be renewed. Furthermore, the President's impoundment of funds allocated for some of the key grant-in-aid programs has raised the question as to whether general revenue sharing really represents new money, or whether it is being viewed by the administration as a substitute. The administration is now giving greater emphasis to the legislation's importance as a way of returning power to the people, rather than as a fiscal panacea. However, experience to date in the priorities selected by local governments raises questions about the validity of the claim that citizens are now more involved in the decision-making process.

There is no question that the proliferation of grant-in-aid programs has resulted in increased red tape, inflexibility, and duplication. Consolidation of programs and greater flexibility of services within a comprehensive model is essential at the state and local levels. At the same time, unless there are clear guidelines at the federal level for goal formulation, problem definition, and equity, progress made in the more reactionary sections of the country will be lost. We are in a period in which the goals of equity and social justice are being retrenched, and in which problems are defined more in terms of measurable units of input and output and quantitative formulae than in terms of people and the human condition.

We are still plagued by a maldistribution of services, resources, and decision-making powers. Revenue sharing attacks only a piece of the problem. There is no guarantee that it will bring a redistribution of decision-making power, and even less guarantee that it will result in a redistribution of resources and services. The strengthening of the states and the localities cannot be at the expense of national power, through which the disadvantaged have tended to find greater equity and social justice.

As the social climate has become more regressive, social work is showing signs of turning inward again and focusing more on method than on social work as a field, a body of knowledge, and a point of view. We are turning to systems theory and to the search for social indicators as well as to better systems of classification. We are sharpening our methodology and improving our social engineering approach. This may improve our ability to describe and evaluate "what-is," but the core of our social problems lies more in the realm of "what-ought-to-be." The revolt of youth, women, and non-White minorities has had a common dynamic, the search for a new meaning in life. As pointed out by Rittel and Webber (1972):

> Each in its peculiar way is asking for a clarification of purposes, for a re-definition of problems, for a re-ordering of priorities to match stated purposes, for the design of new kinds of goal-directed actions, for a reorientation of the professions to the outputs of professional activities rather than to the inputs into them, and then for a redistribution of the output of governmental programs among the competing publics.

There is need for more dialogue and debate on what ought to be, and for greater focus on identifying the barriers which prevent us from closing the gap between these ideal objectives and what is. Only in this way will there emerge a clearer definition of our social problems, and only then will the structure, organization and function of social services become meaningful in the broader sense.

NOTES

1. See Kahn (1973) for an extensive bibliography.

2. White House press release, February 16, 1887.

3. White House press release, January 14, 1954. For a more comprehensive look at the changing role of government, see Schottland (1971: 1437-1445).

4. See Congressional Record (1964); President's Committee on Juvenile Delinquency and Youth Offenses Control Act of 1961 (1962); Cloward and Ohlin (1960); Marris and Rein (1967); Economic Report of the President (1964-1967); Council of Economic Advisors (1964-1967); Kahn (1969: ch. 2); and Powledge (1970).

5. Again, no effort will be made to spell out the details of the legislation in this chapter. See Taylor and Williams (1960) and Department of Housing and Urban Development (1967).

6. More specifically, the Heineman Commission recommended that the program be initiated at a level providing a base income of $2,400 to a family of four, that the benefit levels be raised as rapidly as is practical and possible in the future, that the basic payment be reduced by 50 percent for each dollar of income from other sources, that federal participation in existing public assistance programs be terminated, that in states where current public assistance benefit levels exceed the proposed initial level of the federal income supplement program, those states pay supplemental benefits to those currently eligible for aid, that coverage under unemployment insurance programs be broadened and benefits raised to provide more adequate protection to workers against unemployment, that manpower and training programs be consolidated and improved, and that programs of birth control information and services be expanded.

REFERENCES

ALLEN, F. L. (1954) "A look back and a look ahead," in H. W. Jones (ed.) Economic Security for Americans. New York: Columbia University Press.

Christian Science Monitor (1972) "A new, new Nixon?" July 19: editorial page.

CLOUGH, S. B. (1954) "The new economic insecurity," in H. W. Jones (ed.) Economic Security for Americans. New York: Columbia University Press.

CLOWARD, R. and L. OHLIN (1961) A Proposal for the Prevention and Control of Delinquency by Expanding Opportunities. New York: Mobilization for Youth.

——— (1960) Delinquency and Opportunity: A Theory of Delinquent Gangs. Glencoe, Ill.: Free Press.

COHEN, N. (1964) Social Work and Social Problems. New York: National Association of Social Workers.

COMMAGER, H. S. (1951) Living Ideas in America. New York: Harper & Row.

Congressional Record (1964) Proceedings and Debate of the 88th Congress, Second Session, House of Representatives. June 16.

Council of Economic Advisors (1964-1967) Annual Report. Washington, D.C.: Government Printing Office.

Department of Housing and Urban Development (1967) Improving the Quality of Urban Life: A Program Guide to Model Neighborhoods in Demonstration Cities. Washington, D.C.: Government Printing Office.

Economic Report of the President (1964-1967) Washington, D.C.: Government Printing Office.

GRAHAM, E. (1967) "The politics of poverty," in M. E. Gittleman and D. Mermelstein (eds.) The Great Society. New York: Vintage.

KAHN, A. J. (1973) Social Policy and Social Services. New York: Random House.

––– (1969) Theory and Practice of Social Planning. New York: Russell Sage.

Los Angeles Times (1974) February 17: section IX, pp. 1, 6.

––– (1972) September 4: section I, pp. 1, 6.

MARRIS, P. and M. REIN (1967) Dilemmas of Social Reform. New York: Atherton.

MOYNIHAN, D. P. (1970) "One step we must take," Saturday Review (May 23).

––– (1969) Maximum Feasible Misunderstanding. New York: Free Press.

OGBURN, W. (1934) "The future of the New Deal," in W. Ogburn (ed.) Social Change and the New Deal. Chicago: University of Chicago Press.

POWLEDGE, F. (1970) Model City. New York: Simon & Schuster.

Presidential Commission on Income Maintenance Programs (1969) Poverty and Plenty: The American Paradox. Washington, D.C.: Government Printing Office.

President's Committee on Juvenile Delinquency and Youth Offences Control Act of 1961 (1962) The Federal Delinquency Program: Objectives and Operations. Washington, D.C.: Government Printing Office.

PUMPHREY, R. (1971) "Social welfare: history," in C. Schottland (ed.) Encyclopedia of Social Work. New York: National Association of Social Workers.

RITTEL, H. and M. WEBBER (1972) "Dilemmas in a General Theory of Planning." Berkeley: University of California Working Paper No. 194 (November). Unpublished.

SCHOTTLAND, C. (1971) "Social welfare: governmental organization," in C. Schottland (ed.) Encyclopedia of Social Work. New York: National Association of Social Workers.

TAYLOR, H. R. and G. A. WILLIAMS (1966) "Comments on the Demonstration Cities Program." Journal of the American Institute of Planners 32: 366-376.

10

SOCIAL SERVICES ADMINISTRATION
IN THE U.S.S.R.

BERNICE MADISON

The transformations that have taken place in the Soviet Union's social services since 1917 have had the effect of changing a backward, punitive system to one that compares favorably with those in other advanced nations. The fact that these changes occurred in the relatively short period of 57 years, in the midst of rapid industrialization and monstrously devastating social upheavals and wars, makes them impressive (3; 6; 12-15; 28-33; 39-40; 46). Many features of the Soviet system have been copied in Communist bloc countries and studied by poor and backward nations that are struggling to pull their populations out of poverty by means of balanced socioeconomic development.

At the same time, it is clear that the Soviet people have had to pay an enormous price in human suffering for these transformations. Seen as high-level abstractions, Soviet welfare goals are similar to the humanitarian aspirations of the entire international community. But there has persisted an ideological dichotomy between goals and means. During the period of Soviet power, means have often been characterized by planned failure to respond to human needs and to provide safe channels for the redress of grievances, by reliance on methods that are exploitative and repressive, and by an almost total suppression of dissent. Because means and ends are interdependent, especially in program administration, this has meant that Soviet welfare provisions have been only partially successful in achieving their stated humanitarian objectives that aim to enhance human dignity and freedom.

BENEFITS AND SERVICES

Social Insurance, Social Security, and Allied Programs

Monetary benefits designed to maintain income are organized into clearly identifiable and widely publicized systems, well known to the population. The two major components are the state social insurance for workers and employees and social security for collective farm workers. Both provide old-age, disability, and survivorship pensions; funeral allowances; cash sickness benefits; and paid maternity leaves. For selected beneficiaries, the social insurance system also furnishes sanatoria passes, special diets, and retraining expenses. The system for collective farm workers is more recent in origin and considerably less generous in benefit amounts.

Unemployment compensation does not exist, nor is there any provision for supplementing the benefits enumerated above. Public assistance, a severely restricted program, is open to a relatively small number of individuals who, in addition to other conditions, must be ineligible for social insurance and social security to qualify. Public assistance is offered in the form of grants or as placement in institutions. A modest system of family allowances has been granting benefits to some children since 1936 (6; 19; 20; 24; 25; 27; 35; 44; 45).[1]

Social Services

Social services are much less publicized and much less available and accessible than are income maintenance provisions, especially in rural areas which still contain 43 percent of the country's population. Many social services are not assigned a clearly designated place in bureaucratic hierarchies and are often offered inconsistently.

For aged and disabled workers and employees who are no longer in the labor force, certain services emanate from that segment of state social insurance which is administered by the Republic Ministries of Social Welfare.[2] Available only to those who request them and called "material-household assistance," these services provide friendly visits, supplemented at times by such help as doing the laundry, shopping, housework, and making sure the pensioner gets his or her special diet.

For workers and employees still in the labor force, services are offered by that segment of state social insurance which is administered by the All-Union Central Council of Trade Unions. These services concentrate on friendly visits and help with "daily living" for the temporarily ill; on facilitating and overseeing job placement for the disabled; assistance with assembling documents necessary for pension and other benefit applications; helping those who seek entrance to sanatoria, health, recreational, and educational facilities; and aid in finding suitable jobs for those eligible for retirement who wish to continue in employment.

Child welfare services are available for children living both in and outside their own homes.[3] Especially important are day-care and extended-day school programs and special schools for educable defective children living in their own homes.[4] The All-Union Ministry of Education administers these programs. Outpatient and inpatient psychiatric children's services are administered by either the Ministry of Education or by the All-Union Ministry of Health. Counselling related to prevention and control of delinquency is provided by local authorities. Some children are sent to summer camps organized for the most part by trade unions.

Services for children not living at home include placement with guardians (for those under 15) and trustees (for those between 15 and 18), who care for them on a long-term or permanent basis; adoption; institutional care in the form of "homes" and boarding schools for normal children; and special schools for mildly retarded children and for the physically handicapped and severely retarded children—all under Education, except the last two groups which are served by Republic Ministries of Social Welfare. Institutional facilities are available for delinquents deprived of freedom. Some of the institution children are sent to summer camps, most of them maintained by the institutions themselves. Child welfare services are concentrated in the larger urban centers (23; 25; 26).

The only agency available for counseling husbands and wives is the divorce court, and only if children are involved. In such cases, the judge must "establish the motives for notice of dissolution of marriage and take measures to reconcile husband and wife" by pointing out to them the importance of the conjugal bond. Nor is any counseling available to divorced parents who experience difficulties in relation to child-rearing, except for some mothers who succeed in making their needs known to "socio-legal bureaus" (25). These bureaus are located in some maternity clinics and child health centers. Here pregnant women and mothers receive free counseling and services to help them with problems arising out of living conditions, employment, and marital relationships (1; 37; 41; 43).

Unmarried mothers have the right to place their children in institutions or to keep them. Paternity may be established by a joint statement of the unmarried parents at a registrar's office; if there is no joint statement, the mother may institute a paternity suit in court. The only help available to her, if she seeks it, is through a socio-legal bureau (22; 25; 26).

Vocational rehabilitation services are provided in all of the country's 15 republics, but only to a limited degree in rural communities. They are administered by the Republic Ministries of Social Welfare and, in the case of the deaf and blind, by the All-Union Societies for the Deaf and the Blind which are supervised by these Ministries (39; 42; 47; 48). Services offer medical care and surgical procedures, prosthetic devices (some with bio-electric steerage), vocational training, and placement in jobs. Jobs are found in six types of settings: for the majority, in regular state enterprises, among nonhandicapped workers; in state enterprises that have special sections for the handicapped; in enterprises run by the All-Union Societies for the Deaf and Blind; in sheltered workshops administered by welfare organs; and at home. The majority of the disabled, like the aged, live at home. Institutional facilities, usually combined with those for the aged, are available for some.

Services for alcoholics are quite extensive since Soviet authorities count alcoholism among the country's serious social problems. Services include "sobering-up stations,"—one-night custodial facilities operated by the local militia; district polyclinics and alcoholism departments of psychoneurological dispensaries which offer treatment on an outpatient basis; "narco-admitters" for inpatient care for up to 10 days; psychoneurological treatment centers for inpatient care for one to three months; and institutions which combine treatment with work for longer stays. All of these services are under Health. Access is through self-referral and by referrals from police, family, friends, employing establishments, trade unions, neighbors, housing committees, and other interested persons. Recent decrees require compulsory treatment for those who commit crimes under the influence of alcohol. This takes the form of incarceration for one to two years in treatment-labor institutions, run by the All-Union Ministry of Internal Affairs. Escape is considered a criminal offense and is punishable by imprisonment.

Psychiatric services for adults, both inpatient and outpatient, are under Health and are concentrated in the larger urban centers.[5] The major component is not the mental hospital but the outpatient clinic. In 1962, only one hospital bed in nine was reserved for a mental patient, compared with one in two in the U.S. in that year, although rates of mental illnesses in the Soviet Union were similar to those in other Western industrialized societies. Work, rather than occupational therapy, commands a central position in the treatment of outpatients. Work is provided either in workshops attached to outpatient clinics or through special arrangements with industrial and other enterprises. This treatment is accompanied by group therapy. It is not known to what extent this model of the outpatient clinic is applied throughout the country, but Soviet health authorities do acknowledge that there is a shortage of beds for psychiatric patients (10; 11).

Services for juvenile delinquents are administered under the local Municipal Commissions on Juvenile Affairs. "Children's rooms" in local police stations attempt to locate families which, because of illness, work schedules, divorce, or other reasons cannot supervise their children and/or arrange care for them. Services may take the form of placing the minor under the wardship of a public spirited citizen who volunteers for such duty, or in a special school for those 11 to 13, or in a special professional-technical school for those 14 to 17, both types being under Education, or rendering some form of help to the family. Local juvenile commissions are also charged with arranging employment for youths who remain unemployed after leaving school. In cases where parents are considered unfit, commissions may institute proceedings to deprive them of parental rights.

The adolescent who commits an offense may remain within the jurisdiction of a local commission, if he is under 14, or under 16, if his offense does not involve "criminal responsibility." Or he may come within the jurisdiction of the court, if he is 16, or between 14 and 16 and criminally responsible. Court disposition may take several forms: the delinquent may be referred to the commission in his community when, for example, it is believed that the service he requires is primarily educational; or he may be put on probation; or he may be sent to a labor colony operated by Internal Affairs. Discharge is accompanied by parole services.

ELIGIBILITY CONDITIONS AND DURATION OF
BENEFITS AND SERVICES

Numerous eligibility conditions—some spelled out in decrees and regulations, others defined by the discretion of personnel—govern access to benefits and services.

Social Insurance, Social Security, and Allied Programs

The right to social security is found in the 1936 Constitution, which declares that "citizens of the USSR have the right to material security in old age as well as in the event of sickness and loss of capacity to work. This right is ensured by a wide development of social insurance of workers and employees at the expense of the state, free medical aid, and the provision of a wide network of health resorts for the use of the toilers." The basic decrees that transform these rights into benefits are legislated by the Supreme Soviet, and interpreted for implementation by the All-Union Department of State Pensions of the State Committee for Labor and Wages.

For workers and employees, eligibility is determined by Republic Ministries of Social Welfare and the All-Union Central Committee of Trade Unions. Contact with beneficiaries is made at these authorities' respective regional or urban departments, through which administration is decentralized. Eligibility of collective farm workers is determined by Republic Collective Farmers' Soviets of Social Security, Republic Ministries of Social Welfare, and the Central Committee of Trade Unions. Decentralized administrative responsibility is lodged in regional and local farm soviets of social security.

Thus, all levels of government—all-union, republic and local—are involved in eligibility determination. The higher authorities are responsible for policy, interpretation, and final resolution of problems, while lower authorities make the initial determinations and deal with applicants and recipients on a continuing basis (34: 45).

Major eligibility conditions in state social insurance for workers and employees may be grouped as follows:

(1) *Old-Age Pensions.* The worker is entitled to an old-age pension at age 60 (55 for women) after a minimum of 25 years' employment (20 for women). Small supplements are granted if there are dependents, if the worker has been with his last employer for 15 years, or if the worker has worked a total of at least 10 years beyond

the minimum qualifying period. Age eligibility is currently lower, by five years, for women who have a work record of 20 years in textiles. Workers and employees who have worked for 15 years in the Far North and in other selected localities, and disabled veterans of World War II and other disabled military personnel also qualify at a younger age. For workers in hazardous occupations, retirement is at ages 50 and 45, with an employment record of 20 and 15 years for men and women, respectively. Mothers of at least five children, each cared for until age eight, are eligible for pensions at age 50, after 15 years of service.

(2) *Disability Pensions.* For pension determination, the disabled are divided into three groups: Group III includes those whose working capacity is substantially lowered and limited, but who are able to continue work if transferred to occupations suited to their physical condition; Group II includes people who have lost their working capacity in ordinary conditions of production for a prolonged period; and Group I includes people who have suffered such severe disabilities that they cannot look after themselves and need constant care and supervision. Required years of coverage increase with age, and in certain cases, a worker must have as many as 20 years of coverage to be eligible for full disability pension. Supplements are granted under roughly the same conditions as for old-age pensions. Reduced pensions are extended to workers who are partially disabled, but such partial disabilities must be extensive.

There is no separate system for work-connected injury or illness. This is covered under the general disability program on roughly the same basis as ordinary disability. However, the level of benefits is slightly higher and there is no minimum qualifying period of employment. Partial disability pensions for extensive work impairments are granted just as for ordinary disability, but there is no pension provision for minor disabilities. Pensions are payable as long as an individual remains classified as disabled.

(3) *Survivors' Pensions.* Benefits are granted to family members of a deceased worker if the member is a dependent and unable to work. The members who qualify are children, brothers, sisters, grandchildren, parents, spouse, and grandparents. The dependent's inability to work may have been caused by disability, age, or the need to care for children under age eight. Children and disabled parents not dependent on the breadwinner at his death become eligible for pensions if they later lose their source of income. Children maintained by both parents receive pensions on the death of one

parent even if the other is working. Adopted children and adopted parents have the same pension rights as natural children and parents. Benefits are discontinued if an adult regains the capacity to work or when a child attains age 16 (18 if attending school).

(4) *Cash Sickness Benefits (temporary disability).* Temporary disability benefits are related to length of uninterrupted employment, age, whether or not the sick person is a disabled war veteran, and whether or not the illness is work-connected. Uninterrupted seniority is often preserved if a person goes to a new job within one month after he leaves his previous one. Benefits apply in the following cases: illness or injury, regardless of the cause; the need to look after a sick member of the family; exemption from work as a carrier of bacteria, or in cases of quarantine; during treatment at a sanatorium; during additional leave given to TB cases; during a temporary switch to other work in cases of partial disability or on medical grounds; during a fitting for an artificial limb and similar cases, when this is done in a hospital. Benefits are payable from first day of incapacity until recovery or pension.

(5) *Paid Maternity Leave.* This leave is 56 days before and 56 days after confinement. For twins or an abnormal birth, it is 70 days after confinement. If the mother's health so requires, leave may be extended. Fifty-six days' leave is also granted to a woman who adopts a newborn child. When confinement does not take place within the prenatal leave but later, the allowance is payable during the whole period of prenatal leave and the postnatal leave is not reduced. Amounts granted depend on length of employment, age, whether or not the mother is a member of a trade union, and whether she is a "best" worker or has been decorated with an order.

Major eligibility conditions in the system of social security for collective farm workers, in existence since 1965, may be grouped as follows:

(1) *Old-Age Pensions.* In 1968, retirement age was lowered by five years, making it the same as that for workers and employees. The employment requirement is also the same: 25 years for men and 20 for women. Supplements are not available.

(2) *Disability Pensions.* In 1965, only disabled Groups I and II were eligible for disability pensions. In 1968, Group III disability pensions were added, but only for injuries and diseases having occupational causes. For this last group, pensions are granted regardless of how long the disabled had worked. For disability resulting from nonoccupational causes, the required period of

employment ranges from one year for those under age 20, to 20 and 15 years for men and women who reach retirement age, respectively. There is no pension for partial disability. Pensions are payable as long as an individual remains classified as disabled.

(3) *Survivors' Pensions.* Eligible survivors are now defined in the same way as are workers and employees; duration of benefits is also similar.

(4) *Paid Maternity Leave.* Eligibility conditions are the same as for women workers and employees. But benefits are more generous for women who are collective farm chairmen, specialists, and mechanizers than for other women farm workers.

(5) *Cash Sickness Benefits (temporary disability).* Such benefits became available in April 1970. Eligibility is related to the same conditions as for workers and employees. The number of working days to be covered is determined by the brigade leader or livestock section manager, along with the trade union social insurance representative. The period of time covered is from the first day of illness until recovery or transfer to a disabled group, but not more than four consecutive months or more than five months in any one year, except in the case of occupational ailments or TB. If a person moves to another farm, with a work interruption of more than a month, the approval of the general meeting of farm members is necessary to preserve employment continuity.

Pensions and Public Assistance

As is often proclaimed by Soviet authorities, the retirement age in their country is among the lowest in the world. The labor needs of the 1960s, however, led Soviet policymakers to reexamine the employment potential of pensioners. The result was a 1964 amendment which granted a flat pension equivalent to 50 percent of the earnings of pensionable-age employees in many industries and occupations; 75 percent for those returning to work in the Urals, Siberia, and the Far East; and full pensions to those still capable of working in arduous and hazardous occupations. In 1969, these measures were broadened to include additional categories of workers.

The system of family allowances introduced in 1936 was improved in 1944. Monthly payments became available to a mother after the birth of a fourth child and all subsequent children, starting in the month when the child reaches the age of one and continuing until the month before he is five. The amount increases with subsequent children. For unmarried mothers, payments start with each child's birth and continue until he reaches age 12.

Only poor persons who are Group I and II invalids, who are not eligible for social insurance or social security and whose responsible relatives are unable to support them, are entitled to help. Under the new family code, promulgated in 1968, responsible relatives include parents, children, stepchildren, and grandchildren. Support payments can be exacted by civil suit if necessary, and are set at levels proportional to the supporter's income. If a person is adjudged needy by the local welfare department, he becomes entitled to a flat monthly grant paid out of republic funds, presumably as long as need exists. The situation of needy farm members is much more precarious because the amount and duration of aid are determined by what a particular farm is able and willing to offer. Needy aged and disabled persons from urban and rural communities, if they wish and if there is room for them, may enter institutions and receive full support. Length of stay depends on changes in the inmates' personal circumstances.

Social Services

Since eligibility conditions for many social services are neither spelled out in decrees nor detailed in regulations, discretion exercised by personnel is often the decisive factor. It determines the scope of friendly visits and activities associated with social services for those seeking entrance to various facilities or post-retirement jobs. More formal arrangements are followed in placing the disabled in jobs and assisting individuals with assembling documents for pension application. The existence of socio-legal bureaus is not mandated; it depends, rather, on the initiative of medical personnel and their perception of social need.

In contrast, services for children are quite clearly regulated. Day-care programs operate under specific directives in regard to intake, staffing formulas, fee scales, and types of facilities that should be made available. In principle, all children under age seven (pre-school age) are eligible, but in fact, preference is given to those between three and seven whose mothers are working. The extended-day school, usually for children in grades one to four and sometimes for those in grades five to eight, is for children who during out-of-school hours are without family supervision, as well as for those who are not making normal progress at school. Findings by school personnel as to the existence of these conditions constitute eligibility for the program. Its objectives are to cut down on dropouts and repeaters, and to prevent delinquency. Enrollment continues until either the home situation improves or the child reaches school-leaving age (23; 25; 26).

For many children, services outside the home involve depriving parents of the right to bring them up. In the view of Soviet authorities, this is a last resort, to be used only when it is clearly established that parents are failing to do what is required, or when they treat their children cruelly or exert a harmful influence on them by amoral or antisocial behavior. If the parents try conscientiously but are still unable to bring up their child properly, there is no basis for depriving them of parental rights. Yet, restraint toward parents must not outweigh the interests of children. Children are eligible for guardianship and trusteeship when both of their parents die, or when the parents are alive but cannot give care because of ill health, mental illness, absence on long trips required by their work, or when they are declared unfit but not deprived of custody. Guardians and trustees must provide a home for their wards. If they are unable to support the ward and if the ward does not possess adequate independent means, the child may receive a support allowance from public funds. Arrangements for "defective" children are identical with those for normal ones.

Adoption regulations require prospective parents to apply through either the Ministry of Health or the Ministry of Education. Adoption is a resource for children who have no parents or who have been deprived of the opportunity to live with their own parents. Eligibility conditions for adopters exclude those who are themselves under guardianship, those whose interests conflict with the interests of the ward, the mentally ill, those deprived of their rights as citizens, and those who have not reached majority (age 18). Differences in race, nationality, or religion are not bars to adoption, and single women, but not single men, can adopt if they have experience working with children.

Homes and boarding schools for normal children are designed primarily for dependent, neglected, and disadvantaged youngsters —children of unmarried mothers, of war and labor invalids, orphans, members of large families, or poor families, and "problem families" (4; 23; 25; 26). Usually parents themselves petition the local Commission on Juvenile Affairs for permission to place the child. Sometimes petitions come from schools, relatives, housing committees, neighbors, or other interested persons—if parents should but do not act. A child remains until either home conditions improve or he reaches age 18.

Eligibility for psychiatric services, inpatient and outpatient, for both children and adults, is determined by medical personnel and continues for as long as the need exists. Upon attaining majority, a child may be transferred to an adult facility which is under either Health or Social Welfare.

For "defective" children, eligibility consists of an official determination with regard to whether the child is indeed defective and the degree and the nature of his defect. This finding is made by expert commissions (at city, district, or regional levels) that include representatives from the local school system, from special schools (if there are any in the community), and physicians—both general practitioners and specialists. When mental retardation is suspected, the specialist must be a psychiatrist. Recommendations concerning pre-school children are made by medical personnel who have had contact with them and their parents from the time they were born. In cases of deafness and blindness, measurements to guide expert commissions are available. In cases of mental retardation, if it is not detected before age seven, no determination is made until the child has spent a year in a regular school where all possible measures to improve his performance have been taken and until it is concluded that his backwardness is caused by mental deficiency of organic origin. Services for educable defective children continue until age 18; services for noneducable but trainable children continues until they are referred to an adult institution for defectives at age 18.

Pre-delinquents and delinquents are eligible for services depending on their age, the type of undesirable or unlawful behavior detected, and the view of their needs taken by the helping persons involved with them. In principle, for those who remain in the community, services continue until behavior improves. For those who are released from institutions, parole continues for an unspecified period; for those who are not released, transfer to adult institutions occurs at age 18.

Eligibility for camping vacations appears to be determined by membership in Young Pioneers and by parents' membership in trade unions. In the case of children living in institutions, opportunity depends on whether or not the institution has a camp of its own.

Eligibility for rehabilitation services is tied into and is part of the process of classifying a disabled person into a disability group and ascertaining the extent and nature of his remaining work capacity. There exists a network of vocational and technical schools and specially equipped secondary training facilities. Criteria for referral to them have not been spelled out and apparently depend on the discretion of welfare personnel.[6]

POPULATION SERVED

Reliable and comprehensive data on the proportion of population who require benefits and services and who are actually receiving them are not uniformly available and in many instances are altogether lacking.

Social Insurance, Social Security, and Allied Programs

Social insurance for workers and employees covers about 65 percent of the population, and social security for collective farm workers about 30 percent. Both systems together constitute virtually universal coverage for the Soviet population. By 1970, extensions in coverage raised the number of pensioners to 40,115,000—double the number in 1959. Especially notable were the gains by collective farm workers, among whom the number of pensioners rose from 8 million in 1966 to 12 million in 1970.

Quite a different picture is presented by family allowances. Because most Soviet parents want to have only one and at most two children and are increasingly able to limit their families to this size, fewer children have been benefiting from the allowance program. In 1966, in the entire country, the number of families with four or more children was only 558,000 or 1 percent of the total number of families. In 1970, only 3,217,000 mothers were receiving family allowances, a drop of 238,000 since 1960. By 1969, expenditures dropped to 438 million rubles per year, of which nearly 10.5 billion rubles were spent on pensions. The allowances' major beneficiaries are youngsters in rural and Central Asiatic communities where large families are still found. That this limited coverage does not represent an adequate response to the economic needs of children is recognized by a proposal scheduled to be implemented in the next five-year plan: it is planned to introduce children's allowances for families whose aggregate per capita income (including all types of income) does not exceed 50 rubles per month. The aim is to lift out of poverty not only those children who are already receiving allowances, but also those who are not now being reached. No information has been released as to how many families and children would qualify.

No data are available on the number of public assistance recipients.[7] Partial and speculative insight into the extent to which current provision is responding to current need may be gained from a Soviet study carried out in 1971. It divided the country into five zones and showed that institutional care was required by 1.4 to 4.0 persons, depending on the zone, for every 1,000 persons in the population. According to the 1970 census, Soviet population numbered 241.7 million. If the average need for institutional care is arbitrarily set at about 2.5 persons for every 1,000, the total needed institutional places would come to about 605,000 (including places for the needy)—as compared with 250,000 places available in 1968. It should also be noted that institutional facilities are very unevenly distributed: of the 250,000 places, the Russian Republic had 173,000 in 1970, leaving a mere 77,000 for the other 14 republics. A lower percentage of farm as compared with city destitute, aged, and disabled can enter institutions. For example, in 1968, in the Russian Republic, inter-collective farm homes accommodated only 2,000 persons—a striking disproprotion when it is recalled that in 1971, 43 percent of the country's population lived in rural areas. Waiting lists of those seeking entry into institutions are common in most republics.

Social Services

Friendly visits and associated activities are limited in extent for those no longer in the labor force, fragmentary information suggests. For example, in a district social welfare office in Moscow serving 55,000 clients, only two of the 50 salaried employees devoted full time to such services. These two directed the activities of 150 activists (volunteers). In Leningrad in 1970, the city's social welfare network had a paid staff of 670, with 40 engaged in organizing and directing social services provided by 435 activists for 800,000 clients, so that the potential caseload for each activist was 1,840 clients.

Nor are there any data that would indicate the coverage of friendly visits and associated activities for those still active in the labor force. From a number of interviews with activists who provide these services, this author believes that the situation is spotty; that is, how much and what is done depends primarily on how the need for help is perceived by particular trade unions and individual activists and the degree of their commitment to the helping function.

For the deaf and blind, in and out of the labor force, similar services are provided by volunteers from their All-Union Societies. Numerous interviews give the impression that in these organizations the effort to extend coverage is more genuine than among trade union and welfare organs, but that in rural communities relatively few of the deaf and blind are being reached. It must also be noted that for collective farm members, friendly visits and associated services are nonexistent.

Family counseling, as already noted, is available for parents only when they reach the divorce court, or when the mother succeeds in getting help at a socio-legal bureau. Yet the need for such counseling is widely acknowledged since Soviet families are falling apart at an increasing rate: in 1950 there were three divorces per 100 marriages; in 1960, there were 10; and in 1967, 30. Of all civil cases coming before the courts in 1967, those arising out of marriage and family relationships made up more than half, of which divorces were 30.6 percent. About half of all divorce cases were initiated in families in which there were minor children. In only one-fifth of them did court reconciliation efforts succeed. Letters from divorced fathers and mothers in periodicals and newspapers, complaining about problems connected with visitation rights, stepfather behavior, alimony and child-support payments, and a variety of emotional and economic deprivations are not infrequent. Courts do not find it easy to decide on custody when the divorcing spouses are at odds, even in cases for which they request recommendations from organs of guardianship and trusteeship. The state, although it concedes the importance of keeping the welfare of children uppermost, is concerned about costs.

As for unmarried mothers, there is no doubt that many need counseling which they do not get. In 1969 it was claimed that even before the 1968 law on marriage and the family, "adoption of illegitimate children by their fathers was not rare," and in 1970 it was stated that "recognition of paternity is accomplished in the majority of cases voluntarily." But in neither year were supporting data produced. A Soviet authority states that court cases to establish paternity are few, because many unmarried mothers prefer to raise their children without making demands on the children's fathers. As far as social climate is concerned, although disapproval of out-of-wedlock births has become less sharp among intellectuals and the young, there is no convincing evidence that these less punitive attitudes are significantly shared by the general population.[8] Numerically, the problem is sizable: in 1970, one out of every ten live births, adding up to 400,000 babies, was illegitimate. It is claimed that this figure represents a drop from the 1950s, but in cumulative terms it means that millions of children still grow up in economically and socially deprived circumstances.

In 1970, there were 9.3 million youngsters in permanent nurseries and kindergartens and 5 million in seasonal facilities. This meant that 50 percent of all urban children were accommodated, while the figure for rural children was only 30 percent. These levels fell considerably below the 65 percent of all children predicted for the end of the decade just three years earlier. In large cities most three- to seven-year-olds are accommodated at first request, but in smaller cities the situation is far from satisfactory. Everywhere the shortages for those under age three are serious. By January 1972, 1 million children were on the list of "pending applications."

Attendance at extended-day schools reached 5.2 million by 1971. This development, within a decade, is impressive. It does not, however, indicate the extent to which existing need is being met. It is known that extended-day programs are unevenly distributed, with very little being offered in rural communities. The fact that juvenile delinquency has been rising in relation to the under-18 population also suggests that there are either not enough of such programs or that they are not doing a good job, or both.

Although adoption enjoys official endorsement in principle, services to adoptive applicants remain rudimentary. Prospective parents must rely on their own efforts to find a child, and they encounter many legal and other obstacles. Soviet physicians report, for example, that children who have been abandoned at maternity homes are not always free for adoption because their mothers often neglect to give the home an official waiver of their rights to the child. Sometimes, they state, a child's birth is not even formally registered until three or four months later, and by that time, the mother's identity and whereabouts cannot be ascertained. Pertinent as well is the fact that when a court grants annulment of an adoption, one of the alternatives open to it is to return the child to its natural parents—an alternative that appears to nullify the adoption concept itself. Its downgrading is also implied by the exclusion of adopted children from the five or more who, if raised to age eight, confer on their mothers the right to retire at age 50 instead of the usual 55.

The complete absence of statistics concerning children living with guardians, trustees, and adoptive parents, and the pervasive silence in the literature about any and all aspects of their lives, suggest that from the official perspective these arrangements are considered relatively unimportant. Inevitably, one is left with the uneasy feeling that at least some of the most disadvantaged children who could benefit by these services are not receiving them.

No statistics are made available on the number of children being accommodated in homes and boarding schools for normal children. It is clear that the original plans, officially announced in 1956, for developing them into mass facilities have been abandoned. This has come about mainly as a result of disillusionment with the qualitative aspects of upbringing received by institutionalized children and because of high costs. A Soviet authority states that per capita annual expenditures is 700 rubles, compared to 170 rubles for extended-day schools and 120 rubles for regular primary and secondary day schools (6: 80).

Services for "defective" children, as already indicated, are separated into those for educable and noneducable (but trainable). The former, according to an estimate by this author, constitute about 88.5 percent of the total. By design, services for the two groups keep them almost totally apart. Many of the educable group live at home and attend special schools. No statistics are at hand, but it is claimed that all of them are accommodated. All of the noneducable and some of the educable are eligible for institutional care. Again, statistics are not published, but it is estimated that in 1970 at least 16 to 20 percent of the children who were adjudged as needing institutional care were not accommodated.

Soviet sources make much of the "widespread participation" of volunteers in delinquency prevention and control. At the same time, numerous Soviet writers state that most volunteer activities occur in a sporadic, inconsistent, and often unhelpful manner. Schools are also supposed to play a preventive role, but in current practice, it seems, preventive work is undertaken after the fact, so to speak —when criminal behavior, attesting to long and chronic neglect of aids to normal personality development, has already shown itself.

Of those who come to trial, approximately one-half of detected cases, 60 to 70 percent, are sentenced to a term in a labor colony (7: 127). The others presumably are either remanded to the Commissions on Juvenile Affairs or placed on probation. Soviet authorities maintain that many youngsters are not referred to commissions when they should be, or are not served adequately by commissions when they are. Many who drop out of school without completing the eight years of compulsory education are not helped to find jobs or to continue their schooling, and many parolees are not reintegrated into their communities. A Soviet study of parolees from one labor colony during 1965-1969 shows that notices sent to commissions requesting that arrangements be made for schooling, jobs, and housing were ignored in more than half of the cases. During the three-year period 1967-1969, only 14 or 125 minors were assigned for supervision to "social upbringers" but, according to the study's author, these unpaid volunteers exerted no influence on their charges because they did not know how. In 1970, of all juveniles who appeared in court in the Russian Republic, 25 to 30 percent were supposedly put on probation, but only 12 percent of them were assigned to probation officers. Recidivists among probationers reach 20 to 50 percent. While these fragmentary data do not show to what extent pre-delinquent and delinquent youth receive the services they need (to say nothing of the fact that there are no published statistics on how many of them there are), they do suggest that both the quantity and quality of services for this group leave much to be desired—a fact widely recognized by Soviet authorities.

Psychiatric services, inpatient and outpatient, are concentrated in the larger urban centers. To what extent they are available to the rural population is not possible to deduce from available infor-mation.

Published information does not show the extent of services for alcoholics. As to effectiveness, Connor points out that, even if statistics were available in much greater quantity than they are, this would be a difficult question. He notes that "while the absolute incidence of alcoholism and related disorders remains unclear, one can easily gain the impression that the problems are on the increase," but he cautions that "estimating effectiveness is a tricky business" (7: 79). The program has its successes and its failures. Connor believes that Soviet specialists will undertake further experimen-tation with new measures in the future.

Since a disabled person cannot receive benefits until he has been examined by a medical-labor expert commission, it may be assumed that such examinations occur in practically all cases. Because of labor shortages and absence of unemployment compensation, it is likely that those judged able to work are either placed in jobs or find jobs themselves. The placement of invalids in special sheltered workshops in industrial enterprises is being extended, providing employment for persons affected with cardiovascular, nervous, mental, pulmonary, and certain other diseases. According to published sources, in April 1970 there were more than 4 million disabled persons working in the USSR. That they are very unevenly distributed throughout the 15 republics is clear from the fact that, in 1969, the Russian Republic had 3.5 million employed disabled. From 1968 data, it appears that the working disabled constituted 50 percent of all disabled, while among Group III invalids, 70 to 80 percent were working.

It is also probable that medical care and reexaminations occur in line with regulations to increase the disabled individual's work ability, and thus to reduce his pension. The output of prosthetic appliances, including perfected miniature auditory equipment, has been greatly augmented in recent years, but it is not possible to estimate how many disabled who need them get these appliances.

In 1970, it was reported that vocational training for the physically disabled was provided in 37 professions, free of charge to the rehabilitant. There is no evidence that psychologically oriented counseling is furnished to any significant degree or regularly. What occurs, if anything, is friendly visiting, as described earlier.

As for camping, in 1970 more than 9 million children spent part of their summer holidays in Young Pioneer camps (6: 84), or approximately one-third of those seven to seventeen years of age, inclusive.

ADMINISTRATIVE ORGANIZATION

All Soviet programs are administered by government, since voluntary agencies do not exist.

Social Insurance, Social Security, and Allied Programs: Benefits and Services

The organization of agencies responsible for administering these programs, with the exception of family allowances, is related to whether the beneficiaries are workers and employees, or collective farm workers. And within these two groups, a further division is made between those who are no longer active and those who are still active in the labor force.

State social insurance for workers and employees who are no

longer active in the labor force is administered jointly by trade union and social welfare organs, the former being primarily responsible for assisting applicants with assembling necessary documents and participating in eligibility determinations; the latter are primarily in charge of granting and paying pensions. Programs for state social insurance employees who are still active in the labor force are administered by the trade unions. They cooperate with welfare organs, primarily in the transfer of workers from temporary to permanent disability status, and with Health, in the area of medical certification entitling people to sick-leave pay and maternity grants.

Social security for collective farm workers is under the general supervision of welfare authorities, while the program of cash sickness and maternity grants is supervised by trade unions. In both instances, initial eligibility determination and payment of pensions and grants are carried out by local collective farm social security soviets.

Family allowances for all children are administered by the Ministries of Social Welfare. Public assistance for workers and employees is also within the jurisdiction of welfare ministries, while assistance for needy collective farm members is administered jointly by the ministries and farm social security soviets.

Republic Ministries of Social Welfare. A typical republic ministry is departmentalized roughly according to program areas which include pensions, family allowances, expert medical-labor commissions, treatment at resorts and sanatoria, job placement of disabled pensioners, provision of privileges for invalids (especially for veterans of the last war), referral to institutions for the aged and disabled, and pensions for collective farmers. Field operations are controlled by regional and district offices which closely parallel other jurisdictional units of government. The local social welfare commissions which grant pensions include as members staff of the district office, trade union representatives, and a representative (usually the fiscal officer) of the local soviet of people's deputies —the local government. These commissions also act as a communications bridge between the trade union organizations and the ministry.

In addition, a ministry may operate homes for the aged and for severely retarded and physically handicapped children, direct prostheses factories, staff programs, and maintain facilities to retrain disabled persons. All ministries exercise a quasi-supervisory function in relation to the Societies for the Blind and the Deaf, and all have auditing functions. A few maintain training facilities for instruction of welfare personnel and research institutes, primarily oriented toward design and utilization of prosthetic devices and improved methods for retraining disabled persons. Some ministries handle welfare matters for autonomous republics.

There exists an informal arrangement for coordinating working relationships between and among the 15 ministries. Although they are presumably equal in status, the Russian Republic Ministry plays a leadership role, especially in research and in the training of personnel; it also speaks for the others to the all-union organs to which they are subordinate or with which they must coordinate their activities, as well as being responsible for international relations of the Soviet Union in social welfare matters. It is not clear to what extent this role assures response to special welfare needs that the other 14 republics may have, or to what extent it maximizes the input they can make toward improving their country's level of human well-being.

In carrying out their functions, the 15 Republic Ministries of Social Welfare must coordinate their activities, constantly and in detail, with the Ministries of Finance, Health, Education, and Agriculture, with the appropriate sections of the State Planning Committee and with the Department of State Pensions of the State Committee for Labor and Wages—all directly under the All-Union Council of Ministers. The Department, in addition to serving in an advisory role, fills a key interpretive function. Its rulings are cleared with all appropriate organs at the center, and then it issues directives that are binding on the Republic Ministries of Social Welfare. In this way, conformity to uniform national welfare policy is assured. The Department is also an intermediary for changes and innovations that may be generated by Social Welfare Ministries. At the republic level, these ministries are under the Republic Councils of Ministers, and at the local level they are responsible to the soviets of people's deputies.

Since social welfare does not have an all-union ministry, there is reason to question whether it can exert the same influence on policy and on the ordering of priorities as do the trade unions, Agriculture, Health, and Education, which culminate in all-union administrations in their respective fields. Certain considerations also raise the question whether the social welfare enterprise is experiencing a relative diminution in importance vis-à-vis these all-union administrations. As already noted, in its efforts to satisfy a labor-hungry economy, the government has permitted certain pensioners to receive full pensions and full wages. This has increased the number of pensioners who remain in the labor force and who, therefore, continue within the jurisdiction of trade unions for welfare purposes —rather than going over to welfare organs. As agriculture becomes more industrialized, an increasing number of collective farm workers will be transformed into "workers and employees," thus adding to trade union rolls.

Trade Unions. The All-Union Central Council of Trade Unions supervises welfare matters, for which it is responsible through regional trade union committees. These committees, in turn, set up social insurance commissions in enterprises with 100 or more employees. At smaller employing establishments, social insurance is administrered directly by factory and local union committees. All are formed on a voluntary basis, from among active union members, and their membership is endorsed by factory and local union committees. The commissions determine the amount of benefit and entitlement to it during temporary incapacity and prenatal and postnatal leave. They decide on the granting of vouchers for sanatoria, prophylactoria, guest houses, rest homes, hiking and mountaineering centers, holiday facilities for adults and camping for children, and dietetic feeding. They check to see that enterprises pay the correct contributions to the social insurance budget.[9]

Collective Farm Social Security Soviets. The present administrative structure stems from the reorganization of Soviet agriculture that took place following the meeting of the Third All-Union Congress of Collective Farmers in 1969. At the lowest level of the hierarchy are the soviets of social security elected by the general meeting of the individual collective farm's members, or at a meeting of representatives of such members. District, regional, area, and republic soviets of social security are formed from collective farm representatives, selected by regional and area soviets of people's deputies and by the Republic Ministries of Social Welfare.

All-Union Ministries of Education and Health. The former is decentralized to republic ministries, regional, district and local schools; the latter is decentralized to republic ministries, regional and city health departments. The involvement of these ministries in psychiatric services for children is described by Rollins as follows:

Under the Ministry of Health are children's psychiatric hospitals and departments for acute and chronic psychotic patients, neurological departments of general children's hospitals, and speech departments in both psychiatric and general pediatric hospitals. Ambulatory services include adolescent departments in psychoneurological clinics and psycho-neurological offices in children's polyclinics. There are some workshops for children and adolescents connected with the psychoneurological clinics. Other services under the Ministry of Health are sanatoria, residential nurseries, and kindergartens.

Services administered by the Ministry of Education include schools for neurotic children, boarding schools for mildly retarded children, schools with special regimes for children with disciplinary problems, and schools for children with speech disorders. Special schools are also provided for children who are disabled with neurological sequelae. There are homes and kindergartens for pre-school children with speech problems or retardation.

[The Republic Ministries of Social Welfare are] responsible for homes for children with severe degrees of retardation who are considered trainable but not educable. There are also homes for idiots and homes for children with physical defects [36: 48-50].

Agencies charged with responsibility for providing services for juvenile delinquents are under the jurisdiction of several levels of government. "Children's rooms" are under local police control. Commissions on Juvenile Affairs operate as an arm of local government, and labor colonies are under the All-Union Ministry of Internal Affairs.

Commissions are empowered to apply certain sanctions to parents or surrogate parents, to issue a public reprimand, to impose the obligation to recompense the damage caused by a minor, or to levy fines. They may request courts to deprive parents of their parental rights, and they may send minors to labor colonies or to special training institutions without the consent of parents or surrogate parents. Commission decisions are made by a simple majority of the members and may be appealed to the district, city, or regional soviet of people's deputies, or to the Council of Ministers of an autono-mous republic whose decision is final.

The functions of labor colonies and their tie in with educational authorities and commissions are currently regulated by the decree of June 1968. Colonies are penal institutions for minors who have been deprived of freedom. Their major task is character reformation, through the use of a penal regimen, socially useful labor, general educational and technical-vocational schooling, and political enlight-enment. There are two kinds of colonies: standard regimen and strict regimen. The standard colonies are for males sentenced for the first time, unless their crimes are especially serious, and for all females sentenced to imprisonment. The two sexes are kept separate. Strict colonies are for males who had been incarcerated previously, as well as for those sentenced for the first time for serious crimes. If a minor reaches 18 while serving his sentence, he is transferred to a labor colony for adults to finish out his term. At least in theory, these colonies are different from adult institutions because, in addition to punitive elements, they possess a more clearly expressed educational character (7: 130).

Agencies that serve alcoholics are likewise within different administrative hierarchies. As already mentioned, "sobering-up stations" are under local police control. The more serious and habitual offender will receive further aid, depending on how far his problem has progressed. Connor explains:

Generally, for diagnostic purposes, three types of alcoholics (or stages of alcoholism) are distinguished in order of increasing severity. The first type includes those who are conscious of the dangers of their alcoholic state and wish treatment. These may be treated with supportive and psychotherapeutic measures, generally as outpatients. Alcoholics unconscious of their problems and not seeking treatment . . . [will be treated] in a hospital setting. Finally the third category includes deteriorated cases who, lacking the desire for treatment and subject to "psychotic episodes," need prolonged care in work-colony treatment institutions. The more serious cases . . . where the person could not function in the treatment labor institutions, are sent to large psychoneurological hospitals or "psychiatric colonies" [7: 60-61].

All are controlled by Health.

Treatment-labor institutions for alcoholic criminals, run by the Ministry of Internal Affairs, are intended to serve not only those who are sentenced to deprivation of freedom, but also "a whole new class of noncriminal but socially disruptive alcoholics, and represent a tougher attitude toward the alcoholic than any yet taken" (7: 66). They impose a regimen of confinement, compulsory labor, and political-educational work. From the wages paid inmates, deductions are made for their food, clothing, and other expenses.

FINANCING OF PROGRAMS

In terms of funding, Soviet social welfare programs may be divided into those that do not require direct payments by the beneficiary of the services, and those that do require such payments.

In the system of state insurance for workers and employees, there is no direct contribution by the insured person. Old-age, disability, death, sickness, and maternity pensions and grants are financed from contributions by employing enterprises which amount to between 4.4 and 9 percent of payroll, according to industry. Expenditures exceeding the employer's contribution are covered by the state out of general tax funds and amount to about 50 percent of the cost. Most of the cost of medical care connected with social insurance administration (such as sanatoria, rest homes, and treatment of work-connected injuries) is financed in the same manner.

In the system of social security for collective farm workers, there is also no direct contribution by the beneficiary. Old-age and disability benefits are financed by a contribution of about 4 percent of each farm's gross annual income. The state covers excess of expenditures over receipts out of general taxation. Maternity and sickness benefits for collective farm workers are financed by each farm's contributing 2.4 percent of the sum paid in wages (including wages in kind), with the state again absorbing the difference. Medical care connected with social security is covered in the same manner.

When aged or disabled pensioners enter an institution, their pensions are discontinued and they receive only pocket money.

The entire cost of family allowances is covered by the state from general taxes. In contrast, public assistance for workers and employees is financed out of republic funds. Such assistance for collective farm members depends upon what individual farms allocate for this particular purpose. Institutions for the aged and disabled, for the most part filled by needy persons and pensioners without families, are financed out of republic funds. Although in principle, a farm may allocate resources for the building of its own and inter-collective farm sanatoria, rest homes, pioneer camps, and institutions for the aged and the disabled, pervasive silence on the subject in the literature suggests that all this is not undertaken on a significant scale.

Payments by parents for day care, extended-day schools, boarding schools, and institutional care for "defective" children are adjusted to the parents' incomes, and apparently cover only a small part of the cost.[10] It is claimed, for example, that of the total spent for the maintenance of children in nurseries, the state pays more than 80 percent, and in kindergartens about 75 percent. In 1971, a Soviet authority stated that for nursery kindergartens and boarding schools, parents pay on the average only 15 to 18 percent of the cost of their children's upkeep. The children of large, low-income families are admitted free of charge, as are children of unmarried mothers with low earnings, children of disabled and war veterans, and children of widowers. In 1970, for example, among parents whose children attended extended-day schools, 10 percent were excused from all payments for the two meals their children were served at school, and 15 percent had their payments reduced.

No direct contribution by consumers is required by the medical care system. Patients do pay for medicines, however. Sobering-up stations charge alcoholics about 10 rubles per night, in return for which the drunken person receives a hot shower or steam bath and a bed for the night. No direct charge for other types of services are imposed.

STAFFING AND MANPOWER PATTERNS

Social work as a profession does not exist in the Soviet Union. Social services are delivered by a multitude of people with different backgrounds and types of preparation. In almost all of the organizations described above, the responsibility for management and supervision is placed on persons with some professional training deemed desirable in their particular settings. Direct services, on the other hand, may be delivered either by trained personnel or by activists. The use of the latter is widespread, in-service training for them is often brief or nonexistent, and frequently the relationship between them and their supervisors is not clearly delineated (21: 25).

Social insurance delegates, about half of whom are women, are trade union activists elected to their office by open vote of the trade and professional groups in the industries and agencies in which they work. They act in accordance with regulations set forth by the All-Union Central Committee of Trade Unions and are accountable to the union social insurance commission in their place of employment. In 1971, it was claimed that 4 million activists took part in the trade unions' work in social insurance.

While the responsibility of an insurance delegate embraces everything that can be subsumed under "constant comradely concern" for the well-being of members in his group, his major task is to help workers and employees who are planning to retire to assemble the necessary documents and to assist those who are sick. In helping the latter, the delegate may make a hospital or home visit, sometimes exposing malingerers, alcoholics, and problem families, and do what seems required in each situation. In addition, he may participate in social insurance eligibility determinations, check work records, help retired workers who wish to continue working to find suitable jobs, and follow up disabled workers placed in jobs at his enterprise. Delegates are supposed to perform their tasks outside of working hours. They receive no pay, but the union's insurance budget provides for prizes of varying amounts, given as a mark of appreciation for good work.

The work of union social insurance commissions is directed by union officials who work as such on a full-time basis and are paid accordingly. In addition, unions appoint representatives to pension and medical-labor expert commissions who receive full wages while carrying out commission functions. These paid workers were described as a "handful" in 1971.

The trade union budget provides modest funds for "training of personnel and social insurance education."[11] Some delegates, usually those scheduled to assume union functions full-time, are granted paid leave to attend a two-month course in social security offered by the Russian Ministry of Social Welfare and, on occasion, by other republic ministries. Most, however, depend on shorter courses and seminars organized by local unions, or conferences and meetings at which experiences are exchanged and discussed. This type of training has increased in recent years. Virtually all of it is directed toward giving delegates and union officials the technical proficiency necessary for administering social insurance.

Welfare Workers. While no specific competence is required to qualify as an "inspector" in a social welfare ministry, preferred training for this occupation is in law and accounting. For physicians assigned by Health to medical-labor expert commissions, specialized training oriented to disabling conditions is considered desirable. This is explained by the fact that they are concerned primarily with determining eligibility for pensions and benefits, and to a relatively minor extent, with the social services aspects of programs within the ministry's jurisdiction. An increasing proportion of new workers comes with these qualifications, but a sizable majority still have only a general secondary education or less. No data on the number of welfare workers are published. On the basis of an estimate made by this author in 1967, the current figure may be 175,000.

For a selected number of welfare workers in key positions, arrangements are made for them to take courses in law and accounting by correspondence, supplemented by paid leaves to attend 30-day summer sessions to prepare for and take examinations. For the rest, some in-service training is made available. These efforts are supplemented by "training letters" and materials in professional journals. In-service training instructors, for the most part, are practitioners with degrees in law, economics, and bookkeeping who emphasize correct eligibility procedures. It should be added, however, that in many regions in-service training is either unavailable or offered only sporadically.

The social services that are provided by the Ministries of Social Welfare are delivered by activists who may be compared to outreach or indigenous workers in the United States. These activists, among them pensioners, are supervised by inspectors in the local welfare offices and, although unpaid, enjoy a semi-official status that lifts them above the client mass. Yet the elements of the inspector-activist relationship are not clear, nor is it possible to say with certainty what activities they are empowered to undertake, how much initiative they are permitted to exercise, or how much authority they wield. Criteria for their selection and in-service training for those selected are not mentioned. The impression is gained that the extent to which their activities meet the needs of beneficiaries is uneven. Some activists maintain a meaningful contact with their clients, giving of their time and effort in a humane fashion and sometimes making referrals to appropriate resources. Others confine their involvement to one-time and perfunctory contacts. It should be noted that activists are almost unknown in rural communities.

In homes for the aged and disabled, medical services are provided by professional personnel. As for other employees, "attendants," their qualifications are not specified. Apparently, it is not easy to get or to keep good attendants as there are a number of complaints about them in the literature. Nor is it clear what kinds of people are preferred as directors for these institutions. In many instances, it appears that these positions are given to party members and retired military personnel, either as a reward for past services, or because they have not done well in other assignments.

All-Union Societies for the Blind and the Deaf. In the early days of their existence, these societies' staffs consisted for the most part of activists. In-service training aimed at raising their political and cultural level, but as the training establishments under the societies' control expanded, the need for translators, braille instructors, and specialists in setting up and maintaining appropriate work situations for these handicapped became acute. The societies began to employ more paid workers, and increased allocations for training. To date, however, the number of qualified paid workers remains insufficient, so that heavy reliance on activists continues, especially in localities far removed from the centers.

Educational Personnel. Since teachers perform child welfare services as well as teaching functions, parents frequently turn to them for advice on child behavior and child guidance, and occasionally for counsel with their own personal problems. Often, educators are guided by theory and research developed and conducted by psychologists, themselves a part of the educational system.

In some areas of the country, primarily in large urban centers, home visits by teachers are fairly common. In others, such as Central Asiatic and outlying republics, they are almost unknown. It should also be noted that as a child gets older, especially in the secondary schools, home visits by teachers become rare. The relationship between the school and the home grows more formal and more strictly confined to educational demands made on the student.

Certain teachers, usually those with at least a secondary education and considerable experience in working with children and parents, are selected to act as children's "inspectors." They deal with nonattendance and behavior problems, investigate complaints of neglect and abuse, and make arrangements for children who cannot remain in their own homes.

Upbringers in institutions for normal children are teachers who are supposed to be more concerned with "living" than with "learning" —that is, with the physical, moral, and psychological aspects of child-rearing. But there is no agreement about what kind of training the upbringer ought to receive and what his skills should be. Some believe that no special training is needed, and that what is required is skill in organizing games and teaching children table manners. Others think that upbringers ought to get qualitatively different training from regular teachers—for example, in using the interview as something more than a friendly conversation—and that they should be skilled in "charting the personalities of their charges" in ways that demonstrate a mastery of psychology (2; 25). It is clear that few of them are offered the opportunity to obtain special training that would stress the psychological aspects of growth and development. Complaints about their shortcomings, and about the difficulty of finding qualified teachers willing to undertake the arduous upbringing task, are not infrequent. Most upbringers are women whose education is much more limited than that of women employed as teachers in the general educational system.

Defectologists. It is universally agreed that for raising and educating children who suffer from mental and physical handicaps the teachers and upbringers should have special training. Progress toward this goal has been accelerated, and special training has moved from a general defectological preparation to specialization in deafness, mental retardation, blindness, and speech defects. This special training follows secondary education and continues for five years, one to two years longer than the regular teacher training course. In order to attract able young people, stipends are 50 percent higher than those paid to regular teachers, and salaries of defectologists are 25 percent higher than those of regular teachers. It is claimed that the interdisciplinary character of the training program makes it possible for defectologists to work effectively with a variety of specialists involved in serving handicapped children. Much attention is devoted to vocational training in addition to teaching specific academic subjects and working with parents in order to interpret to them the meaning of their children's handicaps (8; 9; 17; 18; 25; 38).

Patrons' and Parents' Committees. Many children's institutions are helped in their work by the so-called patrons' committees. These are made up of volunteers from various enterprises, the Party, the Young Communist League, other social organizations, and interested individuals. At present the better functioning patrons' committees are divided into subcommittees, each concentrating on a specific area such as education and child-raising, "culture," housekeeping labor, or health and physical education. A program, formulated jointly with the institution's director is drawn up, and all activities are supervised by him.

Parents' committees, closely supervised by school personnel, are composed of parents who are considered as having been successful in raising their own children. Their terms are staggered and extend over a period of eight or nine years. Lengthy, uninterrupted participation is believed desirable because it permits the parents to become thoroughly acquainted with the teachers and children and assures a continuity of interest. Their activities are similar to those of patrons' committees. These volunteers may visit children's families in order to ascertain why the child is not doing well in school. This may be followed by measures thought appropriate in the particular situation, including contact with various "collectives" of which the parents may be members (trade unions, the Party, and so on) in order either to pressure them to change their ways or to seek relief for some from extra responsibilities which leave little free time with their children. The formation of parents' committees in boarding schools is often an arduous task, because these parents tend to divest themselves of responsibility for their youngsters.

To what extent these committees are effective, both quantitatively and qualitatively, in meeting the needs of children is impossible to determine. Qualifications for membership are very general and members receive no special training. That they do not exist everywhere is obvious.

Medical Personnel. Professionally trained medical personnel play an important role in many segments of the social services delivery system. Physicians, including specialists, have a determining function in medical-labor expert commissions. It is primarily their recommendations that serve as the basis for classifying individuals into disability groups, prescribing treatment and follow-up, and placing those with work capacity in jobs. Likewise, physicians' and psychiatrists' participation is required in decisions concerning the education and treatment of "defective" children and adults.

Within the network of medical facilities serving the entire population, teams of pediatricians and "patronage" nurses make up a group of paid staff, part of whose function is to provide social services to children. The training of a patronage nurse is identical to that of a medical nurse; the difference in title reflects the focus of the former on the home and of the latter on work in the clinic. These teams operate out of district clinics and are responsible for approximately 1,000 children of all ages living within their geographic unit. In principle, they care for these children from birth to adolescence, become familiar with their health needs and home conditions, and are frequently able to influence their social situation by family counseling.

If a child's development is hindered by social problems facing the mother, and if a socio-legal bureau is available, the team may refer the mother there. Patronage nurses in this setting work under the supervision of attorneys, reporting to them on home conditions and needs.

Friendly visits and associated activities in the homes of mothers who may be sick themselves, or whose children are sick, are undertaken by activist committees attached to clinics and other medical facilities serving women and children. They are under the supervision of medical personnel, and their only qualification is interest in helping others. Again, it is not possible to say to what extent they meet the need that exists. They receive no training.

Workers in Juvenile Delinquency Programs. The character of delinquency prevention activities by volunteers was described earlier. The organizational forms of these efforts include parents' committees, assembled on the basis of residence or place of work; volunteers attached to the children's rooms of police stations and to the Commissions on Juvenile Affairs; big brother programs; and volunteers forming street patrols. No in-service or other kinds of training for these groups, or for activists who serve as probation and parole officers, are provided.

Teachers and upbringers in labor colonies, who are in the most constant contact with inmates, are

> called upon to strike an effective and delicate balance between coercion and persuasion. For a person with psychological and pedagogical training of a high order, this is a difficult enough task; but as of July, 1965 ... there was no single school in the USSR devoted to the preparation of personnel for work in juvenile labor colonies. Presumably, some training is available in the Ministry of Internal Affairs' schools for its own workers, especially in Moscow, where pedagogically and psychologically trained staffs are present, but this training is directed toward more general preparation for a variety of functions in corrective-labor institutions in general. Soviet teacher-training institutions have devoted little if any attention to the preparation of personnel (for labor colonies for juveniles) [7: 138-139] .

Outside of particular occupational skills, few of the instructors have any pedagogical training.

ASSESSMENT OF OUTCOME

Assessment and accountability procedures are not built into all programs that have been described, despite the fact that many are massive in character and, in the aggregate, importantly affect the lives of large segments of the Soviet population.

Assessment Through Research

With regard to state social insurance for workers and employees, social security for collective farm workers and allied programs, not a single piece of research has been published that would address such questions as adequacy of benefits, levels of living at which beneficiaries maintain themselves, living arrangements, the extent and character of employment patterns among retired workers, the role of saving, ownership of property, and wages paid retired workers in augmenting income—or many other aspects that would shed light on the actual living conditions of pensioners. And yet it is known that, if the current average pension of workers and employees were to be spent wholly upon foodstuffs, it would not suffice to purchase more than 30 percent of the "scientifically determined norms of nourishment." At least one-half of all pensioners exist on a per capita income level of less than 50 rubles a month—below the official "minimum of material well-being."[12] In view of this, the failure to provide supplementary income as a part of ongoing programs seriously diminishes their ability to meet minimum standards.

The limited ability of family allowances to meet the economic needs of children at a level required for normal growth and development has been mentioned.[13] While studies are being conducted in relation to a more extensive and presumably more effective system that is being proposed, none has been published so far. Although the current system has been in existence since 1944, not a single study concerning any aspect of its operations or of its significance for family life has appeared (27).

Especially disturbing in this context is the total silence in regard to public assistance, either in statistical or quality of life terms. Rare references to emergency, one-time grants for such items as a winter coat suggest strongly that destitution among this group of aged and disabled, especially when they cannot gain admission to an institution, reaches dangerously low levels.[14] Nor are there any studies describing institutional care for the aged and disabled, with all its psychological, emotional, and physiological implications. Architectural models are available that are either being considered or used in constructing institutions.

Given the Soviet emphasis on the therapeutic value of work, spurred by a labor-hungry economy, it is not surprising that research activity oriented toward vocational rehabilitation is in evidence. Although statistics on the number of disabled in the three groups are not published, sporadic studies examine "indicators"—devices to determine the pattern of invalidity as it changes over time. The major function of the Central Scientific Research Institute of Expertise on Work Ability and Organization of Labor, created in Moscow in 1930 and located within the Russian Ministry of Social Welfare, was and still is to show how "methods of work must change" in order for more disabled to be placed in jobs. Research in prostheses is conducted by the Moscow Institute, its affiliate in Rostov, and a similar institute in Leningrad, as well as by a few of the larger prostheses-manufacturing establishments. As for the All-Union Societies for the Blind and the Deaf, research in some of the enterprises under their control centers on job specifications and working conditions for optimum employment of these handicapped. The research activities of the Rehabilitation Center for Deaf Mutes in Pavlovsk include teaching methods for the development of skills applicable in a large variety of professions and occupations. The Kiev (Ukrainian Republic) Institute of Gerontology, founded in 1968, is the only one of its kind in the Soviet Union. It is within the jurisdiction of Health, and it heavily oriented toward research in the physiological and psychological aspects of aging. It considers expansion of institutional care for the aged in the near future as the most feasible solution to their problems, although it is realized that most aged could remain in their own homes if supportive services were made available. Not a single study exists with regard to friendly visiting and activities associated with it, either for those in the labor force or out of it.

As already indicated, there is no literature about children who have been adopted or placed with guardians and trustees. The same is true of illegitimate children and their mothers. As for institutional care for normal children, considerable literature exists, but none of it uses the scientific method to assess its impact on the social, emotional, and intellectual development of its charges. Not a single research effort is devoted to following up the children after they leave. The same situation obtains in regard to "defective" children. Personnel involved in their education and care claim that most find jobs in enterprises and on farms, but no studies are cited to prove these claims. Nor is it considered important to research the situation of these children when they try to make their way on the outside as people, rather than only as producers.

Relatively extensive research has been carried out by the Institute of Defectology in Moscow, an affiliate of the Academy of Pedagogical Sciences of the Russian Republic, concerning children with physical (other than orthopedic) and mental handicaps. Its major emphases include a medical-oriented understanding of the handicapping condition, its significance in limiting the child's ability to function in learning and working, ways of assessing this significance, and methods of educating and training the child to achieve his maximum potential. The emotional and social meaning of handicaps, both for children and their parents, is not explored as such, and even indirect reference to it is rare. Evaluative and follow-up studies are not reported.

Connor cites alcoholism-connected studies, mostly by medical and legal personnel, that explore public opinion, describe alcoholics, ascertain the proportion of juveniles and adults who commit crimes under the influence of alcohol, and show the role of drunkenness in divorce (7: 43-49). But little information is available on the success of therapeutic approaches used in noninstitutional treatment. With regard to outcomes in treatment-labor colonies, Connor finds it difficult to evaluate the very few statistics on cures reported since the criteria for a "cure" are not specified.

Although statistics on juvenile delinquency are not adequate, authorities are obviously deeply concerned with both its magnitude and its characteristics. In the past five years, descriptive studies of delinquents have appeared more often than in earlier periods, and more criticism has been voiced about the work of responsible agencies. In April 1971, the USSR Academy of Pedagogical Sciences convened the first all-union "scientific-practical" conference on the problem of preventing delinquency and reeducating delinquents. Some data are now available on characteristics of delinquents, such as their age distribution, level of education, progression in unlawful behavior, and personality patterns. There is also a 1969 study comparing crime among minors in the city and in the countryside —said to be the first of its kind in the Soviet Union. Research has been done on the proportion of secondary school children who use alcohol and the relationship of this usage to delinquency. Some exploration is at hand about the connection between delinquency and "fatherless" homes. But nothing has been published concerning the adjustment in society of probationers and parolees that would yield meaningful insight into their life situations. Seeing recidivism as the mirror of shortcomings in treatment efforts, Connor finds that "statistics on recidivism are fragmentary and in many cases some-what contradictory, but they illustrate some of the persistent problems of the system in dealing with juvenile delinquents" (7: 141).

In her book on child psychiatry in the Soviet Union, Rollins reviews 18 studies published there since 1959. Only two of them, both concerning childhood and adolescent schizophrenia, are of the follow-up variety. Neither indicates what effect treatment had on social functioning except to say that 56 percent of the patients were unable to work when seen 10 to 18 years after treatment (36).

Assessment Through the Appeals Process

As is generally recognized, the appeals process often yields data and insight into how well or poorly social services are fulfilling the purposes for which they are created. Inadequacies of coverage, inappropriate or harsh eligibility conditions, and a multitude of weaknesses in the quality of administration may be brought to light.

In the Soviet Union, nothing has been written about the appellate process in social services. Upon being questioned, administrators in welfare organs reply that, although the dissatisfied individual may discuss his case with the district office, he rarely if ever is invited to do so. The appellate process permits him to present his case either to the local soviet of people's deputies, or to take it through the social welfare hierarchy, culminating in the Republic Ministry of Social Welfare. In both instances, after review, the case is returned with comments or recommendations to the local commission, which is the ultimate arbiter. As to judicial appeal, in theory the affected individual can take his or her complaint to court, but usually this is said to be unnecessary because at some point the situation becomes "fully understood by him." No cases of judicial appeal are on record. A similar situation exists in the system of social security for collective farm workers, with the local social security farm soviet being the body to which all complaints are eventually returned. In social insurance matters for those active in the labor force, appeal is available through the trade union hierarchy and is finally returned to the local social insurance commission. Again, no court cases are on record.

Parents who become dissatisfied with services, either in the educational or health systems, usually try to settle their grievances by discussion with the local authorities. Complaints can be made to higher organs, and are reviewed by them, again with recommendations being made to the local organs.

Only sporadic and fragmentary data on complaints appear. In contrast, financial accountability is constantly emphasized—both in relation to a strict adherence to eligibility conditions (in order to detect fraud and eliminate overpayments) and in the form of reports concerning expenditure of funds allocated for specific purposes, required by financial organs. The fact that dissatisfied applicants and consumers of services exist is shown by sporadic accounts in social welfare literature, highlighted by occasional stories in the press when reporters follow up newsworthy situations in a muckracking style.

As the Soviet Union moves through the decade of the 1970s, its leaders seem somewhat more willing to recognize that in the twentieth century, the choice of socioeconomic institutions and policies must be based on the maximization of human well-being. They appear to find it advisable as well to view this maximization as an ongoing response to human needs, rather than to postpone it until an uncertain communist millenium. It is possible, therefore, that future Soviet welfare provision will narrow the dichotomy between ends and means, and will move the nation's social service system toward its stated humanitarian objectives more directly and con-structively, especially from the point of view of the individual. This possibility is enhanced by the fact that so far, Soviet society has not been able to make good on its promise that it would create human relationships so just and satisfying that social problems would wither away. Nor has it produced programs that have dealt with these problems more effectively than the programs of other nations straining under the exigencies and pressures of rapid technological development.

NOTES

1. Mothers' wages—seen by Soviet demographers as a way to raise the birthrate, as well as help implement equality between men and women—were widely debated in the Soviet press (16: November 1968, January, March, April and August 1969) and rejected, to an important extent because of pressure by "leading" Soviet women.

2. Soviet government has three levels: state or all-union, republic, and local.

3. Since 1968, "own homes" have included those provided by "factual upbringers" —persons who intended to and did raise the child on a permanent basis but are not related to the child by birth or through adoption. They are required by law to provide support and, in return, the children whom they are raising are equated with biological offspring.

4. In the Soviet Union, retarded and physically handicapped children are called "defective."

5. A Soviet authority wrote in 1973 that "One very important social problem is to even out medical service levels in city and countryside, as well as those of the different . . . republics. . . . Village hospitals, some of them with only five beds, are as yet inadequately equipped and staffed. What tells especially badly on the level of medical service in the countryside is shortage of transport facilities" (6: 138).

6. The Rehabilitation Center for Deaf Mutes in Pavlovsk, established in 1963, is administered by the All-Union Society for the Deaf. This society works with the Academy

of Sciences in connection with the methods they use to rehabilitate the deaf, the Health as to the patient's medical problems, and with Education with regard to the student's educational and training goals. It is a leader in its field and appears to serve in a consultnat capacity to various undertakings aimed at improving the ability of the deaf to work and study.

7. An estimate by this author in 1963 suggested a ratio of roughly one public assistance recipient to every ten pension beneficiaries. For several reasons, this ratio would probably be lower today.

8. The only violent crime category in which women predominate is that of infant murder. Soviet studies show that 87 percent of such offenses are connected with unwed motherhood, and that 92 percent are committed during the birth process itself. Crimes of this type are said to be on the decline (7: 152).

9. In addition, with the labor protection commissions, they study working conditions, and in conjunction with management and medical workers, they work out and put into effect measures for preventing sickness and injury (5).

10. A somewhat surprising feature of the fee scale for day care is its regressive character: the higher the parents' earnings, the smaller the proportion of earnings they contribute.

11. In 1971, unions spent only slightly over 0.1 percent of their budget for organizational purposes which include training.

12. The size of pension varies between 50 and 100 percent of former earnings (and is weighted in favor of the lower wage earner) except for the higher paid workers, for whom the maximum-benefit provision results in a ratio lower than 50 percent.

13. Some notion of the value of family allowances—four rubles per month for the fourth child, with payments rising progressively to a maximum of 15 rubles for the eleventh and each additional child—may be gained by relating them to the 1971 average monthly wage of 126 rubles for workers and employees, or to the minimum monthly wage of 70 rubles.

14. Flat grants range from 10 to 20 rubles per month, depending on the republic of which the person is a resident. The Soviet poverty line would require 50 rubles per month.

REFERENCES

1. Abramova, A. A. "Razvitie zakonodatel'stva ob okhrane truda zhenshchin" [Development of legal provisions concerning protection of women's labor], in N. G. Aleksandrov, ed., Novoe v razvittii trudovogo prava v period mezhdu XX i XXII s ezdami KPSS [New features in the development of labor law between the 20th and the 22nd conference of the Communist Party]. Moscow: 1961.
2. Akademiia pedagogicheskikh nauk RSFSR. V pomoshch rabotnikam shkol-internatov; dokumenty i materialy [Academy of pedagogical sciences of the Russian Republic. To the aid of workers in boarding schools; documents and materials]. Moscow: 1956.
3. Aralov, V. A. and A. V. Levshin. Sotsial'noe Obespechenie v SSSR [Social security in the USSR]. Moscow: 1959.
4. Bondar, A. D. and A. F. Pacheko, eds. Pervye shagi. Shkoly internaty [First steps. Boarding schools]. Moscow: 1958.
5. Brown, E. C. Soviet Trade Unions and Labor Relations (Cambridge, Mass.: Harvard University Press: 1966).
6. Buzlyakov, N. Welfare the basic task. Five-Year Plan 1971-1975 (Moscow: Progress Publishers: 1973).
7. Connor, W. D. Deviance in Soviet Society. Crime, Delinquency, and Alcoholism (New York and London: Columbia University Press, 1972). Reviewed by Bernice Madison in Annals of the American Academy of Political and Social Science, vol. 404 (November) 1972, 299.

8. D'iachkov, A. I. "Osnovy sovetskoi sistemy obucheniia i vospitaniia anomal'nykh detei" [Bases of soviet system of education and rearing of abnormal children], in Tezisy dokladov tret'ei nauchnoi sessii po voprosam defektologii, 22-25 Marta 1960 g. [Theses of the scientific reports on questions of defectology at the third scientific session, March 22-25, 1960]. Akademiia Pedagogicheskikh Nauk RSFSR. Moscow: 1960.

9. Dul'nev, G. M. and M. I. Kuz'mitskii, eds. Obuchenie i Vospitanie Umstvenno Otstalych Detei [The Education and Upbringing of Mentally Retarded Children]. Moscow: Academy of Pedagogical Sciences of the Russian Republic: 1960.

10. Field, M. G., "Approaches to Mental Illness in Soviet Society: Some Comparisons and Conjectures," Social Problems, vol. 7, number 4 (Spring): 1960, 277-297.

11. ――― and J. Aronson, "Soviet Community Mental Health Services and Work Therapy," Community Mental Health Journal, vol. 1, number 1 (Spring): 1965, 81-91.

12. Iniutin, G. K. Chto daet trudiashchimsia novyi pensionnyi zakon [What the new pension law gives the toilers]. Moscow: 1956.

13. Karavaev, V. V. Sotsial'noe strakhovanie v SSSR [Social insurance in the USSR]. Second edition. Moscow: 1959.

14. Komarova, D. P., ed. 50 Let Sovetskogo Sotsial'nogo Obespecheniia [50 Years of Soviet Social Welfare]. Moscow: 1968.

15. Krasnopol'skii, A. S. Osnovnye printsipy sovetskogo gosudarstvennogo sotsial'nogo strakhovaniia [Basic principles of Soviet state social insurance]. Moscow: 1951.

16. Literaturnaia Gazeta [Literary Gazette]. Weekly newspaper.

17. Luria, A. R., ed. The Mentally Retarded Child. Essays Based on a Study of the Peculiarities of the Higher Nervous Functioning of Childoligophrenics. Translated from the Russian by W. P. Robinson; edited by Brian Kirman, New York: 1963.

18. ――― and V. I. Lubovskii, eds. Metody issledovaniia detei pri otbore vo vspomogatel'nye shkoly [Methods of investigation for selecting children for auxiliary schools]. Moscow: 1964.

19. Madison, B., "Contributions and Problems of Soviet Welfare Institutions," Social Problems, vol. 7, number 4 (Spring): 1960, 298-307.

20. ――― , "The Organization of Welfare Services," in The Transformation of Russian Society, Aspects of Social Change since 1861, Cyril E. Black, ed. Cambridge, Massachusetts: Harvard University Press: 1960, 515-541.

21. ――― , "Welfare Personnel in the Soviet Union," Social Work, vol. 7, number 3 (July): 1962, 57-69.

22. ――― , "Russia's Illegitimate Children Before and After the Revolution," Slavic Review, vol. XXII, number 1 (March): 1963, 82-96.

23. ――― , "Welfare Services for Children in the Soviet Union, 1945-1963," Child Welfare, vol. XLII, number 7 (July): 1963, 319-331.

24. ――― , "Social Welfare: Soviet Model," Social Service Review, vol. XXXVIII, number 2 (June): 1964, 191-205.

25. ――― , Social Welfare in the Soviet Union. Stanford, California: Stanford University Press: 1968.

26. ――― , "Social Services for Families and Children in the Soviet Union Since 1967," Slavic Review, vol. 31, number 4 (December): 1972, 831-852.

27. ――― , "Soviet Income Maintenance Plicy for the 1970s," Journal of Social Policy, vol. 2, Part 2 (April): 1973, 97-117.

28. Mil'man, A. Sh. Upravlenie zdravookhraneniem i sotsial'nym obespecheniem v SSSR [Administration of health services and social welfare in the USSR]. Baku: 1960.

29. Narodnyi Komissariat Sotsial'nogo Obespecheniia RSFSR. Sotsial'noe Obespechenie za Piat' Let, 30 Aprelia 1918 g.-30 Aprelia 1923 g. [People's Commissariat of Social Welfare, Russian Republic. Social Welfare during Five Years, April 30, 1918-April 30, 1923]. Moscow: 1923.

30. ――― Sotsial'noe Obespechenie v RSFSR k Desiatoii Godovshchine Oktiabria [People's

Commissariat of Social Welfare. Social Welfare in the Russian Republic at the Tenth Anniversary of the October Revolution]. Moscow: 1927.

31. ——— Sotsial'noe Obespechenie v Sovetskom Soiuze [People's Commissariat of Social Welfare, Russian Republic. Social Welfare in the Soviet Union]. Moscow: 1936.

32. ——— Ocherednye Zadachi Organov Sotsial'nogo Obespecheniia, Materialy Vserossiiskogo soveshchaniia rukovodiashchikh rabotnikov sotsial'nogo obespecheniia, Mai 1945 [People's Commissariat of Social Welfare, Russian Republic. Current Tasks of the Organs of Social Welfare, Materials from the all-Russian conference of leading welfare workers, May 1945]. Moscow: 1945.

33. Okhrana Truda i Sotsial'noe Strakhovanie [Labor Protection and Social Insurance]. Monthly Journal.

34. Osborn, R. J. Soviet Social Policies: Welfare, Equality, and Community Homewood, Illinois: The Dorsey Press: 1970.

35. Rimlinger, G. V. Welfare Policy and Industrialization in Europe, America, and Russia. New York: John Wiley & Sons: 1971.

36. Rollins, N. Child Psychiatry in the Soviet Union. Preliminary Observations. Cambridge, Massachusetts: Harvard University Press: 1972. Reviewed by Bernice Madison in Social Work, vol. 18, number 5 (September): 1973, 124-125.

37. Rumiantseva, M., A. Pergament, and G. Gromova Spravochnik zhenshchiny-rabotnitsy; prava zhenshchiny po sovetskomu zakonodatel'stvu [A book of references for the woman worker; the rights of women in Soviet law]. Moscow: 1963.

38. Shif, Zh. I. and A. N. Smirnova, eds. Opyt otbora uchashchikhsia vo vspomogatel'nye shkoly [Experience with selecting children for auxiliary schools]. Moscow: 1964.

39. Sotsial'noe Obespechenie [Social Welfare]. Monthly journal.

40. Sotsial'noe Obespechenie i Strakhovanie v SSSR, Sbornik ofitsial'nykh dokumentov [Social welfare and social insurance in the USSR. Manual of official documents]. Moscow: 1964.

41. Sovetskaiia Iustitsiia [Soviet Justice]. Monthly journal.

42. Sutiagin, P., ed. 30 let VOG [Thirty years of the All-Russian Society for the Deaf]. Moscow: 1957.

43. Sverdlov, G. M. Prava grazhdan v sem'e [Family rights of citizens]. Moscow: 1963.

44. U.S. Department of Health, Education and Welfare. Social Security Administration. A Report on Social Security Programs in the Soviet Union. Washington, D.C.: Government Printing Office: 1960.

45. ——— The U.S. Social Security Mission to the Union of Soviet Socialist Republics. Washington, D.C.: DHEW Publication No. (SSA) 73-11901 (February) 1972.

46. Vlasov, S. N. and A. V. Levshin Sotsial'noe obespechenie kolkhoznikov [Social Security of collective farmers]. Moscow: 1960.

47. Vserossiiskoe obshchestvo slephkh v tsifrakh, 1955-1959 [The All-Russian Society for the Blind in figures, 1955-1959]. Moscow: 1959.

48. Zhizn' Glukhikh [Life Among the Deaf]. Monthly journal.

NOTES ON THE CONTRIBUTORS

DANIEL THURSZ is Dean and Professor of the School of Social Work and Community Planning of the University of Maryland at Baltimore. He has served in this capacity since 1967. Prior to that time he was the Associate Director of VISTA, the United States Domestic Peace Corps, established as part of the Office of Economic Opportunity. He has held a number of important positions in social welfare and has been a leader in the National Association of Social Workers in the United States. Born in Morocco, Dr. Thursz has maintained close links with several centers of social welfare development throughout the globe.

JOSEPH L. VIGILANTE is Dean and Professor of the School of Social Work at Adelphi University in Garden City, New York; he has served since 1962 in that capacity. Prior to joining the Adelphi University faculty in 1955, Dr. Vigilante was a caseworker and a child welfare worker in New York and Wisconsin. He has served as a consultant to a number of state and federal agencies in the United States. He served as President of the New York State Association of Deans of Schools of Social Work and has been active on the national level within the National Association of Social Workers in the United States as well as the Council on Social Work Education.

HODA BADRAN holds a Master's degree in social work from the Kent School of Social Work in Louisville, Kentucky, and a doctorate of social welfare from Western Reserve University in Cleveland, Ohio. Presently a Professor at the Higher Institute of Social Work in Cairo, Egypt, she has been seconded to the UNICEF Office for the Eastern Mediterranean Region. Dr. Badran has worked both in the United States and in Cairo in a variety of social work assignments. While in the United States, she served as a research consultant to the National Urban League in New York City.

SATTAREH FARMAN-FARMAIAN received her B.A. and M.S.W. degrees from the University of Southern California. From 1953 to 1958 she worked for the United Nations in Baghdad as a social welfare training expert for the Middle East. In 1958, she returned to Teheran to establish the Teheran School of Social Work, which she has directed since its founding. She is also a founder of the Family Planning Association of Iran and the Community Welfare Centers of Iran. Miss Farman-Farmaian is on the faculty of the Social Science Department of the University of Teheran and is a member of the Board of Trustees of several agencies devoted to social welfare in Iran. She frequently represents her country on international committees and at international conferences concerned with welfare problems and population.

DAVID MACAROV is a director of the Joseph J. Schwartz Graduate Program for training community center directors and senior personnel, which is jointly sponsored by the Schools of Social Work and Education at the Hebrew University of Jerusalem. He holds a Bachelor of Science degree from the University of Pittsburgh, a Master of Social Work from Western Reserve University, and a doctorate from Brandeis University. He is a member of the Editorial Board of the *International Journal of Social Economics* and author of *Incentives to Work* and *The Short Course in Development Activities.* He has conducted a series of conferences in Europe for teachers of social work under the auspices of the International Association of Schools of Social Work and the United Nations.

ELLEN B. HILL received her Master of Social Work degree from Adelphi University in 1957. She has also studied sociology and social philosophy at Heidelberg University, the Sorbonne in Paris, and Stanford University in California. She has worked in national and international social welfare organizations, including the American Social Health Association, the United Nations Office of the High Commissioner for Refugees, and the United Nations Development Program. Since 1961, she has served on the faculty of the CEPAS School of

Social Work of Rome University and is a consultant to the Research Institute in Social Services of Rome. Mrs. Hill is a member of the International Sociological Association and Secretary of the Research Committee on Innovative Processes in Social Change of that organization.

MARIO CORSINI is a graduate of the CEPAS School of Social Work of Rome University. He has been the Editor of Italy's main professional social work journal, *Rivista de servizio sociale,* since it was founded in 1961, and he is the author of many articles on social policy. Mr. Corsini is a board member of the Italian Section of the International Social Welfare Conference and Chief of Social Services of a regionally sponsored center for the aged in Rome.

H. GLENNERSTER is Senior Lecturer in Social Policy at the London School of Economics. He graduated from Oxford University in 1959 with a degree in philosophy, politics, and economics. Following a number of years as a member of the staff of the Research Department of the Labour Party, he joined the London School of Economics in 1964, where he has been responsible for a number of research projects on educational finance and planning. In 1972 he was a Visiting Scholar at the Brookings Institution and has recently completed a comparative study of social services budgeting and expenditure control in Britain and the United States.

SOPHIA WOJCIECHOWSKI is a Professor at the Adelphi University School of Social Work. She obtained her M.S. degree in Economics from the University of Warsaw in Poland and her M.S.W. degree from Columbia University School of Social Work in New York. Her previous activities include a variety of research positions for the Polish Ministry of Welfare. She served as a Social Affairs Officer for the United Nations in New York and has been a consultant with the American Counsel for Emigrés in the Professions. She is a Fellow of the American Ortho-Psychiatric Association.

ÅKE ELMER holds a doctorate in social policy from the University of Lund in Sweden and has served as Director of the Graduate School of Social Work and Public Administration in Lund since 1966. He has served as Secretary for Social Legislation in the Swedish Government and has held a number of governmental positions in the city of Lund, primarily in the field of social administration.

NATHAN E. COHEN completed his undergraduate work at Harvard University, where he also received his doctorate. He served as Chairman of the National Council on Social Work Education, which was the forerunner of the present Council on Social Work Education. He was the first President of the National Association of Social Workers and the President of the National Conference on Social Welfare in 1964. In 1963, he was appointed Vice President of Western Reserve University, a post which he held until his departure for California in 1964, where he assumed the post of Professor of Social Work at the University of California at Los Angeles. Later on, he served as Dean of the School. At present, he is the Director of the Doctoral Program and a Professor of Social Policy.

BERNICE MADISON was born in Central Asiatic Russia, but received most of her education in the United States. She has a B.S. degree from Northwestern University in Illinois, and her M.A. and Ph.D. are from the University of Chicago. Dr. Madison has worked in county, state, national, and international social welfare organizations, including UNRRA, the U.S. Children's Bureau, and, during World War II, the Office of Strategic Services. While with UNRRA she administered the largest program for displaced persons in Germany. She has taught at the University of Oregon, the School of Social Welfare at the University of California at Berkeley, and at present is a Professor of Social Work at San Francisco State University. She was the only woman and the only non-government member of a Health, Education and Welfare Department delegation to the Soviet Union sent to study that country's social welfare system in 1971.

SUBJECT INDEX